RALPH McGILL

RALPH McGILL
Editor and Publisher

Vol. I–Ralph McGill at Work
Vol. II–Ralph McGill Speaks

CALVIN McLEOD LOGUE
UNIVERSITY OF GEORGIA

Moore Publishing Company
Durham, North Carolina

RALPH McGILL, EDITOR AND PUBLISHER, VOL. I
Copyright © 1969, by Moore Publishing Company, Durham, N.C.
Manufactured in the United States of America
Library of Congress Catalog Card Number: 71-97784

VOLUME I

RALPH McGILL
AT WORK

Calvin McLeod Logue

Kudos and Eulogies

The New York Times, February 5, 1969:
McGill was that rare person, a crusader with a sense of humor. He had strong convictions and a rigorous conscience, but he also understood human nature and human failings... Knowing and loving his native South, he understood that the highest act of love toward any region or people is to tell the truth. He was an admirable craftsman, the master of a pungent, colloquial style.

Time, February 14, 1969:
For four decades his daily column caressed the South with his love, lashed it for its faults, served as its conscience. Surveys repeatedly rated him as both the region's best-liked and least-liked writer——but always the most read. Even his haters could not ignore him, because, as one of his admiring colleagues put it: "Mac had guts when it took guts to have guts."

Citation accompanying the American Education Award for 1969, presented posthumously by National Education Association:
The calm, consistent courageous voice of Ralph McGill has been heard throughout the land, pointing

the way for a new South and a better world. For thirty-eight years, as reporter, editor and publisher of *The Atlanta Constitution*, he has spoken in simple terms but thunderous tones of the American Dream and our regional and national shortcomings in making it a reality for every man. Throughout the years he has demonstrated the human qualities of great-ness——humility, courage, unlimited capacity for friendship and belief in the infinite worth of every human being.

The Rev. Martin Luther King, Sr.:
I have known no man more devoted to the ideas and principles for which he stood and lived.

Roy Wilkins, Executive Director, NAACP:
Ralph McGill was a spokesman for the real South and for the nation in urging thoroughly American solu-tions, grounded in flexibility, justice and consti-tutional equality for the vexatious problem of race relations.

President Richard M. Nixon:
There is a kind of courage which not only calls forth praise from friends, but also elicits respect from adversaries. It was this kind of courage, intellectual and moral, which distinguished Ralph McGill. Proud of the deepest traditions of his Southern heritage, loyal to the concepts of integrity and honor which are the pride of his region, he brought to journalism a sense of responsibility and a devotion to truth.

Former President Lyndon B. Johnson:
His eloquent voice was the voice of nation's conscience. America, which needed him so much, will
miss him deeply. Ralph McGill was a brave and good
man, a forceful and effective fighter for human rights,
and a journalist who lived by the noblest traditions of
his profession.

Senator Edward M. Kennedy:
American journalism has lost one of its legendary
figures...and American society has lost one of its most
compassionate and tireless citizens. With his wisdom
and his understanding and his faith in the brotherhood of man, he helped draw Americans together at a
time when others were trying to drive them apart. I
know how President Kennedy respected and admired
Ralph McGill, and how much Robert Kennedy
esteemed his counsel. I was fortunate enough to
know his friendship, and to value it.

Chief Justice Earl Warren:
Ralph McGill was not only one of the great journalists of our day, but was a great American in every
sense of the word. Every line he wrote was in the
interest of a better America.

ACKNOWLEDGMENTS

Appreciation is expressed to Mrs. Christine Burroughs and her staff for help in getting material through interlibrary loan at The University of Georgia, to Miss Dora Byron of Community Educational Service for providing information about speeches given at Emory University, to Eugene V. Grace, M.D., president of Moore Publishing Company, for his advice and interest in the book, to Miss Grace Lundy for her cooperation, and to Mr. McGill for permission to draw from his column and his speeches. Some of the materials in this book can be found in my articles in *Journalism Quarterly, Southern Speech Journal, Nieman Reports, Speech Monographs*, and *North Carolina Speech Journal.*

PUBLISHER'S NOTE

When Cal Logue consented to let us publish his manuscript on Ralph McGill we were gratified.

From the beginning we have tried to move our company in the direction of needed, worthwhile publications.

Here is a man who filled the pages for a most worthwhile book. Ralph McGill was praised by the world, hated and loved by his own people of the South. He was in all respects a Southerner, born and raised in the South, always close to the morality of his region and speaking to its conscience with his whole self.

McGill knew the power of words. Moreover, he felt that it is incumbent upon those who deal in words to be humble. He pointed out that words could be fashioned into weapons. McGill also knew the beauty of words as he showed in an article on Winston Churchill:

> ——when he rose to have his say and the full light played upon him, he came alive.
>
> ——He rarely looked about. But the words came on and on and for anyone who had an affection for words, they were like notes from some great symphonic arrangement with now and then a trumpet solo...His words purred and rolled like summer thunder.

When I read these and other words and was subdued by their beauty and power I agreed with Dr. Logue that we should not edit the speeches, even those transcribed from tapes. So they are left as they came to us, for all posterity to study and criticize and admire. To change the subtlety, the courage, the grammar would have been presumptuous on our part.

For this book we are grateful for the opportunity to publish it, to Calvin Logue for his accurate and searching endeavor and to all those who help us bring it to the reader.

Most of all we are grateful to Mr. Ralph McGill for having passed this way.

To
Andrew
Michael
Mary Jo
Polly
Hanchey

Preface

There were many Ralph McGills, almost enough to go around. How one saw him usually reflected as much the observer as the observed. Persons with the press often saw him chiefly as "a reporter," in some sacred sense of the word——a "high calling." Some pictured McGill as a promoter and preserver of racial integration and felt somehow if he would go so would this terrible threat to tradition. Upon McGill's death, for example, some "hate letters" went to the *Constitution*, and one person called to ask "what time the resurrection services would be held." Persons who admired McGill's long struggle for social justice described him in such terms as: fiery editorialist; kindly, even gentle person; great patriot and a powerful writer; conscience of the South; a builder and a conciliator; having bulldog tenacity; and a nagging voice.

It is difficult to composite this uncommon man. Reg Murphy, newly appointed editor of the *Constitution*, argued that "too many men have tried to picture McGill as soft and gentle. He was no such thing. He spoke like a man and he acted like a man." Shortly before quitting the *Constitution*, Bruce Galphin concluded that "people who knew him only from the printed word have their own stereotypes of the man. It is doubtful that either admirer or critic has the true picture from the words alone. For the traits of concern, of generosity, of rollicking laughter, of stern dedication undergirded his writing but were more readily visible in deed than in print."

Time felt that McGill served as "conscience"of the South, but "as the *Constitution's* editor, and particularly as its publisher since 1960, McGill proved too kindly to crack the editorial whip..." The Columbus (Georgia) *Enquirer* concluded: "Amiable and easy-going in person, Ralph McGill was a different man in the cold, clear print of his column. A dogmatic exponent of his own viewpoint, he was reluctant to concede that any other viewpoint had validity, and he had difficulty distinguishing between bona fide villains and people who merely happened to disagree with him. But without question, he was the most honored and influential Georgia journalist since Henry Grady...and in reality he was a much larger figure in his time and his nation than Grady ever was." In his *Gothic Politics in the Deep South*, Robert Sherrill shamed McGill for "working up a fine back-scratching relationship" with Herman Talmadge. "First," continued

Sherrill, "it must be remembered that editor McGill was never more than one step, at best, ahead of the community, not three steps. And sometimes he sounded right in step. In that era, at least, he believed the FEPC, the anti-lynching bill and the anti-poll tax bill to be unconstitutional, and said so." The *New York Times* editorialized: "Ralph McGill was that rare person, a crusader with a sense of humor. He had strong convictions and a rigorous conscience, but he also understood human nature and human failings... Knowing and loving his native South, he understood that the highest act of love toward any region or people is to tell the truth. He was an admirable craftsman, the master of a pungent, colloquial style."

Now a personal word: When I began this research five years ago I had no firm opinions about Ralph McGill. Having been raised and schooled in Alabama, I had often heard that "he's Georgia's problem." Quite often, however, I found that he was treated much like some social disease——not to be discussed in public. This may have been related to another surprising discovery, that there were many people, in and outside the South, who had never heard of Ralph McGill.

This book was completed before Mr. McGill's death. Other than the preface and a very few additions, such as the date of death, nothing has been changed. Indeed, Mr. McGill and his secretary were kind enough to look over the complete manuscript. And even though my comments certainly are not always favorable, his only suggestion was that I add "the early 1950's" to the period when he "was not always free to write what he wanted to write." After reading the many personal tributes to McGill and after sitting in the packed pews with other funeral goers and singing "O God Our Help in Ages Past," there was a strong desire to go back and change or delete. But one who studies the life and works of Ralph McGill knows better than to do that.

Obviously I have not attempted to write a complete biography. Little, for example, is said here of McGill's battles with Eugene Talmadge and other important events. My focus is more upon the man, and experiences are used mainly as a means of understanding something of the character of the man.

Some of the following material has appeared in *Nieman Reports, Southern Speech Journal, Speech Monographs,* and *Journalism Quarterly.*

Cal M. Logue

Contents

ONE

AMERICAN FROM THE SOUTH

Expelled from Vanderbilt University shortly before graduation because of his willingness to express unpopular beliefs, Ralph Emerson McGill continued to speak out for more than forty years. Most of that time this Georgian was with the *Atlanta Constitution,* as assistant sports editor, sports editor, associate editor, editor, until his death on February 3, 1969, as publisher.

Mention of a few of McGill's honors and awards reveals the nature of the career this world-famed journalist enjoyed in an era which reached from horse-and-buggy and lynchings to space capsule and school desegregation. In 1953 the Press Club of Dallas and Southern Methodist University cited McGill for "distinguished service as a crusading editor and writer." Two years later he was recognized by the English-Speaking Union for "outstanding contributions to British-American relations." In 1957 McGill was cited by The University of Missouri for "distinguished service in journalism." He received the Pulitzer Prize for editorial writing in 1958 for "long, courageous and effective editorial leadership," and the Medal of Freedom in 1964, the highest civil honor the President can bestow. Although he earned no bachelor's degree, McGill owned honorary

11

doctoral degrees from at least nineteen universities, among them being Columbia University, Brown University, and Brandeis University. When Harvard University conferred an honorary degree on McGill the citation read: "In a troubled time his steady voice of reason champions a new South."

If some persons were pleased by McGill's pursuits, just as many were repulsed. On one occasion this outspoken journalist counted six shots in his mailbox and, on a different day, discovered a bullet hole in his window. Finding garbage on his front lawn, listening to abusive phone calls, and receiving threatening anonymous letters were the least of McGill's concerns. The Columbians once issued a directive that he be beaten. The Ku Klux Klan often named McGill "southern-enemy-number-one."

Not all of McGill's opponents, however, spoke from behind sheets and masks. Some used more sacred robes to muffle McGill. As late as 1963 "thirteen thousand copies of the official newspaper of the Episcopal Diocese of Atlanta" were "sold for scrap because of an interview in which" McGill "charged the local Episcopal leadership with 'hypocrisy' in its relationship with Lovett School."[1] Like a prophet in his own home, McGill was denied use of both a Superior Court room and school facilities in Columbus, Georgia, in 1959 because, as one Commissioner claimed, McGill's address was "an effort on the part of the Atlanta newspapers to ram their opinion down the throats of the people in this county."[2]

It is not difficult to determine why some individuals and institutions were maddened by McGill. He "called his own shots" and they often found their mark. For example, after the infamous replay of the civil war on The University of Mississippi campus in 1962, McGill fired: "Not all the perfumes of Araby will wash clean the political hands of Mississippi's Governor Ross Barnett."[3] In 1968 McGill, noting that William Fulbright of Arkansas had "voted against every civil rights measure to come before the Senate," chided the Senator for practicing a "selective political morality." In that same column McGill pictured former Governor George Wallace as "Alabama's political evil."[4] As early as 1946 McGill dared to write:

Here in the South, the demagogues are very free indeed with "Communist" charges... Any person who declares the Negro has a right to fair treatment in the courts and at the hands of police, which

12

he too often does not have; who asks that he be given a fair share of housing, parks, education and public health; who suggests he has a right to use his skills in industry——that person is sure to be called a "nigger lover." He also is sure to be charged with favoring social equality...and, of course, he is a "Communist." He also will be charged with having violated Southern traditions, with fouling his own nest...[5]

Although he was known most and will be remembered best for his involvement in civil rights, McGill did not limit himself to any one cause. He discussed any issue which seemed important to him at a particular time, whether politics, poetry, economics, social problems, morality, labor-management, foreign affairs, cooking, Churchill, history, or the press.

To understand McGill one must know that he was at once devoted to and critical of the South, and he was the latter because of the former. Listen as McGill speaks to Southerners about the South:

We love the South. It is a love that comes easily. We love the South with a fierce, protective passion such as parents have for a crippled child... Our love is deep and based on emotions that drive us to positions unstable and ofttimes untenable. Our South is a child crippled by discriminatory rates and tariffs; an orphan child whose parents of wealth and culture were killed on the field at Appomattox... I would like to make a testament of faith in the South...there is deep in the soul of the South the courage and courtesy that survived the wounds; the rare, bright flower that was not twisted by defeat or occupation; the intelligence that knows we must move with time and does not want to be let alone... There is willingness to toil and sacrifice and believe in God. And willingness to go on with strong, sure legs if only they will quit pulling a blind-fold over our eyes. There is an eagerness to be just and fair; to build a better world and drown in the creek every litter of the bitch called ignorance.[6]

The University of Notre Dame recognized that McGill "knows the South as no Northerner, however sensitive, can ever know her, knows her nobility as well as her savagery, her gentility and her shabbiness, her terrors and her nightmares, her conscience and her torn spirit."

13

Although he was both in and out of the South McGill was not blind to her faults. He was an American from the South, not a *Southern* American. McGill confessed that he "could not...describe a 'typical' Southerner... I am very much afraid my typical Southerner would be a typical American... In fact, I think the sooner we quit thinking of ourselves as regionalists and begin thinking of ourselves as Americans, the better off we will be."[7] "The Southerner," however, "who loves his region must love it enough to fight for it. He must love it enough to vigorously denounce and oppose all those who seek to say the American dream of justice and opportunity for all Americans is not a Southern dream too."[8] While few had the capacity to love the South as McGill, a still smaller number could criticize that region so intimately:

Let us admit that, with a few exceptions, we restrict Negro employment to the least rewarding fields of work. This denial is based entirely on prejudice. Let us admit that while lynchings have almost disappeared, the Negro does not receive full and equal justice. There are many kinds of lynchings, some mental. Let us admit that our failure to provide equal educational opportunity is in the national spotlight of Supreme Court decisions. We...have repeatedly insisted we want to be fair to the Negro. Let us admit that the record shows we have not. Have we been willing to give him a fair share of our municipal funds?...we will fail if we do not see that the best weapons we have...are not political secession, but honest and just action. We can give to the Negro a right to work... We can give him education and political rights... States' rights also means States' responsibilities.[9]

In the last column that McGill saw in print, on February 3, 1969, the day of his death, he wrote: "Our segregated system of education for generations has been, and is, viciously unjust. It has had a disease that weakened all education——white and black. It has sacrificed generations of all children——white and black——to instruction of inferior quality... There are heavy percentages of high schools in all Southern states that do not offer curriculums that prepare children for admission to the state technical and engineering schools. This situation has existed for decades. We have preferred to sing 'Dixie' rather than see the facts and correct them."[10]

14

NOTES

ONE

[1] *Atlanta Constitution*, October 2, 1963, p. 1.
[2] *The New York Times*, April 1, 1959, p. 14 (AP).
[3] *Atlanta Constitution*, October 2, 1962, p. 1.
[4] *Atlanta Constitution*, May 30, 1968, pp. 1, 19.
[5] *Atlanta Constitution*, April 29, 1946, p. 6.
[6] *Atlanta Constitution*, July 8, 1946, p. 6.
[7] *Atlanta Constitution*, April 13, 1946, p. 4.
[8] *Atlanta Constitution*, July 7, 1949, p. 10.
[9] *Atlanta Constitution*, February 9, 1948, p. 6.
[10] *Atlanta Constitution*, February 3, 1969, p. 1.

TWO

A DEMOCRAT IS BORN

To understand McGill's concern for persons who had been exploited, to appreciate his broad knowledge, and to comprehend his partisan political perspective, one must look to his childhood background, his formal education, and his adult experiences (subjects discussed in chapters two, three, and four).

Born on February 5, 1898, McGill lived the first six years and most summers until he was sixteen in a "somewhat isolated Calvinist farm community located some twenty miles upriver from Chattanooga."[1] This lasted until the young Tennessean could graduate "from 'busting middles' to the responsibility of 'plowing around corn.'"[2] He learned to "run a reaper" and to "tie corn for fodder."[3] The environment on this six-hundred acre farm near Soddy had considerable influence upon McGill, including his attitude toward Negroes.

Because there were few Negroes near his small farm in East Tennessee, McGill was exposed to little overt racial prejudice. Soddy was a "farm trading center turned into a small mining center by the discovery of coal"; thus, there were fewer plantations requiring cheap labor. "We always raised a few acres of wheat on our place,"

16

McGill recalled. "It was nine miles from a post office and was bottom and hill farm land along the Tennessee river. We never knew cotton. We ran to corn, wheat, mules and horses."[4]

McGill, then, simply did not see a great deal of discrimination. Any help on the farm was recruited "from the white tenants on the place."[5] "I remember when I saw my first Negro I thought at first it was a coal miner," McGill wrote. "But I was a boy then, come maybe once a month to the town."[6] He stated further that, "having started out in life somehow with no prejudices against people as people——at least none I can remember——I have always liked people."[7] He did not "recall any of the preposterous or vicious racist demagoguery met with in later years. It could be heard in states to the south of us but we largely escaped it. It would not be honest to be smug about this. There were few Negroes in East Tennessee. Middle Tennessee had no history of racial agitation of politics."[8]

McGill's stay on the farm gave him a love and a feel for language. This rural background affected the style and content of his writings and speeches. Celestine Sibley, writer for McGill's *Atlanta Constitution*, found that his "columns reveal the farm boy who is alive to the beauty of his land, writing of 'the acrid, nostalgic smell of wood burning beneath the weekly washday pots; the pine-and-oak smoke from the chimneys of farmhouses fighting with the smell of wet plowed earth.' "[9] In a speech planned for the American Seed Trade Association in Chicago on December 5, 1958, McGill wrote: "As a young boy I have ridden a horse to the mill with a sack of corn in front of me. I remember yet the nut-sweet smell of the mill, the warm feel of the stones and of the meal itself as it fell into the bin."

When asked by journalism students how they could learn to write, McGill replied that it is good to be "a teller of tales who can put into them the language of persons and the feel of the soil and the people. It also is a fine thing for a writer...to have an eye for trees and hills and birds and animals and a memory for smells and sound."[10] McGill also advised that "the heritage of the hills is independence, and as far as I'm concerned I have my share, and value it very highly indeed."[11]

In discussing the influence of his family, McGill told how "in 1822 a new group of settlers arrived at the valley, having come down from North Carolina... They were farmers.. These were my people, the families of William McGill, William Clift, James Wallace and James McCree..."[12] Because of "inadequate schooling," McGill's father abandoned his dream of becoming a lawyer and became a "good salesman" of heaters. Following his father on "turkey stalks" and political campaigns, McGill learned the importance of books, gained respect for government, and developed a love for politics.

McGill learned to read at the age of five: "It was my father who early encouraged me to read. Books were few at the farm. Most of them were religious in theme, including collections of Presbyterian sermons. I could read well before I entered the first grade, an event delayed by an illness... My father taught me... He was a hardworking, kindly man. There was a streak of stubbornness in him, as well as brooding, but these moods were always short. He was pretty much the Calvinist Puritan and was inclined to be dogmatic in his views. If he ever took a drink I never knew it, and if he ever used profanity I never heard it. Yet I never had even a light spanking from him, though I deserved many."[13]

McGill was taught to respect the United States government, an attitude which later strongly influenced his stand on controversial social problems. He wrote: "Perhaps because of my 'raising,' I have had from boyhood-on what amounts to a reverence for the Supreme Court and its place in our life, for the Presidency as an office, and the Congress as the voice and representation of the people."[14]

McGill's father introduced him to politics, the subject he would love most as an adult. McGill witnessed the returns in 1908 when William Howard Taft defeated William Jennings Bryan. It seems ironical that it was while accompanying his Republican father that a Democrat was born: "When I was a boy of about ten years of age my father...encouraged me to visit the polls on election day... Woodrow Wilson won me completely and I became almost a fanatic follower of the Princeton teacher. I cast my first vote for the presidential Democratic nominees in 1920——Cox and Roosevelt——and against Warren G. Harding. I have never cast anything but a Democratic vote since and do not anticipate any other course in the future."[15]

While McGill's father encouraged his interest in reading and politics, his mother was the source of strength at home. Her influence was not as obvious, so more difficult to define. However, she "raised" McGill "to be polite"[16] and kindled the flame of moral concern that motivated him in years to come. "At home," he concluded, "my mother was the guiding force, but so quietly that it was years before I realized it... She encouraged and inspired. She was always a believing person. She had a personal faith which sustained her and others."[17] It was probably his mother's measured sustenance which helped motivate McGill to such topics as that discussed at the 1960 Lovejoy Convocation: "But, let us return to our central theme, which is the spirit of man and his capacity to believe——this was what characterized Lovejoy and others like him——he believed. He had values. His mind was not withdrawn on the issue. It believed."[18]

McGill's "Aunt Molly" told him, "I don't know what talent you have for writing, but if you have any you got it from your grandfather...on your mother's side."[19] After she had quoted some of grandfather's gems, McGill decided it was best to forget any influence this flamboyant relative may have had. McGill probably was closer to reality when he attributed his own achievements to "hard work."[20]

As a young boy McGill developed a love for books which he never lost throughout his long career. "I am one who actually hid in a barn loft to read the Dick Merriwell story," McGill reflected. "I read the Buffalo Bill stories and the Wild West paper novels in the same study——the barn loft... They weren't bad books...and I am convinced the propaganda of those stories and books had an effect. Right always triumphed. Honesty emerged as the best policy. Integrity and fair play were strong assets."[21]

Moving to Chattanooga at the age of six, McGill read hungrily until the doctor prescribed more outdoor activity because of his "excessive thinness" and "digestive illnesses."[22]

I read prodigiously as a child——two books per day, fetched tied to the handlebars of my bicycle from the library two miles from my home. I did that until they locked up what books I had and sent me back to my grandmother's farm from whence I had come to town...there was a flood of the Alger and Henty books. There were the Barbour books, *Treasure Island, Robinson Crusoe*. There were the Deerfoot books and, finally, the *Deerslayer* and *Ivanhoe, Lorna Doone and Vanity Fair; The Tale of Two Cities, David Copperfield, Oliver Twist*. There was always a flood of books. I read undirected. I read books about Irish kins, being enamored of Ireland. I read everything about Indians I could find and wished I had been one. I missed many books I should have read. But I was drunk with books. I went on to the War Between the States... I developed a great passion for the Confederacy, and many bloody-nosed fights had I in defense of that Lost Cause. I read with pressing eagerness all the books I could get on that war. I got then, and have enlarged since, an immense dislike for Jefferson Davis and complete hero worship for Stonewall Jackson, Robert E. Lee and Nathan Bedford Forrest. I think if I had to pin down the books that most influenced my very young life and the years that came hard on the heels of that first reading of Alger, Barbour and Henty, I would have to say they were the books of Stonewall Jackson and Lee. I got from them, and from my Welsh and Scottish ancestry, too much sentiment; an ability to weep at sad movies and over moving pieces of poetry or passages in books and at grief generally, a mixture of naivete and reality, a belief in loyalty and a liking for causes. And also the bitter fact that high ideals, devotion to duty and honor are not, in themselves, passports to victory.[23]

After moving to Chattanooga from his grandmother's mule farm, McGill had several jobs which proved to be good training for one who would later lose himself in the struggle for human rights: "The summer of collecting 'small, mean bills, some of them damned old and mean' was a fascinating one. Fritz and Wiehl was an old, highly respected company, selling the usual line of drugstore supplies... I was fourteen and a half years old and not, certainly, a commanding figure. But they did not need one. All they wanted was someone to present the bill as a reminder and argue for payment... The summers as a salesman in a haberdashery store were interesting and easy... I learned the peculiarities of tastes in ties, shirts, and underwear. I also became acquainted with the vanity of the male animal."[24]

McGill's "summer job in 1918" was with the United States Marine Corps at Parris Island, South Carolina; he found this training to be "more valuable" "than any one or even two years of schooling" he "ever had." "It was rough and tough," he continued, "but out of it I got more understanding of discipline, order, cooperation and people than I ever got from college or lower grade school... If you went through Parris Island nothing much would ever worry you. I know that I built roads, worked on garbage trucks, cleaned up after horses, asked permission every time I wanted to go to the gentleman's powder room... But when it was all done and months had passed and I could evaluate it, I knew it for what it was——the best schooling a man could have."[25]

Working on a roofing crew in 1919 was McGill's "best and most rewarding summer job." This work provided McGill an opportunity to associate with members of the Negro race, an experience he had not known before. The young lad who then expressed concern for his Negro boss, Charlie White, would one day speak out for that man's entire race; he would not "forget": "By midsummer I realized I had become very fond of Charlie and he of me... In my last week on the job we both began to talk sadly of my quitting to go off to school at Nashville... He knew I had to have a job there and that I would have to borrow some money... Charlie insisted he would bring the old truck out and take me and my trunk down to the station... 'Don't forget me,' he said. 'I'll never forget you, Charlie,' I said... He stepped back, reached in his inside coat pocket, and took out an envelope. 'Don't you open this till you get on the train,' he said... When the train was out of the station, I opened the envelope. There was a folded five-dollar bill and a scrawled note. 'For my helper to spend at school,' it read. It was then I wept."[26]

As for religious training, McGill was exposed to Calvinism both at home and in the "white, clapboard Presbyterian Church."[27] He recalled "the earnest voice reading from the Bible...hesitating over words...mispronouncing the Biblical names...faltering in the middle of the sonorous prose stretches...and the terrible sleepiness which came with the voice, rising and falling in the Sunday morning scripture readings. But, now and then, someone would be there to read who would make the words come alive and bring out the full majesty of the King James version prose, and then it would march and stir and trumpets would sound."[28]

At the Presbyterian church in Soddy, McGill experienced his "first doubts about the accuracy of sermons." He admitted, however, that "even the most daring of us shuddered at the thought of spending eternity in flames comparable to the consuming sulphur fury of the Soddy, Tennessee, coke ovens."[29] "The Calvinistic services," he remembered, "were hot with the fires of an eternal hell and perfumed by sulphur and brimstone. They were never mild sermons, as I recall... The sermons were long. A man who couldn't preach hell-fire and damnation for a good hour was regarded as weak and slothful and likely to let sin get the best of things. The Presbyterian faith in those days was sterner than now, I think, and debated infant damnation and the awesome, predestined ends of man."[30]

While these early religious experiences did influence McGill, at the same time, he apparently rebelled against much of the strict doctrine. McGill, later an Episcopalian, wrote: "Being Presbyterian born...I know worry and the remorse of conscience. The hot breath of Calvin often is a blow torch on the seat of the pants of my immortal soul. I am a restless rebel who cannot regularly endure the shackles of organized religious services. The utterances of most divines make me dance with impotent rage or angry denial of their conclusions."[31] "Whether it is because the hot breath of Calvin has been on my neck since birth or whether I have got too much sense, I never could endure night clubs or gambling as a way to spend money."[32] It is interesting to note, however, that neither Calvinism nor good sense kept McGill from whiskey and being a "wild" reporter in Nashville; though, in later years, he largely gave up drink.[33] Also, the "hell-fire and brimstone" sermons did not keep McGill from his childhood pranks. "Reviewing my youthful life," he wrote, "I was astounded to discover that I, too had been a vandal... I recall that once we took the wheels off old man Penny's wagon and hid them under leaves back in the woods... It was I, too, who invented the most efficient method of bringing somebody else's watermelons out of the patch... I was, at the time twelve or thirteen years old... I was in those days, very expert at hitting with a rock the large glass insulators they had on telephone arms... I don't know why I did those things and I suspect I didn't know then, unless because it was just for the thrill."[34]

NOTES

TWO

1 Ralph McGill, *The South and the Southerner* (Boston: Little, Brown and Company, 1964), p. 47.
2 *Atlanta Constitution*, September 18, 1951, p. 1.
3 *Atlanta Constitution*, July 7, 1946, p. 10.
4 *Atlanta Constitution*, August 14, 1950, p. 1.
5 *South and the Southerner*, p. 64.
6 *Atlanta Constitution*, June 19, 1948, p. 14.
7 *Atlanta Constitution*, September 23, 1949, p. 14.
8 *South and the Southerner*, p. 109.
9 *Saturday Evening Post*, 231 (December 27, 1958), 51.
10 *Atlanta Constitution* May 7, 1948, p. 12.
11 *Atlanta Constitution*, August 30, 1951, p. 1.
12 *Atlanta Constitution*, May 2, 1947, p. 12.
13 *South and the Southerner*, p. 38.
14 *Atlanta Constitution* February 22, 1958, p. 1.
15 *Atlanta Constitution*, September 13, 1949, p. 12.
16 *Atlanta Constitution*, March 8, 1948, p. 6.
17 *South and the Southerner*, pp. 44-45.
18 Speech delivered at Colby College, Waterville, Maine, November 10, 1960
19 *Atlanta Constitution*, May 23, 1947, p. 10.
20 *Atlanta Constitution*, May 1, 1946, p. 6.
21 *Atlanta Constitution*, February 1, 1952, p. 1.
22 *Atlanta Constitution*, October 12, 1947, p. 12B.
23 *Atlanta Constitution*, September 1, 1947, p. 8.
24 *South and the Southerner*, pp. 59-62.
25 *Atlanta Constitution*, September 4, 1947, p. 8.
26 *South and the Southerner*, pp. 63-68.
27 *Atlanta Constitution*, April 14, 1949, p. 16.
28 *Atlanta Constitution*, December 18, 1949, p. 4.
29 *Atlanta Constitution*, June 19, 1949, p. 2D.
30 *Atlanta Constitution*, April 14, 1949, p. 16.
31 *Atlanta Constitution*, February 18, 1947, p. 8.
32 *Atlanta Constitution*, November 21, 1946, p. 24.

[33] George Barker, *The Nashville Tennessean Magazine*, November 5, 1961, p. 10

[34] *Atlanta Constitution* January 13, 1948, p. 4

THREE

THE STUDENT

Leaving the farm at the age of six, McGill "went first to the Fourth District School" in Chattanooga, "a large, ugly, square two-story building with gravel-covered playground."[1] While there he recalled "being mightily stirred one day...when the third grade was let out..for the purpose of going out to Warner Park to see the first airplanes to appear..."[2] "At the age of twelve," wrote McGill, "I engaged in a fist fight on the shoe-scuffed playground...in defense of Jefferson. I have forgot what the canard was, but the fight was hot."[3] Training at the Fourth District School proved to be of particular importance: "One year," McGill stated, "we had a new principal, Professor John Counts. He...announced that for every class from the fifth grade on, the final period each Thursday afternoon would be given to reading. Children should read more, he said... So, then and there, he read us a chapter from *She*, by H. Rider Haggard... I was then in the fifth grade, so our class had three years of this. Under his stimulation we read *Treasure Island* and a number of the Henty books. Now and then Professor Counts would drop by to read a page or so, or listen to one of us——or he would ask questions. Looking back, I cannot be sure that all of us enjoyed the reading.

But there were enough of us who did to create excitement... The Henty books gave me my first interest in foreign history and I shall always remember them, and Professor Counts, with gratitude...three years later...we were pointed out as an exceptional class. Three or four of us were trying to write stories and poems."[4]

Of all McGill's schooling, he probably benefited most from his stay at McCallie School. The young farm boy was quite overwhelmed by the activities at that private institution for boys: "From the elementary school in Chattanooga I moved up to the McCallie Preparatory School where I managed to make the football squad, was accepted for the drama and literary clubs... I was like a bird dog puppy, running happily about scaring up coveys... I remember no frustrations in all the four pleasant years, save in Dr. James Park McCallie's math classes."[5]

McGill captained the 1916 football team at McCallie. Earlier that summer he trained "by doing a lot of hard work and some bicycle riding on Sundays to build up the legs. Two of us rode bicycles from Chattanooga to Atlanta. And back again."[6]

In addition to football, basketball, baseball, and track, McGill also took part in the Boy Scouts, speech and drama activities, began his writing career, continued his consumption of books, and enjoyed a liberal education.

Speech activities consisted of oratory, declamation, debate, and discussion. During his first year, McGill won a gold medal in oratory, "giving an original paper with the imposing title 'America's Position Untenable.' "[7] In 1917, his senior year, McGill won the "city declamation medal," causing the *McCallie Pennant* to name him "champion orator of the city."[8] The *Pennant* also reported that senior McGill "has won several oratorical medals," the Oratorical Medal in 1914-15, the Inter-Prep Oratorical Cup in 1915-16.[9] The *McCallie Alumni Journal* in 1947 summarized McGill's accomplishments: "Thirty years ago in the spring of 1917 he graduated from McCallie after a record which presaged his present ability both as a speaker and writer. He won the orator's medal in both 1915 and 1917 and in between the two years he won the inter-prep orator's cup in 1916." [10]

Active in the Interscholastic Discussion League, McGill represented McCallie in a discussion of "The Manufactories of Tennessee." Members of the League performed at Baylor School,

Chattanooga High School, Central High School, and the Girl's Preparatory School.[12] What was the nature of these discussions? W.G. Davies, who, in 1917 was the editor of literary societies for the *Pennant*, wrote that McGill "represented McCallie in discussion groups held jointly with other high schools in Chattanooga on assigned subjects."[13] Dr. J.P. McCallie, President of the Board of Trustees and Co-founder of McCallie in 1905, insisted that "the Discussion League was not winning a medal or a decision of 'Winner' but for investigation and intelligent presentation of current topics of interest."[14]

M.W. McGill, a first cousin of Ralph's and a classmate at McCallie remembered that Ralph "was rather active in the debating society."[15] "When I was a kid at McCallie School," wrote McGill, "I was trying to...make the debating and declamation teams."[16] He deliberated while a member of the Daniel Webster Literary Society, an organization of which he was vice-president in 1914 and secretary in 1915. The *McCallie Pennant* described the nature of the literary societies, but it should be remembered that McGill did not enter McCallie until he was fifteen; consequently, he would not have benefited from the Uncle Remus or James Fenimore Cooper groups:

The literary society work is the one activity of the school in which all of us...take part. When we first come to McCallie, we are assigned to one of the smaller societies, either the Uncle Remus or the James Fenimore Cooper Society. Under faculty supervision we're coached and encouraged to make efforts to debate in public, to declaim and to read aloud in an interesting manner, so that, after we are promoted to the larger societies and have had a few years experience, we are prepared to try our literary abilities among ourselves and before the public with other schools.

The importance of the literary society work may readily be seen from the fact that the men who represent McCallie in inter-scholastic debates and oratorical contests have had from three to five years preparatory experience in the literary societies. These men are usually taken from the Daniel Webster and the Len White societies, the societies which are made up of the boys in the High School classes from fourteen years up.

The men who were picked to represent the best literary talent of the school this year were elected to the Inter-Preparatory School Senate of Chattanooga. They were Messrs. Ralph McGill, Eugene Tatum...from the Webster Literary Society...[17]

McGill also "memorized a dozen or so poems, mostly Kipling's, for reciting at the weekly sessions of the Daniel Webster literary club."[18] "In our school plays and literary club discussions," he continued, "we enlisted the cooperation of the young ladies from the downtown girls preparatory school."[19]

The shy young farm boy learned to love the stage. Active in the Dramatic Club for three years, he was selected "Best Actor" in 1916, playing the role of Jones in "What Happened to Jones."[20] In 1915 he was Casey Jones, a college politician, in "Aaron Boggs, Freshman." McGill wrote: "I saw every play I could and there was then a good road season even in cities as small as Chattanooga. I saw some of the celebrated actors; John Drew, David Warfield and Robert Mantell are the three I remember best."[21] Earlier McGill recalled other performers: "From the peanut gallery I saw Cyril Maude in 'Groumpy,' Otis Skinner in 'Mister Antonio,' and John Drew in 'Major Pendennis.' Drew, I think, was the most polished actor I ever saw. Robert Mantell in 'The Merchant of Venice' remains with me yet as a deeply moving performance."[22]

McGill considered the "annual school play" to be "a profitable educational course. A young Chattanoogan, Robert Straus," he continued, "had had a few small comedy roles on Broadway, but he was not a great success, and for three springs he coached our drama club. In my last two years he gave me the lead role. The senior year it was in "What Happened to Jones," and we took it on the road to two small nearby Tennessee towns. The role required me to kiss one of the young ladies. (See picture.) We were, in our town at least, an unsophisticated generation, and for me, with my preposterous shyness, the awkward kiss at each performance was agony."[23] McGill recalled playing in " 'Brown of Harvard,' 'A College Town,' and so on... I was a shy and self-conscious boy, and in the plays when I had to kiss a girl I nearly died. It had to be really done the night of the real play."[24]

McGill devoted considerable time to writing, both in English class and for the *McCallie Pennant*. Lewis Berkeley Cox, McGill's English

"What Happened to Jones" was quite an experience to a teen-ager of long, long ago. I remember Ralph vividly, and how chagrined I was that I could never seem to know him better. He was very personable, so good-looking and intelligent, but wasn't a bit interested in girls. It didn't occur to me that he could have been shy.

Margaret H. Dowd
April 7, 1969

teacher in 1914, reported that "according to my recollection, Ralph wrote exceptionally well then for a boy of his age. Especially if the class were given an opportunity to write on a subject of each student's own choosing, Ralph would almost invariably come up with the most interesting story of any boy in the class. His grades, as I recall the situation, were hurt by weakness in spelling and punctuation, but his ability to express himself vividly was outstanding."[26] In Cox's English class, McGill's grades were seventy-eight, first term, and seventy-seven, second term.[26] W.G. Davies, McGill's classmate at McCallie, agreed that McGill would invent an interesting story. Davies wrote that "In Caesar class, second year Latin, I remember he fixed up a dummy of the front page of a newspaper, written in latin——headlines and all."[27]

In 1916 McGill was made local editor of the *McCallie Pennant* and, in 1917, he was "humorous editor" of that publication. At the age of sixteen, McGill wrote the first of at least two short stories for the *Pennant*. Writing about "Old Peter," the most unpopular professor in school who finally gave his life to rescue a student, McGill revealed two traits which were to remain part of his newspaper columns and speeches. First, "Old Peter" revealed emotional concern for people and, second, the story demonstrated McGill's interest in working with words:

Old Peter

"Old Peter will be the boot-black,
When it comes, when it comes"—

The almost sacrilegious wording of the old campmeeting song, "The ship of Zion" came floating over the campus. To the demand of, "Who will be the leaders when she comes?" the students had placed the name of the most popular professor as captain, but when they had reached the rank of "boot-black," Peter McIntyre, the most unpopular professor in school, had been placed there. McIntyre, "Old Peter" stood in the window of his darkened room and listened to the song. He knew to whom the boys were referring. How could they know that he longed to enter into their life? They saw only the stern gray-haired man, relentless in his adherance to the laws of the school. He could have had the song stopped but instead he only turned sadly away from the window. The boys did not understand!

In another part of the building, a boy––a school leader––was silently packing for a week's vacation, by order of the faculty. Several times before he with other friends had slipped away after lights were out and had visited the village. He had been warned and the night before he had been seen by "Old Peter" as he went into his room. It was an accident that he had been caught: McIntyre happened to be looking out of his door and saw, down the dimly lighted corridor, Johnson entering his room. The boys, however, thought he had waited up, just for that purpose.

Singly, by two's, and in groups Johnson's friends came in to express their sympathy and most of them added to their statements that "they thought Old Peter had played him a dirty trick." And Johnson hearing this gradually began to believe it to be true. He forgot all past offences, and thought only of the last. "Seems as though he might have let it pass this time," he muttered.

The next morning as he left college he met McIntyre. The professor stepped up and held out his hand. "I'm sorry, Johnson," he said, and Johnson took his hand and muttered something and then passed on. Sorry he thought to himself, not so'as you'd notice it.

At the end of the week Johnson came back. The school rejoiced, for wasn't the boy upon whose shoulders rested the burden of pitching his school out of the hole, back?

The regular routine went on. The team––undefeated so far––was developing. But of late the coach presented a worried face. Johnson was the cause. He wasn't sick; only too finely trained––he couldn't sleep well.

It was the day before the big game. That night while the college slumbered, fire broke out in Scott's hall. Hundreds of the students stood on the campus powerless. When the fire reached the laboratory it spread more quickly. Suddenly it was reported that Johnson was absent. The cry went up, "Where's Johnson? Where's Johnson?" McIntyre started. He was the only man there who knew that the boy was sleeping from the effects of some powders given by order of the coach!

Some one dashed toward the building. As he neared the steps the fire flashed up brightly, and by its light the boys saw McIntyre––"Old Peter," saw him so plainly that they could distinguish [sic] the gray fringe around the edge of his hair. He disappeared in the building. The students stood tense with expectancy.

McIntyre dashed on up flight after flight of steps. At last he reached the pitcher's room. The boy lay unconscious on the bed. McIntyre picked him up and started to the window in order to reach the fire escape. He thought he would smother but at last reached the window. He covered the boy's face and started down with the body across his shoulder. The hot iron burned his hands and his head was whirling. To the students he seemed to barely move. At last he reached the bottom and was relieved of his burden. "Here's your pitcher, young men," he said, and then fell unconscious into the arms of a student.

Those were his last words, for in that great rescue he had inhaled flame and gasses and at dawn, despite the efforts of the physician, his soul took flight.

The next day his body lay in state in the chapel. When the boys filed through, Johnson was with them. His face had been covered, and with his hardier constitution he had soon revived.

As he paused by the body of his rescuer his shoulders shook with uncontrolled sobs. "Fellows," he said brokenly, "I guess 'Old Peter' will be the captain when she comes." And almost involuntarily they sang:

> " 'Old Peter will be the captain,
> When it comes, when it comes,"——

and the words as they floated softly out the windows sounded almost sacred, as the fellows paid tribute to "Old Peter."

—Ralph McGill[28]

At McCallie McGill continued to read widely and with enthusiasm. "In elementary and secondary school years," he wrote, "I frequently rode the two miles from our suburb to the Chattanooga Carnegie Library for books..."[29] "In my first autumn at McCallie," he continued, "Woodrow Wilson became my hero. I read all of his writings I could find...I...had discovered the Waverly novels. Somehow I never had any direction in my reading. I read hungrily, with darts here and dashes there. It was an odd mixture, Opie Reed, Lafacadio Hearn, Whitman, Shakespeare, Frank Norris, Ralph Henry

Barbour, Owen Johnson, Robert W. Service, and of course, Emerson's essays and poems. The novel which made the greatest impression on me in those days was Norris's *McTeague*."[30]

As for teachers who influenced him most at McCallie, McGill named "...chiefly Spencer McCallie, in history, and Clarence Rothwell Wilcox in English."[31] In describing Spencer McCallie's classroom technique, McGill concluded that "he was one of those rare men with a genius for teaching. He could stir the imagination of his students. I still remember how he looked in class and the things he said about the Romans, the Greeks, the Spartans, the Phoenicians, Persians and others out of the dusty past... In teaching Bible history he was equally as good. He taught them as men, and as seen by their contemporaries. Professor, as we called him, was a rare man."[32]

It was Clarence Wilcox, said McGill, who assisted with "...the athletics,...the dramatic club, the school paper" and the "debating and declamation teams... He taught me football, baseball, track and elocution with at least moderate success, but he was a miserable failure as a teacher of algebra and geometry."[33] On one occasion McGill wrote, "I never had an English teacher in prep school who gave either inspiration or direction. The result was, and is, that my reading has large gaps in it."[34]

This writer asked McGill to describe Wilcox's method of teaching public speaking. He answered: "I don't know that he had any special techniques, except to put us up there, and have us declaim or recite something you yourself had prepared... Dr. Wilcox would always have a critic, one of the faculty as a critic, and he would criticize your enunciation or perhaps...an error in pronouncing a word, or an error in grammar. The critic at the end of your talk or declamation would then get up and give this orally so that the whole group could get the benefit of the criticism."[35] W.G. Davies added that Wilcox "encouraged both original orations and memorizing of great" speeches. He recalled particularly Wilcox's interest in "the dramatic reading of Dan McGrew."[36]

While at McCallie School McGill recalled that he had done poorly in "Dr. James Park McCallie's math classes" and in algebra and geometry.[37] Official transcripts show that McGill did best in English and French, and poorly in solid geometry, German, and trigonometry. (These records also reveal that McGill studied the following subjects: In 1913-14, algebra, English, ancient history, beginning Latin, spelling; in 1914-15, algebra, Caesar (second year Latin), English, German, spelling; in 1915-16, English, French, plane geometry, German, spelling; in 1916-17, solid geometry, trigonometry, American literature, second year French, physics, and botany.)

After McCallie School, McGill's formal education continued at Vanderbilt University in 1917. "When I went off to college," he recalled, "I had twenty-five dollars in cash and a job waiting on tables to enable me to eat. I had a laundry route and did a few other jobs to get through those first two years."[38] McGill also remembered "...a thin, shy, worried youngster who got off a day coach [in Nashville] one autumn morning... Before that year was done I was to patch my own pants, to suffer terribly from self-consciousness, but from the moment I got there life seemed to expand for me, the horizons lifted, and living became an adventure and fun."[39]

McGill maintained that "hero worship for an older cousin who had graduated from Vanderbilt Medical School had persuaded him to register in the pre-medical department. No one counseled me."[40] Earlier McGill wrote: "I wanted to be a doctor...and would have been could I have found the money."[41] After one year at Vanderbilt, he joined the U.S. Marine Corps, returning to the College of Arts and Science in 1919. He discussed this period of his life: "I grew up lucky. Despite the fact I was a wide-eyed kid right from behind the plow handles, I came to know in Southern cities Italian families who took me to their homes above their restaurants and taught me to like real spaghetti, raviolis, food cooked in olive oil and garlic-flavored——and to listen to Caruso records, and the family sitting there, tears running down their faces as they listened. By the time I was seventeen I had friends who were German, Jewish, Italian and Greek. I knew the sour Greek soups and the resin-flavored retsina. When I went off to the Marine Corps almost thirty years ago...I left my fraternity pin with a Jewish girl. It just never occurred to me to dislike someone because of his race or religion. So, I think I was lucky. A lot of silly things got into my head when I was a kid, but dislike for people wasn't one of them."[42]

When fall arrived, McGill "had been out of the Marine Corps for five months. That spring" he took his "discharge and caught the "train from Quantico, Virginia, with high hopes."[43] McGill then enrolled in law school where he "sat at the feet of Judge Ed. Seay, an

34

erudite, somewhat eccentric man whose subjects were wills and real property."[44] "As an unreconverted ex-Marine in 1919," he wrote, "the law bored me. At the time I considered myself to be one of the lost generation, discovering Mencken, Sandburg, and all the new poets and novelists of the time... Anyhow, I did not gain ten yards on torts, and failed of a first down on contracts."[45]

This maturing farm boy became increasingly independent. For example, the student newspaper reported that in the spring of 1920 "there was a demonstration at a Vanderbilt track meet in which Tom Sims, Ralph McGill, and other students appeared in overalls as a protest against clothing prices."[46] Once, McGill let his "enthusiasm for Shaw lead" him "into an experiment with vegetarianism. For a month," he recalled, "I ate only vegetables and cheese with milk and water as my only beverage. This lasted, I think, one whole summer, in which I suffered often from that disease known politely as 'summer complaint'... From that time on I have eschewed vegeterianism as I would communism or Fascism. But I...have never left Shaw the writer."[47]

At Vanderbilt, McGill continued to participate successfully in sports. For example, when McGill was a freshman a reporter wrote, "McGill will start at guard today despite his handicap of weighing only one hundred fifty-two pounds."[48] He "was one of those footbare guards in the days when pulling the guards out in interference was assumed to be hot stuff."[49]

Oral work at Vanderbilt was closely connected with McGill's literary interests. Public speaking was limited to a few talks as a representative for the Sigma Chi social fraternity.[50] Critic Allen Tate, classmate of McGill's at Vanderbilt, recalled that McGill "had a very pleasant personality," but did not "remember him giving a public speech." "I believe I thought then——and his career confirms it——that he would become a powerful journalist rather than a 'creative writer.'"[51] Two experiences stimulated McGill's interest in declaiming poetry: Professor Edwin Mims' freshman English class and a literary group called The Fugitives. In freshman English, McGill wrote that "we memorized and we read aloud. Professor Mims enjoyed reading to the class. As he read his eyes moved back and forth, like a man watching a tennis match on a miniature court, seeking to find a nonattentive face... It was, all in all, a good class for stimulating one to read poetry and to memorize it. The very first day's assignment was to learn the part of Tennyson's 'Ulysses,' beginning, 'Come my friends, 'tis not too late to see a newer world.' I can say them yet. But we heard almost nothing of contemporary poetry... He wrestled mightily with young minds of the small towns of Tennessee and adjoining states, seeking to make them 'see' and 'feel.' "[52]

Professor Mims, continued McGill, "...hammered Tennyson, Milton, Keats and Shelley into us by demanding that we memorize great chunks of lines from Idylls of the King. And I could reel off Il Penseroso and L'Allegro without hesitation. Dr. Mims was a demanding man. He would, when he did not see a look of awareness on the faces before him, call them out by name, ask them to stand, and denounce them as having the emotional reactions of an oyster. 'Don't you see that?' he'd shout. 'Can't you feel that?' "[53]

In his freshman year, McGill won a prize given by Mims to the student who "memorized the most lines of poetry." These exercises helped develop what Newsweek called McGill's "prodigious memory."[54] When asked, for example, if his memory had been especially helpful in speaking, McGill replied: "Yes, it has been very helpful... I can think of four or five times when I would be talking and it would seem to me that a line or so from a poem might be helpful, and I just pull that out of my memory——it wouldn't even be in the manuscript at all——and throw it in."[55]

McGill's interest in literature and declaiming was also stimulated by his association with The Fugitives, persons who rebelled against Mims' reluctance to discuss contemporary poetry. Although McGill was never a member of that group, he was a close friend of several of its members. "Many a night," he stated, "I have argued...over one of Shaw's prefaces"[56] "...and read poetry until dawn."[57] "Looking back from the sixties to the twenties," he wrote, "the Fugitives are seen as the best symbol of the South's campus response to the many motivations of rebellion, of flight from the tyranny of the Southern Brahmin. Poems were written in class, pages from proposed new novels were read along the paths between classes. They were fine sunlit days... Vanderbilt had no course in writing novels, poems or plays. For me, the nights with Merrill Moore and Stanley Johnson provided the most stimulation to read and think."[58]

It was not until he "was a sophomore" that McGill "discovered contemporary poetry."[59] Stanley Johnson, a young English professor, provided shelter and motivation: "Edwin Arlington Robinson," related McGill, "was introduced to me years ago in the flat of an English teacher at Vanderbilt University. We used to gather there at night and read poetry aloud. On this night the teacher read 'Mr. Flood's Party.'... I met, too, 'Richard Cory' and 'Miniver Cheevy' and 'Reuben Bright'——and all the rest of Robinson's poems."[60]

McGill "recited or read aloud at the slightest excuse."[61] In 1946, more than twenty years after Vanderbilt, McGill received a long-distance call from an old colleague, asking where a certain poem could be found. "If anyone," said the caller, "could tell us where to find this poem you could." The phone call caused McGill to reminisce: "Time was when I would recite at the drop of a hat and, as they say, find the hat to drop. I once knew thirty-seven of Kipling's poems and about that many of Mr. Service's ballads...at the end of my freshman year I knew two thousand lines of Tennyson... I got to be a sort of poetic Sinatra of my time and generation, able to recite as long as the party or the night lasted. I never made them swoon, but still that call was a pretty good tribute... After more than a quarter of a century there was someone at that party in Chattanooga who was in school with me and remembered hearing me recite 'Cynara.' "[62]

McGill's love for drama caused him to go off Vanderbilt's campus in search of the theater. "After the First World War," wrote McGill, "when I was at Vanderbilt University and working part-time on the *Nashville Banner*, [Fritz] Leiber's troupe came often to Nashville. [Bobby] Straus was playing the lead comedy roles. I carried spears, was a messenger in *Macbeth*, and in *Hamlet* once filled in as the second gravedigger. I was wild to be taken on. Straus arranged a talk with Leiber. 'First, let me tell you,' he said, 'that you do not have the voice for it. You can never play the really big parts.' We looked each other in the eye for a moment, and then I thanked him, and went out blinking back tears. It had been a great dream."[63]

McGill pictured his role in *Macbeth* and explained in more detail why his voice was unsuited for the stage: "I reached my peak as a great [tongue-in-cheek] dramatist when I was chosen by Fritz Leiber for a stage part in the tragedy *Macbeth*. At the moment when Macbeth stands defiant, confident that he shall not suffer defeat until Birnam wood moves against him, a messenger comes to warn him the English troops are near, and Macbeth shouts: 'The devil damn thee, thou cream-faced loon. Where gottest thou that goose look?' I was the messenger, and the fact that friends in the gallery tittered at that 'cream-faced loon' line did not dispel the magic of it. Later I came back again to bring word that Birnam wood was on the move. The critics, careless fellows, overlooked my art, being provincials... Leiber was my beau-ideal. He would have taken me with his troupe, but he talked to me plainly, telling me that my husky voice would never do for real dramatics. So I went back to my reporting beat, sighing over a lost dream."[64]

Because McGill changed from medicine to law and then to a more general course of study, he was exposed to a variety of subjects. The Registrar at Vanderbilt wrote that "Mr. McGill entered the...College of Arts and Science in September, 1917." After his tour in the Marine Corps, McGill "returned to the College of Arts and Science for the 1919-20 academic year. In those years," the Registrar continued, "only two years of liberal arts work were required for entrance into Law School. He was enrolled in the first year class of the Vanderbilt Law School" in 1920-21.[65] Requirements for first-year law students consisted of contracts, torts, bailments and carriers and public callings, agency, criminal law, common law pleading and practice, and personal property.

He refused to take one course "because the man holding the chair of economics had been personally endowed by a retired manu-facturer and was a paid speaker seemingly at the beck and call of certain groups." Consequently, admitted McGill, he "deprived" himself "of the fundamentals of economics."[66] Besides Mims' English course, McGill also took biology, political science, chemistry, an advanced English course in Chaucer and Shakespeare,[67] and German.[68] McGill lasted at Vanderbilt until shortly before grad-uation, so he must have fulfilled many of the courses required for the B.A. degree: Latin, Greek, Mathematics, English, Chemistry, History, Philosophy, three hours in a science: chemistry, or Physics, or Biology, or Geology.[69]

"It was Dan McGugin," stated McGill "who taught me most in those days. He was the coach and he was also a great reader of books, student of people and their ways, and expert in American history, and a profound admirer of the ancient Greeks and their ways... He was a wonderful man, kind, gentle, and understanding."[70] The

38

editor of the *Vanderbilt Alumnus* asked McGill to "reminisce about teachers who stimulated" him at that university. He responded: "From Dr. Mims I got an accelerated interest in poetry and in memorizing it. From Doctors [George Pullen] Jackson and [George] Mayfield I received an impetus to learn about Germany and France, their literature and art. And from Reinke I learned to know and recognize the keen blade of truth and its place in life... [He] gave me what mental discipline I possessed when I left there... He taught me the value of doubt——and to ask 'How do you know that's true?'...my idea of a teacher is one who sparks the interests and imagination...causes a man to try and keep on learning all his life. That's what Reinke, Mims, Mayfield, and Jackson did for me. They were never just classroom teachers."[71]

Increasingly at Vanderbilt, McGill's "energies, after bitter frustration with verse, turned to the weekly student newspaper, the *Hustler*. A column idea," McGill recalled, "was submitted and accepted. It ran column one on page one and quickly involved me in discussion and controversy. Some of the latter led to blows, but it was fun. There was an excitement in getting the four pages ready for the paper. We made an all-night job of it, talking and arguing on a variety of unrelated subjects."[72]

McGill's writings plus his growing independence helped get him expelled from Vanderbilt a few months before graduation. He wrote:

Now and then I sit back and reflect that I started in this business as a writer of humor in a college newspaper and was one of the founders of Vanderbilt University's first humor magazines. In fact, Mr. Tom Sims (whose name you see on the cartoon strip "Popeye") and I once got out two consecutive issues of the magazine without any help, writing all the alleged jokes, articles and comment. I continued on my merry way, with quip and jest, defying loathed melancholy, until one bright spring day when the University officials took a very funeral view of some humor by Mr. Sims, another gentleman, now a distinguished Texas physician, and by me. I later was told that even the Chancellor laughed in private until tears ran down the furrows of his sorrowful face. But when he talked to me there was no suggestion of a smile at the corners of his mouth. My cause was done no good by the fact that in the college paper of that week I had turned to serious subjects in a ringing editorial accusing the university administration of embezzlement. I still think I was technically right, in that the provision of a will had been ignored [McGill argued that certain funds were supposed to have been used in constructing a student lounge]. All of this, however, had the same effect upon the bloom of my university career as does the visit of a family of very hungry boll weevils to the lovely green boll of the cotton plant. I turned thereafter to serious subjects, like making a living, and left the quest of laughter to others whose buoyant spirit had not been crushed by a university chancellor with a voice like a shovel scraping on wet concrete.[73]

George Barker, writing in the *Nashville Tennessean Magazine*, related McGill's account of one other extra-curricular activity: " 'I got hold of a bunch of prom invitations that were about to be mailed by the Beta Theta Pi,' McGill recalls. 'Now, in those days the Betas were a bunch of stuffed shirts. I was a Sigma Chi. There was only one thing to do...' McGill sent the invitations to individuals who definitely didn't figure in Nashville's social order of things. It got kind of sticky for Ralph after that. To make a long story short, the university gave him the gate in April of 1921, a couple of months before he was to have graduated."[74]

"I don't know really what happened to me at Vanderbilt," McGill concluded.

It was a great experience and a thrilling one, and I recall feeling most of the time a high peak of excitement and inspiration. I was trying to write. I did very well in Dr. Edwin Mims' English courses. I even had a favorable comment on two or three poems, but I never got anywhere with poetry. I knew and was closely associated with about two thirds of the Fugitives, but since I was not a poet, I was not a member of the group. None the less, I was very closely and intimately associated with Merrill Moore and Stanley Johnson...

We used to get together a great deal and listen to music, but mostly read poems and plays aloud. Stanley's wife, who was assistant librarian at Vanderbilt, and another friend or two would join us in taking parts, and we frequently would get together and read a play. Howard Odom and Paul Green at the University of North Carolina were then writing and we began to talk about their material...

I was out of school in the year 1918-19 and did not get back until the fall of 1919... I borrowed enough to pay the academic tuition and had a few jobs, but I was not too interested in anything except English. That year I got on the staff of the student weekly, "The Vanderbilt Hustler." I was also elected to the sophomore literary fraternity. I was a part of a group in this fraternity which founded a Vanderbilt humor literary magazine called "The Jade." The society's emblem was green jade scarab...

In order to work in the mornings, I entered law school because the classes didn't begin until one o'clock. I wasn't cut out for law either. Toward the end of the term I attended only one class with regularity. That was because I liked the personality of the teacher. He was a prominent lawyer in Nashville...

I really don't remember too much about the courses and guess the least said about them, the better... I read prodigiously... I roomed next door to Robert Penn Warren for a while. He was working while we talked. Most of the training I got was, I suppose, inside the classroom.[75]

Interest in newspaper work led McGill to a part time job and, eventually, to a career. "Two of the fraternity chapter alumni worked on the Nashville *Banner*," he wrote. "One day...I filled in... This was my first newspaper job, and it was agreed it would be a regular one... That summer I was also a part-time police reporter, and held minor assignments. The pay was seventeen dollars per week. I can still recall the intense excitement and the pleasure of those days. I knew then I had found what I wanted to do."[76]

NOTES

THREE

1 Ralph McGill, *The South and the Southerner*, p. 43.
2 *Atlanta Constitution*, March 6, 1950, p. 8.
3 *Atlanta Constitution*, April 18, 1947, p. 12.
4 *South and the Southerner*, pp. 43-44.
5 *South and the Southerner*, p. 54.
6 *Atlanta Constitution*, August 6, 1947, p. 6.
7 *South and the Southerner*, p. 55.
8 *The McCallie Pennant*, 1917, p. 13.
9 *The McCallie Pennant*, 1917, p. 13.
10 *The McCallie Alumni Journal*, July, 1947, p. 14.
11 *The McCallie Pennant*, 1915, p. 45.
12 *The McCallie Pennant*, 1916, p. 45.
13 Letter to this writer from W.G. Davies, November 21, 1965, Chattanooga, Tennessee.
14 Letter to this writer from J.P. McCallie, January 15, 1966, Chattanooga.
15 Letter to this writer from M.W. McGill, Bursar and Assistant Treasurer, Davidson College, November 16, 1965, North Carolina.
16 *Atlanta Constitution*, July 18, 1949, p. 12.
17 *The McCallie Pennant*, 1917, p. 72.
18 *South and the Southerner*, p. 55.
19 *South and the Southerner*, p. 54.
20 *The McCallie Pennant*, 1916, p. 35.
21 *South and the Southerner*, p. 57.
22 *Atlanta Constitution*, June 30, 1951, p. 1.
23 *South and the Southerner*, pp. 56-57.
24 *Atlanta Constitution*, November 8, 1949, p. 10.
25 Letter to this writer from Lewis Berkeley Cox, April 28, 1966, Avon, Connecticut.
26 Official transcript, McCallie School.
27 Letter from W.G. Davies, November 21, 1965, Chattanooga.
28 *The McCallie Pennant*, 1914, p. 29.
29 *South and the Southerner*, p. 63.
30 *South and the Southerner*, pp. 55-56.
31 *Atlanta Constitution*, April 20, 1949, p. 12.

32 *Atlanta Constitution*, October 22, 1949, p. 4.

33 *Atlanta Constitution*, July 18, 1949, p. 10.

34 *South and the Southerner*, p. 56.

35 Taped interview with McGill, December 29, 1965, Atlanta.

36 Letter from W.G. Davies, November 21, 1965.

37 *South and the Southerner*, p. 54.

38 *Atlanta Constitution*, July 7, 1946, p. 10.

39 *Atlanta Constitution*, April 14, 1950, p. 22.

40 *South and the Southerner*, pp. 70-71.

41 *Vanderbilt Alumnus*, March, 1952, p. 12.

42 *Atlanta Constitution*, January 27, 1947, p. 8.

43 *Atlanta Constitution*, December 19, 1961, p. 1.

44 *Atlanta Constitution*, December 19, 1961, p. 1.

45 *Atlanta Constitution*, December 23, 1946, p. 8.

46 *Atlanta Constitution*, August 23, 1948, p. 8.

47 *Atlanta Constitution*, August 15, 1946, p. 10.

48 *Atlanta Constitution*, October 15, 1950, p. 1.

49 *Atlanta Constitution*, September 25, 1947, p. 12.

50 Taped interview with McGill, December 29, 1965.

51 Letter from Allen Tate, July 12, 1966, University of Minnesota, Minneapolis.

52 *South and the Southerner*, pp. 71-72.

53 *Atlanta Constitution*, December 20, 1960, p. 1.

54 *Newsweek*, LIII (April 13, 1959), 102.

55 Taped interview with McGill, December 29, 1965.

56 *Atlanta Constitution*, August 15, 1946, p. 10.

57 *South and the Southerner*, p. 74.

58 *South and the Southerner*, pp. 85-86.

59 *Atlanta Constitution*, December 20, 1960, p. 1.

60 *Atlanta Constitution*, February 14, 1952, p. 1.

61 *Atlanta Constitution*, December 20, 1960, p. 1.

62 *Atlanta Constitution*, September 6, 1946, p. 12.

63 *South and the Southerner*, p. 57.

64 *Atlanta Constitution*, August 6, 1947, p. 6.

65 Letter to this writer from William O. Batts, Jr., October 7, 1965, Nashville.

66 *Atlanta Constitution*, October 2, 1946, p. 6.

67 Letter to this writer from Ralph McGill, November 29, 1966, Atlanta.

68 *Vanderbilt Alumnus*, March, 1952, pp. 8 & 12.

69 Letter to this writer from Mrs. Janice Sowell, secretary, Registrar's office, Vanderbilt University, August 8, 1966; plus photographic copies of graduation requirements from official publications.

70 *Atlanta Constitution*, April 14, 1950, p. 22.

71 *Vanderbilt Alumnus*, March, 1952, pp. 8 & 12.

72 *South and the Southerner*, p. 76.

73 *Atlanta Constitution*, April 25, 1948, p. 8B.

74 *Nashville Tennessean Magazine*, November 5, 1961, pp. 10 & 20.

75 Letter to this writer from Ralph McGill, November 29, 1966, Atlanta.

76 *South and the Southerner*, p. 76.

FOUR

BECOMING A JOURNALIST

McGill began his newspaper career with the *Nashville Banner* "as a glorified copy boy whose chief chore was to take the play-by-play detail of the baseball game over the telephone."[1] McGill's "first newspaper interview as a young and wide-eyed reporter," he wrote, "was a gentleman who had attempted suicide with a shot gun and failed, by the narrowest of margins; my second was with Will Rogers, the cowboy humorist, and my third with Rebecca West, the British novelist."[2] He met Mrs. Carrie Chapman Catt when he was doing "chores on politics about the Tennessee State House. It was," McGill continued, "when Tennessee's Legislature put women's votes on the legislative calendar that Mrs. Catt and others came down to lobby. She was a fine, able woman, and because she was able and not afraid of little, mean minds and their gossip, she was the subject of many jokes... I was in the legislative hall when Tennessee gave women the right to vote by becoming the key state to ratify the nineteenth amendment... Today there is not a politician anywhere who is not fearful of the women's votes."[3]

Writing about Edna St. Vincent Millay, McGill stated that he, too, "was a poet not long out of college and I was her servant. Had she

45

asked for the Golden Fleece I would have sought it... She was there to give a reading of her poems and that afternoon in the hotel suite she recited some which were never on a program... One I asked her to write down and sign for me, which she did... I have never seen it anywhere else. Without Millay saying it, with gestures, it lacks something. I recall it inexactly, but it went something like this:

'See that man standing there,
The one close there by the stair?
No, not him. The one in blue serge pants.
Well, he was born in Paris France.' "[4]

The rebel whom Vanderbilt could not tame found reporting in Nashville more to his liking. There were whiskey, fights, adventure, discussions, and an exciting time in general. McGill, who in no way could be grouped with the fearful, wrote that "all but the more timorous reporters kept loaded pistols in their scarred old desks, along with a bottle of bourbon whiskey."[5] More than twenty years after Nashville, McGill reminisced: "I see by the papers where the Columbians' strong-arm boys have confessed they had been instructed to waylay me and give me a fatal slugging... In my time I have been threatened with shooting, with having my place blown up, and with being slugged and beaten by hired thugs, but, somehow, I never really believed it... So, I never carry anything of a defensive nature save my good right arm, which isn't as good as it used to be... When I was around twenty-three years old, reporting politics in Tennessee, things were different."[6]

All this time McGill continued "developing the vice of reading anything and everything."[7] "On the *Banner*," he recalled, "four of us found an evening or so each week on which to read plays out loud, with the parts assigned. We discovered Eugene O'Neill. We read Russian plays, all of Ibsen's... The new novels were devoured and discussed. I can yet remember the impact of *Jurgen Main Street* and *Babbitt*...we were stirred by the new ideas, the new poets and novelists."[8]

McGill's bosses on the *Banner* were blunt, yet effective teachers. For example, McGill recalled his "first time at a typewriter in the news room... The city editor called me to the desk and told me to get the story on a run-away horse and wagon which but a few minutes before had terrorized Church Street... Along the way were basked in cars, mostly Model T Fords. I wrote it as the rebellion of the horse against the machine age——a desperate decision to attack and take the consequences. I wrote this because I had been reading Sherwood Anderson. It was an imitation, I hoped, of his style. The city editor looked at me curiously. 'College stuff, eh?' he said. And went to work with his pencil."[9]

The managing editor, described McGill, "was a gaunt, tall and cadaverlike man. Legend has it he did not take his corn pipe out of his mouth when he went to bed. His name was Marmaduke B. Morton. He had been schooled by Henry Watterson on the old Louisville Courier Journal. He was a hard and unyielding man, but a good teacher. 'As in religion, so it is in newspaper writing,' he would say. 'There are just two great commandments. The first one is that a man writing should put the fodder down where the stock can reach it. And the second is, don't lie to yourself.' The first commandment calling for simplicity of expression isn't always easy. The second is the most difficult of all, because there are times when the easiest way out is to lie to one's self and pass on the lie to those who read."[10]

Major Edward Bushrod Stahlman groomed McGill for political reporting. Persons reading McGill's column and his speeches will recognize Stahlman's influence in the way McGill involved himself personally with his subjects. When Stahlman died in 1930, he "had been owner and publisher of the *Banner* since 1885. In all those years," maintained McGill, "the paper mirrored not so much the news as it did his personality and convictions... It was his custom to pick a young reporter from the staff and make a political writer of him as a backstop for the veteran who ordinarily covered the state house... I had been so selected... We reporters all loved the Major because he was such a reckless and courageous fighter."[11]

"There is something of the Major in me," confessed McGill. "I do not hold with his extreme, almost compulsive partisanship. But I believe in being strongly partisan on issues which require a choice... Also, it seems important that newspapers should have, as the Major had, an acute sense of right and wrong... There comes a time in all controversies when one must hit the issue right on the nose... Sometimes it is better to spar for a while or back away for a good look. But finally the issue must be hit hard."[12]

"Although *The Banner* in 1923 made him acting sports editor, he continued to handle occasional political stories."[13] "He originated a popular, Will Rogerish column called 'I'm the Gink,' and branched into political writing with prodigious energy."[14] McGill wrote: "Chance had taken me from cubbing in politics to sports. I went with reluctance, but that ended when I saw Ki Ki Cuyler and Richbourg and LeBourvea run and hit."[15]

McGill's first love, however, continued to be politics. Tennessee politics taught him "that a polite political campaign was entirely ineffective. But the most valuable lesson I learned," said McGill, "was that if you get in mud——you will get muddy——and if you do get muddy it is a mistake to try to scrape it off. That only smears it. Let it dry and it will fall off, because it isn't real. It is just political mud.[16]

McGill recalled "lying behind a log once on a Tennessee hillside while bullets whined over" him "and through the woods... I had gone along with a sheriff's force to cover a great still raid. I was a young reporter then and too naive to know the reason for the raid was that city policemen were running this still and cutting in on an area supplied by stills the sheriff was interested in. We caught two city detectives. I learned fast."[17]

George Barker, after interviewing McGill for the *Nashville Tennessean Magazine*, discovered that he had been "a wild, energetic reporter in Nashville during all the Roaring Twenties. He was young and undefeated and wrote about everything he could find——sometimes murder in the morning and sports in the afternoon. 'It was a good time and a good place to be a young newspaperman,' he says. 'Nashville was loaded——bootlegging, gambling, vote rigging. Society was really high...' "[18]

In 1929 McGill moved to Georgia where he became assistant sports editor of *The Atlanta Constitution*. "It was April 2, 1929," recalled McGill. "At ten a.m., I walked into The Constitution feeling excitement and anticipation."[19] (On September 4, 1929, McGill married Mary Elizabeth Leonard.[20]) Later promoted to sports editor, McGill gained valuable experience by meeting all kinds of people and treating all kinds of subjects under the guise of sports. For example, in 1935, in his massive sports column, "Break of the Day," McGill wrote: "If I had all the wealth in the world I would arrange for at least four things: All the babies and children in the world would have all the milk they needed to drink; and nobody's sister would ever be in need; and every young boy would be taken to see that log hut on a Kentucky hillside in which Abraham Lincoln was born and every person in these United States——all the 120,000,000 of them, would be given a chance to look into the face of Franklin D. Roosevelt and see him smile and hear him speak."[21]

The sports page also became a training ground for language development, often holding religious themes. When in Pasadena, California on December 31, 1935, McGill previewed the Rose Bowl football game: "They are tenting tonight on the old camp ground and tomorrow afternoon they will have at it in the famous Rose Bowl of concrete, topped with blossoms, to determine whether Stanford or Alabama shall be the football champions of the season."[22] [Alabama won.]

In 1937, because of a series of articles on farm tenancy and share-cropping, this Sports Editor won a Rosenwald fellowship which proved to be a turning point in his career. "I was one of about forty of about eight hundred fifty seeking them," wrote McGill. "It was one of the finest things that ever happened to me, and the most valuable. I was considered because I had been writing some articles on the farm problems of the South and on the need for cooperative marketing for the small farmers. I received a fifteen hundred dollar fellowship. *The Constitution* granted me leave and also helped me. I had sold historical articles which brought in another fifteen hundred dollars. This enabled me to take my wife and go to Scandinavia where I diligently visited, lived with, and wrote about the farm marketing problems and methods of small farmers in countries with a population akin to that of Georgia. I also visited, and spent time in the rural schools and I have been gratified by the fact that our own rural school program is turning more and more toward the intelligent one they had——designed of, for and by rural people... I managed to travel on the continent, visit Great Britain and to have the great luck to catch on with the German movement into Austria."[23]

McGill returned to Atlanta in 1938 as associate editor of the *Constitution*. No longer expected to mention sports with at least some regularity, McGill discussed every imaginable topic: politics, religion, economics, military, raising bees, Eisenhower's speech improvement, ancient Greece, the press, education, Andrew Jackson, poker, the 4-H Club, television, foreign affairs, the Negro vote, and sports. *Newsweek* noted that "McGill displays an awesome reach as a columnist. With equal facility, he has discussed the adventures of an alcoholic bear, the misadventures of a prominent politican, and agricultural problems in the interior of India."[24]

To arm himself for his daily column, McGill continued to travel and study. As a vacationing sports editor in Cuba, McGill took time out to cover the Batista revolution.[25] McGill recalled how "on February 21, 1938, we watched the parade of Hitler and his hierarchy along streets guarded by the SS troops, to the Kroll opera house across from the burned out Reichstag. I heard him speak. It was the day he practically announced he would go into Austria. The next month I saw him in Austria and again heard him speak. The unbelievable decorations, the hysteria, the ferment, the secret meetings with people to whom I had letters..."[26]

McGill's "first Atlantic flight was in early 1943 when the sea lanes hid hostile submarines and war flamed on the continent of Europe and in the skies above it."[27] On May 12, 1954, in Manchester, England, McGill told about his "eleventh such crossing."[28] In 1938 and on several later occasions McGill saw Winston Churchill address the House of Commons:

I...heard him, like a prophet of old crying in the wilderness, warn against the course of appeasement pursued by the Chamberlain government. Again, during the war, I heard him in the House of Lords, where Commons met after their own historic chamber was bombed out. And a few days after the Queen returned in May 1954 from an arduous and important journey, he put the resolution of congratulations, loyalty and affection... About us in the gallery sat men from the African colonies... There were Indians too...and some Chinese, Burmese and others from Ceylon. There were Lords and Ladies present, and many commoners and alien visitors, for when it was known Churchill was to speak or answer questions, the galleries filled early.[29]

McGill became editor in 1942 and publisher in 1960. In 1945 McGill was one of three representatives sent by the American Society of Newspaper Editors on a forty thousand mile tour of world capitals to "examine conditions affecting freedom of the press."[30] McGill climbed Mount Fuji in Japan,[31] and interviewed King Farouk of Egypt "in his palace at Cairo."[32] On his way back to India in 1951,

50

McGill concluded that "If I had my choice, I'd rather have a look at India than any one country."[33] He observed the military government in postwar Germany, covered the Nuremberg trials, and witnessed the United Nations charter meeting in San Francisco, California. "Bethlehem was, to me, wonderful," thought McGill. "It was, one plainly may see, an old caravanserai into which the travelers of those days drive their animals and put down their bedding in the next stall. No one knows in which stall it was The Christ was born——although they have picked one——but it is THE place. You feel it and know it and even the guides seem less offensive there. You wanted to kneel down there and pray and you felt tears in your eyes and a very great humility."[34]

This Georgian also traveled throughout the United States. His newspaper column often began with such statements as, "In the past three weeks I have ridden by car or flown by plane over much of Georgia and the South."[35] To study the candidates and the issues, McGill accompanied such men as Franklin D. Roosevelt, Robert A. Taft, Adlai E. Stevenson, Dwight D. Eisenhower, John F. Kennedy, Lyndon B. Johnson, and Richard M. Nixon. Celestine Sibley summed it up when she wrote that "a combination of luck and all-encompassing curiosity has time and again landed McGill where the news was breaking."[36] "Character builds itself out of a man's experiences,"[37] added McGill. "Whatever traveling I have done, and whatever and all I have seen, have taught me just two things——humility and the awful truth of the uncertainity of things."[38] "Experience teaches one," he continued, "that at least a certain amount of integrity and courage, and some sort of spiritual quality, are good things for a man to have inside him... Travel and study and experience teach one, not to be too sure about the answers, and to know that humility is a comfortable garment which wears well and is becoming. If I have learned anything, it is never to be too sure about things. It is best, I think, always to be a seeker, and never to stop and say, 'This is all.' "[39]

After joining the *Constitution*, McGill accepted many assignments and responsibilities which added further to his wealth of knowledge and experience. A few of these are simply listed here: chairman of the local Selective Service Board in Georgia, 1940-44; War Labor Board's advisory committee for Georgia, 1942; Advisory Board of the Children's Bureau, Department of Labor, 1942; Southern

Council for Regional Development, 1943; special adviser to the director of State Department's International Information Service, 1945; Georgia state chairman for the thirteenth annual celebration of American Brotherhood Week, 1946; chairman of a committee of educators, editors, publishers, and civic leaders, formed to further legislation for the State Department's overseas cultural relations program, 1947; worked with President Eisenhower and leaders in business, labor, finance, publishing, and education, 1953; national chairman of the newspaper committee for Brotherhood Week, 1957; national education committee to study use of tape recordings and other devices for education, 1958; member of John F. Kennedy's twenty-one-member advisory committee for Labor-Management policy, 1961; member of the Commission on Goals for Higher Education in the South, 1961; Fair Campaign Practices Committee, 1964; traveled extensively by request of the United States government. He also served on the Advisory Committee on the Arms Control and Disarmament Agency, the board of trustees of the Carnegie Endowment for International Peace, and the Ford Foundation's Board for the Advancement of Education. *Constitution* writer Celestine Sibley pointed out the influence of McGill's vast experience upon his credibility: "Sometimes he is referred to as the conscience of the South, and in Atlanta his function is frequently summed up in the words of one subscriber who said simply: 'He does my thinking for me.'... Those who say he does their thinking for them say it without apology because they know that no matter where the news is breaking, the chances are that the *Constitution* editor is either there or has been there and knows, first hand, the issues involved."[40]

McGill considered reading to be his "chief vice."[41] "To the point of being unsocial to a fault," McGill preferred reading to bridge, gin rummy, poker, dancing, and smoking. "Having had the hot breath of Calvin on my neck since birth," he commented, "I grew up under the impression that dancing and card playing were sinful. This made it necessary for me valiantly to try both... There is no more sin in the ace of hearts than in a pack of rook cards... I could never understand why anyone would play any card game when it was possible to talk or read. I think it much more sensible to invite guests and issue each a good book to read until midnight than to sit playing a card game."[42]

"Since I try to read about three books each week and have a great deal of trouble finding the time to do so," wrote McGill. "I have to pick and choose. Therefore, most of my reading is nonfiction and much of that is selected deliberately with the idea of trying to learn something from it."[43] McGill liked to read because he believed "we should take from the past that which gives us strength and courage and to use both to face the problems of today and tomorrow which also require strength and courage."[44] "In this day and time," he argued, "it is necessary to do a lot of reading, much more than ever before... It is this adult generation, with its pattern of thought and its culture, developed of that past, which meets with the modern technology of a world swiftly industrialized by the steam engine, the gasoline and diesel engines. This is one reason it is more difficult for us, who in the space of a generation have come from the coon-skin cap and the percussion-cap rifle, to jet-propelled, radio-controlled weapons and the atomic bomb and atomic energy, to work efficiently with the mental tools we possess... The past always seems to have been more simple... But we aren't going back and we are going on." [45]

"I prowl around with my reading," claimed McGill, "without much plan or reason except trying to learn something, and that way you come across a mixture of books and articles and end up not learning too much, I guess."[46] Quite often, however, McGill spoke in behalf of that which sounded most logical, like planned study, but really believed his own way to be best. "I do not know whether planned reading is superior to just reading," he asserted. "I think perhaps planned reading may be best, but to do so causes one to miss much. And who is to do the planning? It may be best just to pitch in and read, putting aside any book which, after getting a third of the way through is still uninteresting."[47]

McGill's favorite sources were the Bible and Stephen Vincent Benet's *John Brown's Body*"; however, he read all kinds of materials. Celestine Sibley demonstrated the influence of the Bible upon McGill's daily newspaper column: "Many of McGill's columns quote the Scriptures and from time to time somebody detects in his own style the measured music of the Old Testament. One visitor's comments on the subject were quoted by McGill in a column: 'An old fellow whose clothes smelled of wood and smoke and mothballs came in and said, 'You must read the Bible a right smart,' 'Well,' I said, 'I do.' But he confessed to the old man that he fled in terror from a cover-to-cover study of Holy Writ but keeps, 'the Book handy to read for relaxation and pleasant roaming about in it.' As a newspaper man he liked its 'good reporting' and marveled that there were 'no bad war correspondents' at the battles described in the Old Testament. His idea of a flawless lead on a news story was the one beginning: 'There was a man in the land of Uz, whose name was Job.'"[48]

Study of the Bible also influenced the language and content of McGill's speeches. For example, in his address to the North Carolina Press Association, July 12, 1956, and again at De Pauw University, April 18, 1958, McGill began: "It is written in Proverbs that a word fitly spoken is like apples of gold in pictures of silver. The beauty of that simile teaches humility, especially to an advertising or newspaper man, whose job it is to use words..."[49]

McGill also quoted often from *John Brown's Body*, as when he delivered his Lincoln Day Address at Cooper Union, New York on February 12, 1960. McGill concluded with: "I like what Stephen Vincent Benet said, in *John Brown's Body*, of Lincoln's trials and his patient search for answers. Wrote Benet:

> 'What is God's will?
> They come to me and talk about God's will
> In righteous deputations and platoons,
> Day after day, laymen and ministers...
> But all of them are sure they know God's will.
> I am the only man who does not know it...' "[50]

McGill's reading habits were quite remarkable. To demonstrate the kinds of materials McGill read, some of the works discussed in his daily newspaper column are listed here, using McGill's labels: H. Allen's *The Forest and the Fort, Bedford Village*, and *Toward the Morning; Death Comes for the Archbishop; Drums Along the Mohawk; Kim; A Farewell to Arms; The Late G. Apley; Appointment In Samarra; Northwest Passage; The Grapes of Wrath; The Heart Is a Lonely Hunter; Look Homeward Angel; Of Time and the River; Web and the Rock; You Can't Go Home Again; Anthony Adverse; Arrowsmith; Gone With the Wind;* E. Merton Coulter's *The Confederate States of America;* Churchill's war memoirs; *Economic*

Geography of the USSR; The Old Man and the Sea; U.S. Camera; Divided We Fought; a picture of Lincoln; Benjamin Thomas on Lincoln; Agnes Demille's *Dance to the Piper* and *Sam Clemens of Hannibal*; Salvadore Madariagoa's *Bolivar*; J. P. Marquand's *H. M. Pulham; Esquire*; Henry Steele Commager's *The Blue and the Gray*; Boris Pasternak's *Dr. Zhivago*; Howard Odum's *Southern Regions of the United States*; Lincoln papers; *Atlantic Monthly*; E. E. Robinson's *They Voted for Roosevelt*; C. Vann Woodward's *The Burden of Southern History, Tom Watson: Agrarian Rebel, Reunion and Reaction, Origins of the New South, The Strange Career of Jim Crow; Thunder Out of China*; F. Perkins' *The Roosevelt I Knew*; Eric Sevareid's *Not So Wild a Dream; The Autobiography of William Allen White*; John Hershey's *Hiroshima*; James B. Conant's *The American High School Today; Would Schools Be Desegregated?*; John Fox's *The Little Shepherd of Kingdom Come*; Erskine Caldwell's *Tobacco Road*; Thomas Hamilton's *Men and Manners in America*; Vergil's *Georgics*; Gunnar Mydal's *The American Dilemma*; Eugene O'Neill plays; Edmund Burke's *Conciliation with America; Mercury*; Sophocles' *Ode to Antigone*; Carl Sandburg on Lincoln; report of the U.S. Commissioner of Education for 1900-1901; 1916 census statistics; University of Georgia Economics Department study on industry; National Education Association's report on support of education by states; newspapers from "all over the nation"; farm publications such as the *Hereford Journal*; intelligence reports; translations of the Soviet press; monitored radio programs; and report published by the University of Tennessee.

In his studies McGill often seemed more concerned with the spirit of his findings than with particulars. For example a Ph.D. candidate in history at Emory University found that "McGill frequently misuses facts or is careless in his use of facts. For example, he is fond of writing how Sam Houston died in 1863, it is difficult to conceive of his advising any course of action in 1865."[51]

McGill's chief concern appeared to be that of understanding his subject matter. Staughton Lynd, of Spelman College, said it well when he wrote in *The Journal of Negro History*, "One aspect of McGill's compassion is a concern not to condemn the (often repulsive) end-products of history before inquiring into their beginning. Whether in clamboring up mountains to find the source of the Chattahoochee River or in tracing the style of the Southern demagogue back to Professor Dew, McGill shows a zest to get at the root of things."[52]

NOTES

FOUR

1 *Atlanta Constitution*, July 30, 1956, p. 1.
2 *Atlanta Constitution*, August 2, 1948, p. 6.
3 *Atlanta Constitution*, July 2, 1946, p. 8.
4 *Atlanta Constitution*, October 23, 1950, p. 1.
5 *South and the Southerner*, p. 91.
6 *Atlanta Constitution*, December 11, 1946, p. 8.
7 *Atlanta Constitution*, August 2, 1948, p. 6.
8 *South and the Southerner*, pp. 76-79.
9 *Atlanta Constitution*, May 30, 1960, p. 1.
10 *Atlanta Constitution*, September 30, 1957, p. 1.
11 *South and the Southerner*, pp. 90-92.
12 *South and the Southerner*, pp. 100-101.
13 *Newsweek*, LIII (April 13, 1959), 103.
14 *Time*, 40 (September 14, 1942), 46.
15 *Atlanta Constitution*, February 17, 1950, p. 8.
16 *Atlanta Constitution*, December 22, 1946, p. 2D.
17 *Atlanta Constitution*, November 10, 1951, p. 1.
18 *Nashville Tennessean Magazine*, November 5, 1961, p. 20.
19 *Newsweek*, LIII (April 13, 1959), 102.
20 Letter to this writer from Grace Lundy, November 28, 1967.

When McGill's wife died on March 21, 1962, the *Atlanta Constitution* carried the following statement: "She was a church and civic leader... She was a native of McMinnville, Tennessee, but spent much of her early life in Nashville, where her father, the late Dr. Thomas A. Leonard, was a dentist... She was a Daughter of the King... She also taught Sunday School... Mrs. McGill was a graduate of Ward-Belmont and Peabody College in Nashville. She majored in home economics, and had planned to become a dietitian. She and McGill were married September 4, 1929, in the Peabody College Chapel on campus... Mrs. McGill was active in the Gray Ladies at the Atlanta Veterans Hospital during the second World War. Mrs. McGill was in demand as a public speaker on several subjects... She was an expert in herbs... One of her talks was entitled 'Plants of the Bible.' Mrs. McGill was known as a fine cook and a gracious hostess...

Besides her husband and son, Ralph Jr., Mrs. McGill is survived by her mother, Mrs. T.A. Leonard, of McMinnville, Tennessee, and a brother T.A. Leonard, Jr., of Richmond, Virginia, who was a star quarterback at Vanderbilt University.

On April 20, 1967, McGill married a second time, to Dr. M: ·· Lynn Morgan. The bride had been engaged in the practice of dentistry for children for twenty-one years and a member of the faculty of Emory University since 1951.

21 *Atlanta Constitution*, January 31, 1935, p. 13.
22 *Atlanta Constitution*, January 1, 1935, p. 9.
23 *Atlanta Constitution*, June 9, 1948, p. 8.
24 *Newsweek*, LIII (April 13, 1959), 102.
25 *Nashville Tennessean Magazine*, November 5, 1961, p. 10.
26 *Atlanta Constitution*, September 2, 1957, p. 1.
27 *Atlanta Constitution*, September 13, 1961, p. 1.
28 *Atlanta Constitution*, May 13, 1954, p. 1.
29 *Atlanta Constitution*, March 25, 1963, p. 1.
30 *Atlantic Monthly*, 177 (April, 1946), 76.
31 *Atlanta Constitution*, August 8, 1962, p. 1.
32 *Atlanta Constitution*, September 5, 1951, p. 1.
33 *Atlanta Constitution*, November 21, 1951, p. 1.
34 *Atlanta Constitution*, March 10, 1946, p. 8B.
35 *Atlanta Constitution*, August 11, 1946, p. 14C.
36 *Saturday Evening Post*, 231 (December 27, 1958), 52.
37 *Atlanta Constitution*, November 1, 1946, p. 12.
38 *Atlanta Constitution*, March 28, 1946, p. 10.
39 *Atlanta Constitution*, June 15, 1948, p. 10.
40 *Saturday Evening Post*, 231 (December 27, 1958), 25 & 52.
41 *Atlanta Constitution*, November 21, 1949, p. 10.
42 *Atlanta Constitution*, May 14, 1946, p. 8.
43 *Atlanta Constitution*, November 24, 1949, p. 18B.
44 *Atlanta Constitution*, June 30, 1949, p. 13.
45 *Atlanta Constitution*, December 9, 1946, p. 6.
46 *Atlanta Constitution*, February 1, 1950, p. 1.
47 *Atlanta Constitution*, November 28, 1952, p. 1.
48 *Saturday Evening Post*, 231, (December 27, 1958), 25.
49 Manuscripts given this writer by Ralph McGill.

[50] Manuscript given this writer by Ralph McGill.

[51] Letter to this writer, June 25, 1966, Decatur, Georgia.

[52] Staughton Lynd, *The Journal of Negro History*, XLVIII (July 1963), 217-218.

FIVE

JUST LEFT OF CENTER

"In the corridor outside McGill's office is a little brass cannon a couple of feet long... At two a.m. after the" 1960 "presidential election, when it was clear that John F. Kennedy had won, the cannon was dragged outside, stuffed with powder and fired. McGill, of course, was the gunner. But he forgot to brace it against recoil. There was a horrendous boom and a terrible kick. When the smoke lifted, McGill's shin was bruised, his eyelashes singed and his face pale. But he was grinning. That's the way the police found him."[1]

Such human interest stories have caused McGill to become a legend in his own time. One who studies all of McGill's works, however, will be more impressed by the extreme seriousness of his career. McGill was aware of this when he wrote: "It occurs to me I have not had any fun in a long time and that I probably have become a bore, going about with a long face and a serious story on my tongue. The banner I have been carrying has written upon it the slogan, 'Life is real, life is earnest.' "[2] McGill used a funny event to reveal his serious nature. "It was an old Southern city where I was once asked down to speak at a Saint Patrick's Day annual dinner... This whole organization, they had a fifth of whiskey between each

60

plate. And there had been considerable drinking before and during the dinner, and so when the time came for me to speak some of them were singing at the tables... They never did get it completely quiet. So I just didn't even attempt to deliver the talk I had written... I just got up and tried to be moderately funny. I'm not very good at being funny. I tell you, I'm a serious minded sort of person I'm afraid."[3] McGill was filled with emotion and a driving concern for humanity. "Of Welsh and Irish descent," he "inherited...a tendency to weep over sad movies, great pieces of writing, dramatic stage scenes, and mournful songs."[4] The result is "to conceal emotion badly."[5] This personal involvement with life moved McGill to search for lasting qualities in people and events. "In all the years I have been coming to New York," stated McGill, "I have been in night clubs but twice and both visits stand out in my mind as painful bores. I like to get by myself and prowl the town, looking in side street windows at places that sell old books or old jewelry or foreign foods. I like to try and find Russian or Greek Orthodox crosses in refugee shops or look at the old Russian icons that have been parted with in great pain and put on the market."[6]

"It would never have occurred to me," wrote McGill on a later date, that "I would be standing on my first day in London blinking back tears all because of a small bouquet of flowers I had left the Navy office...and was engaged in a walk. At Hyde Park corner...there is a great and heroic monument in marble with bronze figures of artillerymen about it. Carved in it is the message that it was erected to the more than forty-nine thousand members of the Royal Artillery regiments who gave their lives in the great war from 1914-18. A section has been added and so carefully was it planned, it seems a part of the original. And on this is written that it is in tribute to the more than twenty-nine thousand members of artillery regiments who died in the second great war. On this there lay a pitiful bouquet of home-grown garden flowers. They were wrapped in a paper sack, with their once gay and pretty blossoms and part of the stems exposed... They looked so small, in their incongruous cheap wrapping there on the great marble pile of beauty and solemnity, and yet they had about them a dignity and a pathos which wrung the heart."[7]

Although McGill responded to life emotionally, he disliked "exhibitionism or loud, pious screams"[8] and writing "personally of family or friends."[9] Recalling a memorial he attended in honor of students at Berry school who had given their lives in the Second World War, McGill declared: "I never like to reveal personal emotions on this page" of the *Constitution* "or anywhere else."[10] "That is a part of me that is not for sale, and I do not use it for street-walking solicitation in my trade. It belongs to me and I honor it as mine. I do not offer it shamelessly in the market place."[11]

To understand Ralph McGill, one must know the nature of his work. "It never occurs to me," he stated, "that my daily routine is of any special interest, but a visiting friend has left emotionally exhausted saying he would crack-up under it. During his visit my wife had anonymous letters abusing me, one suggesting I was in love with another lady, an occasional drunk was abusive over the phone and still others called up for advice and help in how to get off the stuff. Kluxers, acting on orders, tried to smear me with a stupid lie, and various persons called to complain or praise comments on politics. People sought help getting jobs. Meanwhile, the mail continues heavy and office callers are at an alltime high with comment and proposals... It had never occurred to me it was anything other than normal. It is always like that... My work and my life have been, and are, a lot of fun. I can't imagine a man who doesn't like to discuss controversial subjects, but who avoids them out of fear of being 'bothered.' It never occurs to me that anyone dislikes me for it and I never met anyone I didn't like, in at least some degree. I like newspaper work and have never had a day when I wasn't eager to go to work... It rarely seems strenuous, and most of it is fun. If I crack up I will be the most surprised of all."

"There are times," continued McGill, "when anyone doing a daily column wishes he were a nature writer... When these writers are introduced at luncheon clubs everyone smiles sweetly... No one ever frowns and whispers to his neighbor, 'I hear he is a little to the left when it comes to Roosevelt and his ideas.' A fellow who does a daily piece which goes down in the market place and walks about, entering into arguments and taking a part in a brawl if necessary, is different. His job is somewhat remindful of one which used to be in vogue at the old-fashioned carnivals. A fellow would stick his head through a hole in a large sheet of canvas For a nickel, you could throw three baseballs at his head... Most of the days I love it in there with my head through the canvas and everyone privileged to pay his five cents and throw three baseballs at said head.... And, even though now and then one of the missiles hits you square in the nose, it still is fun. At least to me. I always have trouble not working up a sort of affection for the tougher adversaries, the ones that fight back the hardest."[12]

Probably reflecting his training under Major Stahlman and the *Nashville Banner*, McGill disagreed with those who "say the best policy is a 'hush-hush' policy. And that the least you say about crackpot organizations the better. I can imagine certain conditions under which that might be true," he admitted, "but mostly I go along with the policy of getting in there and firing both barrels——after you have something to fire... To fight them you have got to get in their gutter and fight with some of their weapons. Including mud, if they use it. You've got to be highly impolite and you have got to know something about them. You've got to call names and know something of their records. The pleasant fact is they always have records. But the point is, you can't be afraid of them. They will try to smear you and everything you say. They will try to terrorize your family and annoy you with anonymous calls. That isn't important if you know how to shrug it off and regard it as part of the game."[13]

Although McGill was able to "shrug off" many of the unpleasantries of public life, he did "not have the disposition to leave problems at the office. I take them home," he wrote, and "wake in the night with them. This is especially true if it be the troubles involving some person who needs an immediate solution. This is not to argue, necessarily, that I am sensitive or kindhearted. I trust I am. But it is merely to say troubles of others trouble me... You wake and remember...how their destinies worked; how many escaped, how many were trapped. And they leave you weary and depressed and sleepless while you wonder."[14]

McGill was "not a professional optimist," but "a worrier and a dreader and a fretter."[15] In 1946, when his candidate for governor of Georgia was defeated, McGill reported that "it made" him "feel pretty sick. It was a bitter pill to swallow. There was very little sugar, if any, on it," he continued. "I don't like to lose... Losing goes awfully hard with me."[16] "I am not by nature nonpartisan," maintained McGill. "I like a political fight as some persons like cake or pie. A political campaign to me is easily the most fascinating and absorbing event which our society produces. And I like to be in there

63

where the plotting and the planning are thickest; to find cigarette and cigar smoke-filled rooms more exhilarating than the pure air of mountain tops. I like throwing punches and rolling with them. I do not bruise easily. The black and blue of political blows goes away in a few days."[17]

McGill contributed to a dialogue on social problems because he was "cursed with a certain sense of responsibility."[18] Though he was basically partisan, he believes that "unless there is some great principle at stake, the higher duty would seem to be to remain aloof and speak for the whole community."[19] It was this willingness to be purposefully inconsistent which distinguished McGill, and frustrated radicals both to McGill's Right and Left. For example, McGill would quarrel bitterly with fellow Georgian and former national president of the White Citizens Council, Roy Harris; nevertheless, McGill respected his ability as a fighter. "I wrote a piece about Mr. Harris a short time ago," argued McGill, "in which I said he was easily the most effective politican in this generation. This caused me to be abused by a number of persons who wished to know why I was lauding such a political 'menance.' Well, I was not endorsing Mr. Harris' works... But I always respect champions, and Mr. Harris is a champ. I also would be less than honest if I did not say that I like him personally, even though violently disagreeing with him, often and publicly. I got to liking him in the days when we were fighting together to elect Ellis Arnall governor. In the last month of the campaign I was with Mr. Harris constantly. Ellis Arnall wouldn't have been elected without him..."[20]

McGill's concern for persons with whom he disagreed can be found in thoughts he expressed about Southerners who were deeply disturbed by a relatively fast moving social revolution. "There is an agony," he wrote, "for millions in the South. Some of the letters one receives go deep in the heart. The angry ones, the abusive scribblings...are unimportant... But there are letters which one sits and reads and reads and puts away to read again. They are from decent, honest, troubled men and women. They are letters to weep over, to pray over. These people are deeply, honestly and irrevocably opposed. They are, more often than not, confused... But one does not even think of criticizing those honestly troubled persons who are in agony of mind and spirit... Changing the long-established folkways and mores of a people is never easy."[21]

McGill "not only permits disagreement from his aides," reported *Constitution* writer Celestine Sibley, "he encourages it. An ardent Democrat and a wholehearted and enthusiastic supporter of Franklin D. Roosevelt, both personally and editorially, he hired some years ago a young man from Savannah who was known to have Republican leanings and was suspect of being, in the McGill phrase, 'a mossback reactionary.' The young man, William H. Fields, advanced rapidly...not because he tactfully suppressed views counter to those of his boss but because he advanced them boldly and argued them with a sharp and caustic intelligence which delighted McGill. In times of great editorial crusades *The Constitution* staff has always had members who were in marked disagreement with the announced policy of the paper, and it never occurred to the editor that they might be sinister borers from within...he welcomed them as sort of friendly whetstones on which to sharpen the edge of his own arguments and persuasions."[22]

McGill could be a patient man. For example, in Moscow when Russian officials gave him a "bad time" concerning "racial violence" in the United States, he "rolled with the punches and never showed any loss of patience or failed to make a full comment."[23] While on a fact-finding tour of Africa for President John F. Kennedy, McGill agreed to answer questions following one of his talks. When young communist rebels tried to anger McGill they were unsuccessful.[24] McGill's self control was dramatized by his reaction to the May 17, 1954 ruling of the Supreme Court which outlawed racially segregated public schools. Admittedly, he was in England when the decision was announced; however, his column continued in *The Constitution*. Although he had been warning for months that the decision would come, he resisted the temptation to say "I told you so." Instead, he waited five months, until October 5, 1954, before really commenting in his column on that historic interpretation. Then he put it simply. "But no matter what the emotions or the likes or dislikes," he wrote, "whatever the states do eventually must come within the constitutional directives. There is only one alternative and that is secession by armed force."[25]

Although McGill attempted to weigh all sides of a problem before deciding on public issues, and to be patient when dealing with people, he of course, was not always successful. "At least one of my faults," he confessed, "which I slowly have been subduing, is that of making quick judgments or decisions."[26] In 1946 when a candidate for the Georgia legislature asked that his statement be published in the *Constitution*, because the man was "tough, ugly, rude, and abusive," his request was denied. McGill repented: "I last lost my temper about twenty-five years ago. Maybe longer. The other day I came close... Ordinarily I am a patient guy, realizing that the weather is hot, tempers strained, and that to a candidate, even to one without a chance, but badly bitten by the political bug, a 'statement' is more important than the Declaration of Independence and the Bill of Rights. I want the gentleman to know I am sorry. And that I am sending out for the book on how to win friends and influence people. I have waited too long to read it."[27]

It is interesting to try to define McGill's role in society. The *Atlantic* labeled McGill a "fearless"[28] editor, "known throughout the South for his fighting heart...and for his two-fisted editorial approach to any bothersome problem below Mason and Dixon's line."[29] The Press Club of Dallas cited McGill for "distinguished service as a crusading editor and writer."[30] The Columbia University Graduate School of Journalism not only awarded McGill the honorary degree of Humane Letters but also lavished praise on the journalist. He was hailed as "spur to the conscience of America, champion of human rights, foe of demagoguery, prophet of the mature Southland, heir to the Chair of Henry W. Grady and Joel Chandler Harris——yours is a voice from Atlanta that speaks to the whole world."[31]

When the *Atlantic* pictured McGill as a "fearless" editor with the "two-fisted editorial," it simply planted the first seeds for a sure-to-be McGill myth. On occasions, such as the bombing of a church or school, he resorted to open battle, but for the most part McGill remained one of the most patient, if persistent, proponents of social change in the South.

The *Atlantic* gave a more accurate assessment when it called McGill "one of the bravest and most balanced liberal editors in the deep South."[32] Without question McGill showed great courage. Besides his decisive stand on human rights in the late 1960's, McGill courageously supported minority groups from the early 1930's to 1954, when few men, north or south, were willing to speak. His methods and policies, however, were more "balanced" than "two-fisted" or "fearless," more like a teacher than a crusader. "In his office last week," wrote George Barker, "McGill denied that he is fearless or particularly strong. 'I worry about my son and my wife,' he says. 'They take a lot of abuse because of me... If you're looking for some dramatic thing that showed me the great truth...you're gonna be disappointed,' he says: 'There isn't anything like that. I never learned about prejudice from my parents and when, in school, I ran into prejudiced kids, I just thought that was a problem of their own——not mine.' "

McGill was not a crusader in the sense of a William Lloyd Garrison. In fact, McGill was convinced that "extremists——in either direction——almost inevitably provide dangerous and damaging leadership."[34] In 1947, he wrote: "I cannot be a good crusader because I have been cursed all my life with the ability to see both sides of things. This is fatal to a crusader. A real, burning crusader must be able to see only his side. I do not criticize this, because much of our progress has been brought about by crusaders. But, unfortunately, they are rough fellows and in their furious laying about, they undo almost as much as they accomplish."[35] In 1965 this writer reminded McGill of that statement, and asked if he had changed his mind concerning his role. He replied that he "would still have to say" that he was no crusader, but that his "indignation has run toward the people" in society "who do the exploiting."[36] On February 14, 1959, *Time* concluded: "Ralph McGill was no crusader. He considered his columns and editorials to be merely common-sense appeals to the humanitarian impulses of his fellow Southerners. A soft-spoken, always courteous man, he preferred understatement. He put down Alabama's Governor George Wallace's 1963 defiance at the schoolhouse door as 'a little man standing alone in his diminishing circle.'... Only when an outrageous act angered him did McGill drop his civility. After the assassination of Robert Kennedy, he assailed the 'abscesses in America's society——the jackals, the cowards, the haters, the failures who hate achievers, the yapping feist pack that tries to drown out truth, those who dislike Jews, Negroes, Catholics, liberals.' "

McGill argued that he lacked the "omniscience"[37] required to conclude his own position to be the only solution to complex social problems. What he did aggressively claim, however, was the right to express his independent judgment. "I belong to no organization representing any cause," wrote McGill. "If I belonged to one I would not feel like sitting down and banging out a piece for the paper about how I disagreed with it. So, I don't belong. I do belong to the Democratic Party, but fortunately a political party is an arena... I also am a Mason, an organization which is committed to the ideal of tolerance and brotherhood... But I belong to no organization committed to a cause. I like to think I have served some causes. I have tried to put my shoulder to whatever worthy wheels seemed in need of pushing. I have joined to get a few oxen out of ditches. I like a fight and I have had my share. I expect to have more... But...I am not a good crusader. I like to call my shots. And aim where I think a shot is needed."[38]

McGill's role, then, in the judgment of this writer, was that of a social critic. "I have always tried to develop a nonconforming mind," stated McGill, "believing such a mind necessary to one whose job it is to comment on events and policies... If man ever becomes tamed, and if he loses the one paramount freedom from which all others stem——the freedom of his mental processes——then all else is lost."[39] When this writer asked Arthur Schlesinger, Jr. for his opinion concerning McGill's role in society, he answered: "I have the greatest admiration for Ralph McGill. He has shown himself over the last generation a newspaper man of exceptional wisdom and courage... In my judgment, Mr. McGill exemplifies as much as anyone in our time the ability of the newspaperman to remain faithful to his craft and at the same time assume a role of creative social leadership."[40]

McGill's role, then, seemed to be that of the social critic who provides creative social leadership. Although he was not a fanatic crusader, McGill worked diligently for certain causes. A few examples will serve to demonstrate the kind of social leadership McGill provided. Writing in support of the "Scottish Rite Hospital for Crippled Children," McGill commented: "I began the story with the line, 'Strong legs will run that weak legs may walk.'... I am prouder of that line than any I've ever written, or will write."[41]

McGill also "became a man with a cause" when he "became a disciple of the Voice of America program and an apostle of the American Information program, including exchange of students, books and educational, factual movies portraying our American scene. I wrote of it," he continued. "I went to Washington and worked for it. I went to Washington and testified for it... I accepted the chairmanship of a national committee devoted to the cause. I spoke for it on 'The Town Hall of the Air.'... I think I am more proud of what little I contributed to that victory than anything else I have done. Now, so help me, I find myself knee deep in another cause——aid to Europe..."[42] In his column on October 25, 1948, McGill warned: "I am going to be hovering around, peering over the shoulder of the cub reporter assigned to do my obituary——which I trust will be many years from now——and if he doesn't have one line in it I am going to scare him right out of the place by writing it in myself. The line I want is this——'He was one of those who worked to save and establish The Voice of America.' "

McGill was best known for his concern for civil rights. He demonstrated an interest in human rights when he first moved to Atlanta. In their book, *Seeds of Southern Change: The Life of Will Alexander*, Dykeman and Stokely concluded that "a young writer on the *Atlanta Constitution* was destined to make one of the most significant contributions to interracial harmony in the South... [McGill] carried on a lifetime of work in ever widening circles to create a climate of rational good will and justice... The call for the Atlanta Conference of April 8, 1943, was sent out in the name of Ralph McGill... Arrangements for the meeting were made through the offices of the Interracial Commission. One hundred and fifteen prominent white southerners attended... On January 6, 1944, under a petition from Rufus E. Clement, Ralph McGill, Bishop Arthur J. Moore, Charles S. Johnson, and Howard W. Odum, the Southern Regional Council was chartered as a corporation by the State of Georgia."[43] *Time* called the Southern Council for Regional Development "one of the most hopeful steps ever to be taken in the United States toward race relations."[44]

McGill, then, served numerous local, national, and international causes. Indeed, when *The Atlanta Constitution* celebrated its seventy-fifth consecutive year of publication in 1942, McGill proclaimed: "I would not like to work for a newspaper which did not have a history of fighting for causes. This was a newspaper founded to fight... One may suppose that, one hundred years or more from today, a research man may be looking through the old files of *The Atlanta Constitution*. He will come across this seventy-fifth edition... I am sure the researcher will find that things have not changed... *The Atlanta Constitution* will have been fighting

69

against untruth, against hypocrisy, and for the rights and the interests of the people."[45]

When providing creative social leadership, McGill worked from a social-political base "just left of center." "I have never said I was a liberal," argued McGill. "I hope I am. I do know I am not a professional, parasitic liberal, making a profession of it and living off 'liberalism,' as are most of the [Henry] Wallace crowd. I hope I am a liberal as I conceive the word to be. As I conceive it to be, a liberal is one on the side of the people. I hope I am... I find myself happily in the middle, a little left of center..."[46] "A syndicated labor columnist whose typewriter is cut on the anti-AFL bias," continued McGill, "wrote a piece the other day in which he referred to me as a 'former liberal.' At about the same time a teacher of political science lamented that I had become a practical politician instead of an idealist... All this interests me no little. I have been keeping down my same old road, a little left of center, as is my custom and belief. I do not have to make a living being a professional liberal, but can center on trying to be liberal, a fact which makes me very glad... But, since I have never attempted to peddle a column to a special audience, I am really shocked and chagrined that anyone should ever have thought of me as having anything but a practical approach to actual political problems as compared with issues. This does not mean I am lacking ideals. I am not. But political problems must be approached with muscle and sweat and a willingness to get things done... All I do is to wind up every day and throw a column for the plate, hoping my control is good... And always, come hell or high water, I expect always to be found in the middle of the road, just a little left of center, highly idealistic about life, but knowing that progress in government comes by politics and that they are practical problems. Noise doesn't rattle me and I know there will always be another time at bat and that sometimes the best rallies come late."[47]

NOTES

FIVE

1 *Nashville Tennessean Magazine*, November 5, 1961, pp. 10, 20.
2 *Atlanta Constitution*, August 4, 1946, p. 2D.
3 Taped interview with McGill, Atlanta, December 29, 1965.
4 *Atlanta Constitution*, July 17, 1951, p. 1.
5 *Atlanta Constitution*, May 2, 1947, p. 12.
6 *Atlanta Constitution*, November 21, 1946, p. 24.
7 *Atlanta Constitution*, August 21, 1952, p. 1.
8 *Atlanta Constitution*, January 26, 1947, p. 14C.
9 *Atlanta Constitution*, August 9, 1946, p. 14.
10 *Atlanta Constitution*, May 20, 1946, p. 6.
11 *Atlanta Constitution*, July 30, 1948, p. 8.
12 *Atlanta Constitution*, January 28, 1949, p. 14.
13 *Atlanta Constitution*, July 17, 1946, p. 6.
14 *Atlanta Constitution*, December 12, 1946, p. 12.
15 *Atlanta Constitution*, July 23, 1949, p. 6.
16 *Atlanta Constitution*, January 2, 1950, p. 20.
17 *Atlanta Constitution*, July 19, 1946, p. 10.
18 *Atlanta Constitution*, September 8, 1948, p. 10.
19 *Atlanta Constitution*, February 29, 1948, p. 2D.
20 *Atlanta Constitution*, August 22, 1948, p. 2D.
21 *Atlanta Constitution*, February 20, 1947, p. 10.
22 *Atlanta Constitution*, September 16, 1957, p. 1.
23 *Saturday Evening Post*, 231 (December 27, 1958), 51.
24 *South and the Southerner*, p. 185.
25 Taped interview carried over WAGA television, Atlanta.
26 *Atlanta Constitution*, October 5, 1954, p. 1.
27 *Atlanta Constitution*, October 27, 1947, p. 6.
28 *Atlanta Constitution*, June 29, 1946, p. 4.
29 *Atlantic Monthly*, 174 (September, 1964), 61.
30 *Atlantic Monthly*, 184 (November, 1949), 64.
31 *The New York Times*, May 3, 1953, p. 85.
32 *The New York Times*, April 16, 1963, p. 32.
33 *Atlantic Monthly*, 197 (April, 1956), 31.
34 *Nashville Tennessean Magazine*, November 5, 1961, pp. 10, 20.
35 *Atlanta Constitution*, August 10, 1955, p. 1.

36 *Atlanta Constitution*, November 4, 1947, p. 10.
37 Taped interview with McGill, December 29, 1965.
38 *Atlanta Constitution*, February 29, 1948, p. 2D.
39 *Atlanta Constitution*, November 4, 1946, p. 10.
40 *Atlanta Constitution*, May 31, 1949, p. 10.
41 Letter to this writer from Arthur Schlesinger, Jr., February 15, 1966, Princeton, New Jersey.
42 *Atlanta Constitution*, November 28, 1946, p. 42.
43 *Atlanta Constitution*, January 21, 1948, p. 6.
44 Wilma Dykeman and James Stokely, *Seeds of Southern Change: The Life of Will Alexander* (Chicago: The University of Chicago Press, 1962), pp. 283-284.
45 Quoted in *Current Biography* (New York City: The H.W. Wilson Company, 1947), p. 414.
46 *Atlanta Constitution*, September 1, 1942, p. 4D.
47 *Atlanta Constitution*, June 24, 1948, p. 4.
48 *Atlanta Constitution*, February 13, 1947, p. 12.

SIX

CONVICTIONS OF A SOUTHERN EDITOR

From the 1930's to February 3, 1969, Ralph McGill worked tirelessly to ensure equal rights for all men: justice before the law, educational and economic opportunity, freedom to vote, and public facilities. To understand McGill's thinking concerning citizens' rights, one must look to his entire career. Since he was usually identified with the struggle of the American Negro, it is surprising to find that it was not until about December 1, 1953 that McGill devoted a sizable number of his *Constitution* columns to that subject.

For convenience, McGill's views on human rights may be divided into three stages. Until the early 1950's he supported and seemingly advocated *separate-but-equal* treatment of the Negro. For example, in 1946 he wrote that " separation of the races" is "the best and only workable system." "There may be," continued McGill, "separation of races and still equal justice before the law; equal opportunity to use one's skills and still not have to mix with other workers; equal opportunity for education, without mixing in schools."[1] "I have never approached" Negro rights, wrote McGill in 1948, "on the basis of abolishing segregation. I do not now... This

73

newspaper and this writer have not, and do not, favor or advocate ending educational segregation. We always have maintained, and still maintain, and have thereby earned the criticism of many of the nation's more liberal and leftwing elements, that any attempt, by law, to mix the races at a rate which exceeds general public acceptance will harm, not help, race relations."[2] As late as 1959 McGill told audiences in Augusta and at Emory University that, "I do not, and have not, advanced a policy of integration. Nor do I have such a policy."[3]

Persons looking from the 1960's at some of McGill's earlier statements may be tempted to criticize his stand on civil rights. By some absolute moral standard, this may be justified. One should note, however, that McGill's particular position even in the 1940's was novel. When he spoke in behalf of separate-but-equal rights for all men, he meant just that. Unlike many, with McGill this was not a palliative proposal designed to ignore social injustices. Every town, county, and state, argued McGill, should provide equal facilities and opportunity for all their citizens. The quotations below are typical of McGill's persuasion in behalf of equitable treatment for the Negro, representing the first stage of his thinking concerning human rights:

[1946] There was too much truth in the revelations about our really awful convict and work camps in many states in the South to invoke denial... Our failure, even today, to give the Negro equal justice in our courts; to make him safe from police brutality; to give him his due in education, in playgrounds and the usual civic facilities such as paved streets, public health, sewers and so on, is another example.[4]

[1948] I am willing to say that the Constitution of the United States reserves certain rights to the States... But I am not willing to say that I am against any effort to bring to the people of the South, or any other region, a full share of human, or civil rights... I am on the side of human rights and believe it the obligation of the South to so be and to positively assert itself.[5]

[1950] We want some leadership in law and in creating in the common school division a program of equalization. If we do not the Supreme Court will be forced to invade the field...[6]

From approximately 1930 to 1950, then, McGill supported separate-but-equal opportunity for the Negro. The second stage of McGill's thinking concerning citizens' rights fell between the late 1940's and the early 1950's. His purpose was to convince his auditors that the South could learn to live with social change which he now considered to be inevitable. A typical statement during this period came on December 1, 1953:

There are those who insist that segregation protects the "integrity" of both races. There are others who believe, with deep sincerity, Negroes are "better off" under it. Conceivably this might be argued with some logic. It does not matter. The world, in the throes of a social revolution which began with the coming of the industrial revolution, and which was tremendously accelerated by two great world wars, has moved on. Segregation by law no longer fits today's world... As a matter of fact, segregation has been on its way out for a good long time and has been breaking down at the edges for more than a generation... Two great forces have been at work on segregation and the problem of race. One is secular, the other religious. The Christians of today cannot help but wince at the full implications, and the jarring clash of his creed, with discrimination against any person because of color... The other influence is secular. Segregation implies inferiority... There are those who say the fish never feels the hook. But, unfortunately, it is not possible to ask the fish. Across two great wars now we, along with other free people, have preached the rights of men everywhere to be free and equal——we have encouraged long-oppressed peoples to rise... An end to segregation——when it comes——will not, of course, force people to associate socially. That will remain, as now, personal choice...segregation is on its way out and he who tries to tell the people otherwise does them great disservice. The problem of the future is how to live with the change.[7]

To prepare the South to live with this social change, McGill wrote increasingly of how "one of these Mondays the Supreme Court...is going to hand down a ruling which may...outlaw the South's dual school system, wholly or in part... I believe it a fact that the average citizen doesn't yet have any idea that such a decision is possible, or that everything indicates that a decision——one way or the other——is close at hand. So, somebody, especially those who have a duty so to do, ought to be talking about it calmly and informatively... The vital point is——there is no reason for violence, whatever the decision. Leadership everywhere in the South must talk about this and make it clear. Anger and violence solve nothing."[8] McGill wrote a less remembered, but very significant column on October 6, 1953, again attempting to prepare his readers for a ruling he knew would come: "Ahead of us stretch years of great constitutional decision. These, when finally made, will bring changes to us, and some will be digested by the body politic only with accompany distress and time... Shortly before noon yesterday the Supreme Court received a new Chief Justice. Governor Earl Warren of California will now join in determining how the empty vessels of Civil Rights, segregation, congressional investigations and their ultimate powers, the constitutionality of portions of the Taft-Hartley Act, of Tidelands oil——and others——will be filled... Governor Warren never once acted without honor and integrity. He is a stubborn man. He has a great respect for law. Most of all he has a feeling for people and their right under that law. Therefore, those who expect him to have any judicial patience with what seems to him to be an inequality of the law or the rights of citizens generally, had best be prepared now to be disappointed in him."

Following the historic Supreme Court desegregation ruling in 1954, McGill's emphasis became compliance with legal and moral law, which meant racially integrated schools, parks, buses, restaurants, movies, hospitals, swimming pools, motels, and jobs. From the vantage point of the 1960's, the complex social issues of the past seemed relatively simple to McGill. This third stage saw McGill argue that segregation as the United States had known it was wrong. There had been no justice and no equity for the American Negro. Week after week McGill wrote and spoke about the economic, social, political, and moral burden which segregation had placed upon the New South. On June 30, 1966, for example, McGill addressed the delegates at the National Education Association convention in Miami Beach:

But it is true, now, that we see, I think, clearly and painfully, how ugly and what a great weight and burden this policy of segregation put upon the southern people and now, by the great dispersal [of persons] into the great industrial cities, upon the whole nation... We see...in my region, which has exported so...many people who never had a chance at education, who never had a chance at skills, who never had a chance to learn to be a voter, who never had a chance to participate in community affairs and learn something of citizenship. We learn, I hope we see very plainly...that this produced the harvest of today, or much of it, and that in this region where we had not enough per capita income, being largely agricultural, for one good school system——at a time when we had seventy-two percent of all the Negroes in America in our region——we chose out of heaven knows what disaster of decision to try to have two systems, when we couldn't really afford one good one.[9]

McGill's ideas relating to social problems, then, changed considerably between the 1930's and the 1960's. To understand why this journalist said what he did during that period, one must know the basic beliefs upon which his statements were based. With this knowledge it becomes apparent that what McGill said in the early 1940's, though different, often grew out of the same basic premises that prompted his pronouncements in the 1960's. Several of his basic premises are considered here. For example, as can be seen in the quotations below, McGill always acted on the assumption that *individuals and governments should pursue policies that are feasible.*

[1948] I am fully aware of the philosophy of leadership, and of pulling for the long view [concerning Negro rights]. But I happen to be alive as of now and the tools with which I must work are the tools of today... This, I know, satisfies no one——not even me. But not being beholden or in politics, I can say it.[10]

[1950]...while all of us know what the objectives are...we should know that while it is noble to die on the barricades, it is better for all concerned to get what one can in the name of progress.[11]

[1957]...moderates are seeking to make some sort of progress. They must learn to run on the fence——not merely sit on it...the moderate develops a sort of technique of survival. He knows just how far he can go in telling his people the truth...[12]

Because of prevailing more during the 1940's McGill believed the only possible way to achieve equal rights for the Negro was through separate channels. By 1949, however, he questioned whether it was feasible to think that the South could afford separate-but-equal facilities. "Have any of our counties," he wrote, "figured what it would cost to provide equal school buildings, libraries, laboratories, hospitals, playgrounds, and so on when they are unable to pay for adequate ones for white people."[13] By 1954, what had seemed practicable in 1940, to McGill, was impossible. He explained this fact to a Daytona Beach audience: "When public education was a matter of one room schools," he stated, "two such schools in each neighborhood were no great drain on the public purse. When a consolidated school building costs several hundred thousand dollars and its technical and vocational equipment is expensive too, here and there, ways will be found to reduce the rigidity of school segregation."[14]

There was a second belief underlying McGill's stand for separate-but-equal opportunity in the 1940's and racially integrated public facilities in the late 1950's. Both policies were based upon legal interpretation, and McGill, as can be determined from his writings below, always believed that *laws should be obeyed*:

[1948] I always have insisted that we, as a region and a people, have been dishonest in our segregation policy... We wrote our laws to say that while the races were to be separated we would provide "separate but equal" educational, travel, recreational and other facilities. This we have not done and no person can insist we have made a fair effort to do so.[15]

[1949] Here in the South we set up, by our own States, laws which said that we would have separate systems for white and Negro, but would make them equal. Would to God we had been honest enough to do so... Our attitudes have been dishonest and wrong.[16]

[1954] [Following the Supreme Court desegregation ruling, McGill wrote that]...whatever the states do eventually must come within the constitutional directives. There is only one alternative and that is secession by armed force. Therefore, every state should be seeking to avoid violence in word or deed and to find a way to live within the Constitution.[17]

[1957] When the due processes of law are exhausted the decision must be accepted as law... Editors, governors, commentators, ministers——all those who speak out——will do well to remember the old text: "Be ill at ease when your words and deeds please the mob."[18]

[1958] [Largely because of this article, McGill was awarded the Pulitzer Prize for editorial writing.] Dynamite in great quantity Sunday ripped a beautiful Temple of worship in Atlanta... This is a harvest...of defiance of courts and encouragement of citizens to defy law on the part of many Southern politicians... It is not possible to preach lawlessness and restrict it... For a long time now it has been needful for all Americans to stand up and be counted on the side of law and the due process of law——even when to do so goes against personal beliefs and emotions.[19]

[1966] There is no question but that had the top political and public leadership of the South given support to the processes of law in 1954 when the U.S. Supreme Court school decision was handed down, the South——and nation——would have avoided the bitter and disgraceful harvest of hate, the murders, the bombings, and the burnings...[20]

Increasingly, as time eroded the customs of segregation, McGill placed less emphasis on feasibility and legality, and more stress upon morality. Underlying all of McGill's writings was the belief that *free individuals have a moral responsibility to oppose wrong*:

[1946] If in our respective communities and States, we are not willing to do the unpleasant jobs, to stand out against what is wrong even though it leads to misunderstanding and criticism, we won't have very happy communities or States.[21]

[1947] Whatever is done must, eventually, meet the test of being right or wrong... We must first be honest with ourselves... We cannot, whatever it be or in whatever field, clothe wrong in the garments of law or emotion and say, "It is mine. You will please let it alone." Moral right is slow and patient... But you cannot escape it.[22]

[1958] The Klan, which prostitutes the cross of Christ by burning it to advertise their meetings and attract the suckers, also exploits Americanism. By paying a necessary sum a fellow can become a one hundred percent American. The Ku Klux mentality also prostitutes the Christian religion by making over the New and Old Testaments into a KKK revised version. This justifies hate and twists the great commandment to love thy neighbor as thyself to apply only to one hundred percent Americans, excluding most Protestants, all Roman Catholics and Jews and colored peoples. To the Kluxer mentality the Christian communion cup must be a Dixie cup.[23]

[1962] The Christian church cannot forever proceed with platitudes and irrelevancies, with fiddle-faddle, with operating huge, rich country club churches which are almost totally unrelated to the lives of the people, echoing with cliches and prescriptions for peace of mind.[24]

Three other basic premises should be mentioned. One grew out of a comparative study McGill made of education in Georgia and Scandinavia, i.e., *education is requisite to individual and community progress.* When he published this research in 1938, McGill wrote that "An educated man with at least some idea of how to rationalize himself with the world about him is better prepared for making his lot a better one and making his community an improved one."[25] Another belief, demonstrated in several quotations already cited, was that *all men should be granted the rights and privileges of full citizenship.*

Until the 1960's McGill basically opposed all federal legislation relating to citizens' rights. Unlike many persons, however, this was not a delaying tactic employed to get around social evils. McGill simply argued that *southern states should ensure the rights and privileges of their* (own) *citizens*:

[1946] Those Southerners who resent what generally is termed "outside interference"...might just as well prepare to make the most of it... We have said to let us alone and we would do the job. Shall we have the moral courage to do it or not? A lot of Americans want to know.[26]

[1948] I want the South to do what is right. I do not want the Federal Government to compel it... I want Georgia and Mississippi and South Carolina and all the others...to do what is just and right because they want to do it, and not because they are made to do so.[27]

[1955] In a limited sense the court [in requiring desegregation of schools within a "reasonable" time] has ordered a program of gradualism... What this will do is exactly what should have been done...restore decision as nearly as possible to the local level.[28]

[1961] We do not need new legislation. This is something we must find the will to do by ourselves... Not until we do this, will the South be able fully to make its great strength and good will felt in the national forces of morality, politics and industry.[29]

McGill, then, worked continuously for human rights for every man. Basic to his views was the importance of legal, feasible, Southern-based, and moral solutions. Although many of his underlying beliefs apparently did not change, the fact remains that McGill's public position on human rights underwent considerable revision between 1930 and 1969. "I've always thought," said McGill, "that in writing you must not get too far ahead of the audience you're trying to reach. I hope it isn't immodest, but I think that I have managed...to keep the readership of a lot of persons, you might say the average reader. And they haven't quit reading. They may dissent violently, but they don't quit reading. And I've deliberately tried to do this, to write persuasively or to provide information for discussion... I've always thought...that a newspaper columnist or editorial writer ought to be something like a teacher, in that you ought to try to stimulate discussion... You ought to write...as persuasively as you can."[30]

McGill also revealed why he did not write some of the things in the 1940's and early 1950's that he later wrote. Before this writer interviewed McGill, he had always found McGill to say, "In my work I have never worked for an ownership which didn't allow me to say what I thought and believed...not only are there no editorial restrictions or instructions, but none have ever been considered or suggested."[31] During this writer's taped interview with McGill, he seemingly made the following statement as an apostrophe to history. "I think that I must say, and I regret to say, but I now will say, namely that...there was a period here [at the *Constitution*] when I had a rather difficult time with some of the management which was opposed to me writing what I wanted to write. This took about three years. I continued to do it, but I, naturally, was handicapped and sometimes couldn't say what I wanted to. And there was this continual unhappy, very unhappy period... It was in the 40's,"[32] and "early 1950's "[33]

While it is true that McGill said certain things in the 1940's designed to hold his readers, and that he apparently was not always free to write what he wanted to, there is one other reason why McGill, as *Time* recognized too, appeared to be "inconsistent"[34] in his daily column. "In the course of the years," admitted McGill, "many of my ideas have changed. I have always looked with pride on the fact that today I find it possible to change my mind when confronted with valid reason to do so... A person should continue to learn as he goes along. If one learns then one changes one's mind. It is quite inevitable."[35] Surely as the nation's customs, laws, economy, political structure, population distribution, and rural-urban environment changed, so did many of McGill's own ideas and beliefs. But it is to McGill's credit that his change of mind was not only an effect of societal shifts but, also, McGill was himself a *mover of change*. His honest appeal for equal (if separate) rights for the Negro in the 1940's, for example, probably was more controversial and took more courage than his approval of the "sit-ins" and the "Dr. Kings" in the 1960's. At least the Ku Klux Klan thought so. Indeed, during this long, socially heated era, McGill was a social critic providing courageous creative social leadership.

NOTES

SIX

[1] *Atlanta Constitution*, June 12, 1946, p. 3.

[2] *Atlanta Constitution*, January 22, 1948, p. 3.

[3] Augusta speech manuscript provided by McGill. That he actually said this before the Rotary Club was emphasized by the *Augusta Chronicle*, February 4, 1959, p. 5. Emory University address was on tape recording.

[4] *Atlanta Constitution*, March 20, 1946, p. 3.

[5] *Atlanta Constitution*, September 2, 1948, p. 3.

[6] *Atlanta Constitution*, September 21, 1950, p. 1.

[7] *Atlanta Constitution*, December 1, 1953, p. 1.

[8] *Atlanta Constitution*, April 9, 1953, p. 1.

[9] Taped recording.

[10] *Atlanta Constitution*, March 1, 1948, p. 6.

[11] *Atlanta Constitution*, February 14, 1950, p. 10.

[12] *Atlanta Constitution*, October 2, 1957, p. 1.

[13] *Atlanta Constitution*, March 20, 1949, p. 14B.

[14] "Open Forum Speech," Florida. Manuscript provided by McGill.

[15] *Atlanta Constitution*, January 22, 1948, p. 8.

[16] *Atlanta Constitution*, November 13, 1949, p. 8B.

[17] *Atlanta Constitution*, October 5, 1954, p. 1.

[18] *Atlanta Constitution*, September 12, 1957, p. 1.

[19] *Atlanta Constitution*, October 13, 1958, p. 1.

[20] *Atlanta Constitution*, January 7, 1966, p. 1.

[21] *Atlanta Constitution*, August 5, 1946, p. 6.

[22] *Atlanta Constitution*, January 3, 1947, p. 10.

[23] *Atlanta Constitution*, January 21, 1958, p. 1.

[24] *Atlanta Constitution*, September 25, 1962, p. 1.

[25] McGill and Thomas C. David, *Two Georgians Explore Scandinavia* (Atlanta: State Department of Education, 1938), p. 12.

[26] *Atlanta Constitution*, August 3, 1946, p. 4.

[27] *Atlanta Constitution*, March 1, 1948, p. 3.

[28] *Atlanta Constitution*, June 1, 1955, p. 1.

[29] *Atlanta Constitution*, February 18, 1961, p. 1.

[30] Taped interview, December 29, 1965, Atlanta.

[31] *Atlanta Constitution*, May 15, 1950, p. 1. In the *Constitution* on

October 4, 1952, p. 1, McGill wrote, "I've been lucky as a news-paperman. I've never yet, in my long span of years, had a publisher who ordered me to write in a certain way. Nor have I ever been directed to slant news or take a position not in accord with my own views. Any sins in those fields are my own." On May 30, 1960, p. 1, he wrote, "Today...in *The Constitution*, shop... there are some changes. Major Clark Howell retires as publisher. The writer [McGill] is honored and privileged to accept his title and place... I worked under 'Papa Howell.' It was he who first put me to writing politics. And after his passing I had the pleasure of being with Clark Howell, his son, who gave me my head, but wise advice too. And, when the Late Governor James M. Cox came, I never once had so much as a suggestion save to tell the truth and try always to serve it. And after him, it was the same. Newspapers are, in essence, the people who get them out. They reflect the purpose and integrity of management."

32 Taped interview, December 29, 1965.

33 After reading this chapter, McGill requested that "early 1950's" be added here; letter from his secretary, November 28, 1967.

34 *Time*, 51 (January 5, 1948), 48.

35 First written in *Atlanta Constitution* column on November 28, 1952, p. 1; then repeated on December 10, 1960. p. 1.

SEVEN

RHETORIC AND POLITICS

Ralph McGill was active in public affairs as a reporter, critic, theorist, speaker, and close observer of twentieth-century politics. From tagging along with his father to witness the returns in 1908 when Taft defeated Bryan, and the battles with Governor Eugene Talmadge of Georgia in the 1940's, to covering Richard M. Nixon's inaugural address in 1969, McGill remained deeply involved in politics. This southern journalist often observed and analyzed the polemics of such Americans as Franklin D. Roosevelt, Harry S. Truman, Dwight D. Eisenhower, Robert A. Taft, Adlai E. Stevenson, John F. Kennedy, Lyndon B. Johnson, and Richard M. Nixon. He helped manage two gubernatorial campaigns in Georgia, those of Governor Ellis Arnold in 1942 and James Carmichael in 1946.

What were McGill's views concerning democratic processes? Although he recorded no systematic theory, he wrote widely about public affairs. Beginning in 1938 McGill penned a signed editorial column in which, drawing from personal experiences, he wrote extensively about politics in the United States and the role of persons who sought to perform within that system. His comments, gleaned from that *Constitution* column and other sources, form what is called here McGill's political-rhetoric. Although the term has fallen on bad times in recent years, rhetoric here refers generally to the business of man as he works and communicates (through newspapers, speeches, etc.) with other men. A specific definition is to be found in McGill's conviction concerning how persons should function within a democratic system.

As noted in Chapter Six, McGill worked from the basic premise that individuals and governments should pursue policies that are feasible. While always "pulling for the long view," McGill argues that he was "alive as of now and the tools with which" he "must work are the tools of today."[1] As "politics is the science of the possible,"[2] contended McGill, so rhetoric is a relative of expediency and probability. "I was on the Chicago Round-Table program Sunday in a discussion of civil rights," McGill recalled. "I had remarked that...while all of us know what the objectives are and are unreservedly for them, we know we must crawl before we walk..."[3] McGill admitted that "there is schizophrenia" in "running with the hare and dropping back, now and then, to see how the hounds are making out" and that there is "great frustration of spirit but there also is Americanism and good politics as well."[4]

It is a marriage between democratic and rhetorical processes which McGill suggested gives birth to progress. This union, McGill asserted, is only possible when all voices and views may be heard. So when many persons sought to deny Henry Wallace a chance to speak in the South, McGill rebutted: "Why shouldn't he speak?... No one has to go to hear him. He has an idea and a policy...he has every right to speak."[5] Because he is convinced that the "progress" and "education" which result from free democratic discussion far outweigh any harm done by extravagant "spellbinders," McGill's theory placed no restrictions on public performers:

I am a great hand to stand up for political license. By that I mean it never occurs to me to deny to the politician his right to make extravagant claims. Some may be deplored. Others may be considered dangerous and unworthy. Some will be down-right lies... But all this is a part of our political system. The candidates, in so doing, are gambling...that the people to whom they are appealing are so ignorant as to be unaware of any real issues; so prejudiced as to wish to hear lies and calumny; so careless about government they prefer mud-throwing to facts... This is the political license of the candidate. If he succeeds it is not he who is responsible. It is his audience. If he is elected he mirrors the majority of the voters[6]

It was with this placing of responsibility that McGill again joined rhetoric and politics. As rhetoric is an index of audience performance, so "politics is a mirror of the people and a measure of their citizenship."[7] Because McGill's political-rhetorical system not only guaranteed but encouraged free discussion, he was concerned with the nature and capabilities of people. Indeed, McGill's views about the parliamentary system and about rhetorical processes were dependent upon a faith in humanity and their ability and willingness to judge; and, if the marketplace of ideas is free and open, ultimately to judge increasingly well.

Although McGill maintained that "Man, generally, is pretty fine,"[8] he found that "by and large the people are not informed and it usually is rather easy to lead them off on false trails by appealing to old prejudices and by smearing an opponent in humorous, yet acid, manner."[9] Asked to write a platform for the Democratic State Convention in 1936, this Georgian would later conclude: "The planks selected are those which are believed to contain the most appeal to the lacks, wants, needs, or emotions of the voters. An emotional one is best. If the people really are aroused about something close to their personal life then that is the 'plank' to stress."[10] McGill learned that the "professional politician knows that the greatest political force which can be unloosed is discontent. It is greater even than the force known as "What's in it for me?' "[11]

What did McGill's theory, then, do about the fact that people are often poorly informed and easily deceived? Faced with only one other alternative, censorship, McGill concluded: "I dislike someone else deciding what is good for me and what is bad for me. I prefer to decide for myself... And I want the privilege of deciding. What is more I think I ought to have it."[12] Besides being an unalienable right, McGill believed that free dialogue was a means of *societal self education*. Persons, McGill argued, should be protected with the arm of "truth." "A free people must be free to discuss and debate——because they have been informed."[13] And, he continued, "our [parliamentary] system not merely permits debate... Ours prolongs it, for years, if necessary. Our process is educational."[14]

Although McGill was willing to put up with questionable appeals, at the same time, he called "for a better breed of politician...and for a better type of campaign."[15] But, he suggested, the achievement lies, not in muffling men, but in encouraging a more responsible public performance:

There are many audiences which delight to have pleasant fleas named "states' rights," or "the danger of state-ism" (whatever that is), scratched very vigorously and often...many of our writers and speakers...scratch the same old fleas of "Southern tradition," "states' rights," "saccharin constructive criticism," "the unholy course of Northern Democrats," "let us alone," "the advancing South," and so on, without ever really saying anything. We are making progress——we are doing some mighty and noble things——but we are doing them largely because of those who keep pointing out the need for them to be done... *We can do with a little more intellectual honesty and less professional flea scratching.*[16]

McGill's definition of an ideal politician-rhetorician derived from his belief, also discussed above, that free individuals have a moral responsibility to oppose social evils. "If a free society is to reach an established goal, across the board," McGill maintained, "it must do so to a great extent through individual decisions. This freedom implies a moral responsibility. This responsibility is that of free business, a free press, free labor, free civic groups, a free bar, and free men... We cannot equate the moral value of the just deed of a free man with the same deed of a state automation. If a group in a totalitarian society acts responsibly——there being no moral choice——there can be no moral credit."[17]

To distinguish between that which is socially evil and that which is good, McGill recommended that "a doubting and inquiring mind is the best mental tool to have... Travel and study and experience teach one...not to be too sure about the answers and to know that humility is a comfortable garment which wears well and is becoming... It is best...always to be a seeker, and never to stop and say, 'This is all.'"[18] The communicator-citizen can "never cease to study, read and learn."[19] Part of this probing should be done in the presence of a reading or listening audience. McGill believed that quite often the communicator could act only as a counselor. Social-political problems often are far too complex, he contended, for any one person to claim ready-made answers. The ideal writer or speaker, then, states his ideas with an attitude of determined inquiry, admitting his limitations yet upholding his convictions. For example, when McGill discussed problems relating to education before delegates at the National Education Association convention in 1966, he confessed: "I don't know the answers. I can't find them yet. I keep looking..."[20] Of course no one, including McGill, would deny that this is an effective way to reveal one's modesty and possible credibility; however, McGill insisted that the ideal communicator must mean it.

This dialectical inquiry between the communicator and his auditors is another link in McGill's political-rhetorical system. The political process is prolonged and educational; the rhetorical, ideally, is a continuous condition of mental inquiry. A rhetoric-of-inquiry, McGill believed, is not only a means to an end, but because the process is never ending, it is a lasting state of mind. Thus, the writer and speaker should "stimulate discussion. You ought to provide, when necessary, what seems to you to be the information pertinent to the question."[21] A person, continued McGill, should encourage "inquiry, more reading, more study, a seeking for more information, and in that sense" the writer and speaker should "occupy the role of a teacher."[22]

The goal of the writer and speaker, then, according to McGill, ought to be one of discovering, first within his own mind and, second, when he confronts his auditors. His purpose should be to prepare himself and the public for wise decision making, "supplying information and interpretative comment which make people think and decide issues for themselves."[23] In doing this one should be "honest and aggressive, not dishonest and apologetic."[24] "The American system...can never be a careful, restrained, regimented, controlled existence," he continued. "Our system demands that we live boldly, adventuring always in the fields of business, the mind and professions."[25] McGill practiced this aggressiveness and honesty in both his writings and speeches. For example on January 3, 1954, prior to the Supreme Court's historic desegregation ruling, McGill told a Florida audience:

In the nation's solemn temple of justice final argument has been made in the case of segregation. Now the nation waits... So, as we wait, history now cries out to us to have a policy of reasonableness which, when the decision comes, will not deliver us into the hands of a few political radicals who will lead the nation again into folly and tragedy of destroying public education and of violence... We must respect the fact of honest differences. But, all of us must be careful never to accept the support of, or give aid and comfort to, the crackpots, the fanatics of the lunatic fringe and those who with maliciousness and hate have only the substance of enmity.[26]

McGill's political-rhetorical system has implications for the person who communicates in public. He believed that the communicator who is, in fact, sincerely concerned with his subject and about society would enjoy some success. This belief grew out of the more basic premise that "Emotional concern for human life is perhaps the one most significant mark of a civilization and civilized individuals... All of us——governments and individuals——must have an emotional concern for individual life."[27] Oratory which reflects this kind of interest McGill called "plain talk," i.e., saying something worthwhile in a clear and unaffected manner. To illustrate that mode of speaking, McGill wrote that President Harry S. Truman "is just a fair-to-middling speaker when he is up there with a manuscript before him. But when he talks from his heart his heart comes through and he sells himself solidly. I have seen him addressing a convention of newspaper editors, most of them hostile," continued McGill, "take them in completely when he put aside his manuscript, turned off the radio connection and just plain talked."[28]

It was J.C. Penney, founder of the chain store which bears that name, who impressed McGill most. His speech was used to demonstrate how a sincere speaker can violate many of the traditional tenets of rhetoric and still be effective. Indeed, McGill implied that disregard for certain cherished canons can be a sign of concern:

Mr. Penney, who is a man of seventy-five years, slight and gray, stood up and began to fumble for words. It was this which first attracted me. "What," I said to myself, "doesn't he know it by heart? Hasn't he got it all down like the rest of them, X plus Y equals Z?"... He talked awkwardly as I have ever heard a man talk, yet he was convincing as orators rarely are. He was not glib. His joke was not too well told. He fumbled around, finding his way through his thoughts. Finally he got going. It was a rambling story of a man [himself] who began with poverty and becₒ ⌐ wealthy through initiative and hard work. It was the story of a moral man... He never avoided God. He was not hostile. He was just a sojourner and a seeker. He didn't have any answers. He didn't have any formula for me or anyone else... He didn't make the mistake which, in my opinion, is the mistake of so many who preach, talking in generalities... Mr. Penney held his audience still and quiet because he was completely and humbly sincere... It was a unique meeting. Men who have heard hundreds of "inspirational" talks, dozens of glib and cheery leaders and who remembered not a word they said, will remember for a long, long time the deeply moving and completely sincere, awkward, halting talk of a humble man who had Christ come into his life.[29]

Such concern for one's cause and his audience, McGill believed, may also be revealed in the speaker's supporting material and his choice of language. Facts, he argued, should not be divorced from feeling. If supporting evidence is to be meaningful it must be thought of "in terms of persons——all kinds of persons——the happy, the free, the untroubled, the ambitious, the frustrated, unhappy, defeated, the neurotic, the unstable, the able, the misfits——the old, the young, the babies——all these are the flesh and bone of statistics. And all these persons have their own individualities, culture, backgrounds, loyalties, and problems."[30]

On the other hand, logically invalid appeals should be recognized as a possible index of insincerity and selfish motives on the part of the public performers. "It is distasteful to Georgians," wrote McGill, "to have the Columbians, a hate organization, to locate in the State... Their audiences are almost entirely good, plain persons of little or no education, of little working skills therefore in a very low-income group. The spellbinders, their fingers itching to get those three-dollar initiation fees, talk to them with a certain logic, about as follows: 'Governor Arnall talks about freight rates. Governor Talmadge is always talking about the farmers. Major Hartsfield is interested in streets and airports. You are interested in bread and meat and a living wage. That's what we are going to do for you.' "[31]

The honest communicator, then, will want to develop a well conceived message McGill warned, however, that the orator's argument must be presented so as to appeal to his auditors and reveal himself as a man of good will. For example, McGill told how Senator Robert A. Taft, after speaking in New Hampshire, was informed by a member of the audience that "they liked what you said, but they thought you were a little too distant and lofty." McGill analyzed: "The American people...want someone who warms them and who causes them to lift up their eyes and their hearts. And the able gentleman from Ohio...has been unable to overcome it with either expediency or logic."[32]

McGill emphasized the importance of language facility. Style, McGill said, can indicate the speaker or writer's intentions. If one is truly interested in counseling wisely with an audience, surely, felt McGill, he will want to be clear and easily understood; yet, "no matter how hard one strives to put the little words, simply and plainly one after the other, one does not always succeed."[33] Language can window the inner worth of a man. Adlai Stevenson, wrote McGill, "never repeats. Each speech, even for a small town, is new. He is too honest a man to give them a hack routine"[34]; "he knows what he is saying because they are his own words and thoughts."[35] Describing John F. Kennedy's speaking, McGill reported that "he had plain words...and few generalities, in what was a tersely eloquent inaugural address... There is a balanced sense of realism and idealism in the new President as his words so well revealed."[36]

Unfortunately the worth of man is not always so virtuous. Although McGill suggested that "one who deals in words" must "of necessity" be "humble,"[37] he found that "very few swords have been beaten into plowshares, but a great many words have been fashioned into weapons."[38] One may "run at random through" the "hate pamphlets" of the "Christian Anti-Jewish Party," continued McGill, and "extract phrases which reveal their technique of incitement: 'Plot, dirty, foul, debauched, vile, vicious, conspiracy, savage, Jew machine, counterfeit Americans, Jewish power, Jewish traitors, invisible government, sinister, subversive aggression'——these are the more familiar words. They are repeated over and over as the old familiar lies and accusations pour from the poisoned pens and minds of those engaged in this weird business."[39]

To debate whether language should serve the communicator's ideas or be studied for itself, to McGill, bordered on the ridiculous. Words can be appreciated both for themselves and for what they can do for an oral or written communication. Recalling his visit to the House of Commons, McGill told how Winston Churchill

came slowly into the House just before the questions assigned to him for answer...his squat figure, with the pink round face. He looked older because he was. It was with obvious effort he pulled himself to his feet. Until he speaks his face is expressionless, cast in the familiar lines. But when he rose to have his say and full light played upon him, he comes alive. When the great organ-like voice began and the close-clipped and rolling words followed one another until they sounded like a symphony, then he really seemed to glow. He stroked the stand upon which notes rested, rubbing the hands back and forth. His hands were pink-white and unusually slim for so heavy and short a man. He rarely looked about. But the words came on and on and for anyone who had an affection for words, they were like notes from some great symphonic arrangement with now and then a trumpet solo... His words purred and rolled like summer thunder.[40]

Words not only can provide pleasure, but also, at the same time aid in persuasion. When analyzing Adlai Stevenson's welcoming speech at the Democratic national convention in Chicago in 1952, McGill wrote that, "quite remarkable for these times, he had something to say... It was well written. It was filled with new phrases which gamboled like lambs at play and with sharp-pointed shafts which went into the hide of the Republican elephant like the barbs of picadors."[41] A few days later, after the delegates had heard Stevenson's acceptance address, McGill sensed that "they knew they had in Adlai Stevenson a man who approaches Woodrow Wilson in mind, thought and command of language. Some few said of his acceptance that it was perhaps too highly pitched for the average man. It was not. The people listened to Wilson and understood him and believed him. Because almost all politicians speak in cliches and in a dull and deadly formula it does not necessarily follow the people will not welcome freshness of phrase and thought, written by the speaker himself, and not prepared for him by a team of speech writing ghosts."[42]

McGill, then, argued that a rhetoric-of-inquiry is intrinsic to the political process of prolonged free discussion, the result being a system of societal-self-education. McGill's theory required his ideal communicator-citizen to be an aggressive searcher, before, during, and after his communication. He will seldom be in a position to end by saying, "This is all." He must forever be, to place Emerson's "American Scholar" in a communicative situation, a *Thinking Man Speaking or Writing*. He ought to be a person with deep concern for human life. Only this kind of individual can wear the "garment" of "humility" required of the teacher-rhetorician, yet be "willing to do the unpleasant jobs, to stand out against what is wrong even though it leads to misunderstanding and criticism."[43] As a realist and close observer of men McGill knew that, because many audiences prefer promisers to seekers, there are other routes to personal success. But if all may speak and all may listen audiences gradually gain in sophistication and speakers and writers are forced to inch toward the teacher-rhetorician ideal. Even so, McGill did not guarantee that his ideal communicator would win immediate results and new friends. Honest inquirers are often "abused as Communists, leftwingers, nigger-lovers and traitors."[44] The only certain reward for the *Thinking Man Speaking or Writing* is "an inner satisfaction of being able to face one's self."[45]

SEVEN

1 *Atlanta Constitution*, March 1, 1948, p. 6.
2 *Atlanta Constitution*, October 2, 1957, p. 1.
3 *Atlanta Constitution*, February 14, 1950, p. 10.
4 *Atlanta Constitution*, October 2, 1957, p. 1.
5 *Atlanta Constitution*, November 15, 1947, p. 4.
6 *Atlanta Constitution*, April 9, 1946, p. 8.
7 *Atlanta Constitution*, June 13, 1948, p. 2D.
8 *Atlanta Constitution*, December 10, 1946, p. 6.
9 *Atlanta Constitution*, January 11, 1946, p. 10.
10 *Atlanta Constitution*, August 1, 1948, p. 2D.
11 *Atlanta Constitution*, June 13, 1948, p. 2D.
12 *Atlanta Constitution*, March 21, 1946, p. 8.
13 *Atlanta Constitution*, January 2, 1959, p. 1.
14 *Atlanta Constitution*, March 1, 1950, p. 8.
15 *Atlanta Constitution*, September 10, 1942, p. 18.
16 *Atlanta Constitution*, March 20, 1946, p. 10.
17 McGill, *The South and the Southerner* (Boston: Little, Brown and Company, 1964), p. 231.
18 *Atlanta Constitution*, June 15, 1948, p. 10.
19 McGill, *Saturday Evening Post*, 224 (November 10, 1951), 34.
20 Taken from taped recording. Also the writer witnessed this address at Miami Beach, Florida.
21 Taped interview with McGill, December 29, 1965, Atlanta.
22 Taped recording of his National Education Association speech, 1966.
23 *Atlanta Constitution*, March 18, 1952, p. 1.
24 *Atlanta Constitution*, October 25, 1948, p. 6.
25 *Atlanta Constitution*, November 20, 1951, p. 1.
26 Speech at the Open Forum meeting in Daytona Beach; manuscript provided by McGill.
27 *Atlanta Constitution*, April 22, 1952, p. 1.
28 *Atlanta Constitution*, May 8, 1950, p. 8.
29 *Atlanta Constitution*, February 24, 1950, p. 8.
30 *Atlanta Constitution*, March 24, 1954, p. 1.
31 *Atlanta Constitution*, November 13, 1946, p. 8.

32 *Atlanta Constitution*, March 21, 1952, p. 1.

33 *Atlanta Constitution*, March 23, 1947, p. 14C.

34 *Atlanta Constitution*, October 10, 1952, p. 1.

35 *Atlanta Constitution*, July 22, 1952, p. 1.

36 *Atlanta Constitution*, January 21, 1961, p. 1.

37 *Atlanta Constitution*, March 23, 1947, p. 14C.

38 *Atlanta Constitution*, August 23, 1946, p. 12.

39 *Atlanta Constitution*, October 15, 1958, p. 1.

40 *Atlanta Constitution*, March 25, 1963, p. 1.

41 *Atlanta Constitution*, July 22, 1952, p. 1.

42 *Atlanta Constitution*, July 28, 1952, p. 1.

43. *Atlanta Constitution*, August 5, 1946, p. 6.

44 *Atlanta Constitution*, January 20, 1959, p. 1.

45 *Atlanta Constitution*, October 2, 1957, p. 1.

EIGHT

THE SPEAKER

In addition to his writing McGill was also a "tireless speech-maker."[1] As a young reporter in Nashville McGill "was invited out to a number of schools to talk about sports or Tennessee politics." It was in Atlanta, however, during the "early years of the depression," that McGill became an active speaker. "I had some friends who were on the faculty at Emory University in political science and economics," he recalled, "and at that time one of the government agencies encouraged communities to set up forum meetings. And I remember going with Dr. Goodrich White and particularly with the late Cullen Gosnell to towns all over Georgia...to make talks at these forums... And then in 1937 I was awarded a Rosenwald Fellowship" which "enabled my wife and me to go to Europe. When I came back there was a great demand from civic clubs and all sorts of organizations to talk about one of these many experiences... I've had many other trips to Europe. I went over during the war. I must have made a hundred talks about various aspects of this."

In 1945 McGill talked in North Carolina, Tennessee, and Kentucky, increasingly upon "Southern subjects."[2] "I make a lot of

97

appearances on platforms outside the South," McGill wrote, in order "to tell the real story of the South. I am proud of what the South is trying to do. I admit our problems, our errors and our failures. But we have a story to tell which is a good one. It makes for better understanding."[3] By the 1960's McGill was one of the most experienced and sought-after speakers in the South. In 1965, Miss Grace Lundy, McGill's secretary, reported that he "turns down quite a few invitations to speak——I would estimate between six and eight hundred a year. In 1965 he made forty talks that I have recorded on calendar. This, of course, does not include tapes he was asked by various radio and television stations to make in Atlanta and in the cities where he would be making talks."[4]

McGill has spoken to all kinds of audiences about all kinds of subjects. Civic clubs and organizations of every kind invite him to speak. Speaking in Bradenton, Florida, McGill reported that he "ran into some trouble trying to explain Georgia's political "predicament to the Kiwanians who overflowed into adjoining halls. It is so difficult to explain that not even Georgians themselves can explain it..."[5] Drawing from his broad experience in raising bees, McGill ran into even more difficulty before a garden club:

"Once upon a time I was called upon to talk on the subject of the bees. I began by saying that their social system was not unlike our own. The female bee, called the queen, is a bit fat, had to be waited on all the time, and the male bees work themselves to death keeping her in the style to which she is accustomed. I was speaking to a garden club, and to my surprise this bit of levity did not roll them in the aisles. I hastily turned to the subject of pollination."[6] He once told a men's Bible class that although "Southerners have a reputation of being Bible-oriented," they often "managed to exclude the Negro from" their "concept of the Fatherhood of God and the brother-hood of man." After "polite applause," one "old man came up to" McGill and insisted: "I just want you to know...that I believe in white supremacy. Even the Bible says as much. I hold with our tradition."[7]

Besides churches, McGill preferred to speak to students, and "hated to turn down school and college groups in particular, as he is highly interested in young people."[8] In 1959 he addressed the Columbia University School of Journalism. In 1961 he told the

Harvard Law School Alumni Association that "since the United States Supreme Court decision of May, 1954, the leadership of the Southern bar has not lived up to its responsibility."[9] The American Federation of Teachers, in 1961, heard McGill say that "we have no way to be sure the abilities and talents of thousands of youngsters now moving toward, or in, secondary school, will become a national asset."[10] Two years later this journalist told members of the National Council for the Social Studies that "educators must take the lead in stemming 'the increasing feeling of alienation from the country's future by extremists, depressed or disadvantaged groups.'"[11] On February 3, 1969, the day of his death, McGill spoke at Booker T. Washington school in Atlanta.

Appearing often on radio and television, in 1946, McGill discussed "displaced persons and Palestine" over radio station WAGA in Atlanta. That same year he traveled to New York "to appear on the Town Hall of the Air."[12] On NBC's "Today Show" in 1959, McGill discussed the difficulty of obtaining news from official sources.

Because of his interest in labor, on May 13, 1946, McGill shared speaking duties with Senator Wayne Morse at the Southern Labor Conference of the American Federation of Labor in Asheville, North Carolina, where he spoke to a racially integrated audience from twelve southern states. The day after that address, George L. Googe, Southern Organizing Director, concluded that, "we are also planning to expand our Public Relations Department... We are taking heed of the fine constructive criticism offered by Ralph McGill...in his address before the conference here. He said we had for years been telling our story in a slipshod manner and we intend to do something about it."[13]

Probably known best for his concern for minority groups, McGill, in 1946, informed two hundred and fifty "delegates from Jewish communities in Georgia, Alabama and East Tennessee" about his experiences in Germany and Palestine. Delegates had met to "plan for a hundred million dollars United Jewish Appeal for refugees, overseas needs, and Palestine." Willington Wright, reporter for the *Constitution*, wrote that "the conference took place in the civic room of the Ansley [hotel in Atlanta] against the background of a huge placard indicating that five million seven hundred thousand Jews had died in Europe as the result of Nazi atrocities... In opening his remarks, McGill first told of his visit to the court at Nuremburg, where twenty-two Nazi leaders are on trial for some of the atrocities of which the delegates heard yesterday. 'I intended to stay there two weeks,' said McGill, 'but I stayed only six days. After that time I had a feeling that here was a sort of frustration, a futile gesture in which we placed the emphasis on the wrong things. The real thing is elsewhere, I thought. For in reality it is civilization itself that is on trial.'... In telling of his trip to Palestine, McGill said he came away with the feeling that Palestine offered the real hope for the displaced Jews of Europe... 'I found that Jews and Arabs are getting along in neighborly fashion,' he continued. The Jews have learned a lot from the Arabs and the Arabs have learned a lot from the Jews. My feeling is that if there were no power politics between Great Britain and Russia there would be no Arab-Jewish trouble in Palestine.' McGill then urged the Jews of America to make this hundred million dollar appeal a success... 'This campaign must not fail. There are thousands of people, young people, who want a place in the world to come, a place where they can live and labor in peace and security. God help the future of the world if we fail them.' "[14]

Many of McGill's addresses relating to human rights tackled what he told a Florida audience was "the largest single domestic problem of the United States," "the nation's thirteen million Negroes."[15] In 1948 McGill spoke to "civic, labor and church leaders from seventy-two Southern cities in eleven states" met "to seek the reasonable and tolerant approach to the problem of civil rights."[16] In his newspaper column for several days after that talk McGill analyzed the speaking occasion, telling first what he had said, then describing the response stimulated by the speech, "I had opposed the timing and the methods behind the Federal legislation as proposed" by President Truman, he wrote, "with an argument which can best be summed up as follows: 'I want the South to do what is right, I do not want the Federal Government to compel it... Changing a jury from the courthouse to the jury box in the Federal building will not change a state of mind.' "[17]

Response to McGill's speech was both immediate and delayed. Right after the talk "two young Negro students came up to me, separately," McGill wrote, "and asked these questions: 1. 'Mr. McGill, why is it the majority in the South do not want the Negro to have justice and a fair chance?' 2. 'Will you tell me, sir, how a liberal viewpoint [like McGill's] can oppose the Federal legislation?' "[18]

Several days later, McGill told of a delayed response to his address:

A young Negro woman, married and the mother of one child, came to see me... She said that she came because of a conversation with her friends, who had urged her to come. I want to put it down, her thinking, exactly as I can. "We read in the papers about your talk at the school and about how they asked you questions and didn't agree with you. We read what else you had to say," she began. "Those people (at the university) wouldn't spit on us. There isn't anybody harder on a common Negro than they... They are a lot more distant to their cooks and maids than white people. So, don't you worry too much about how they acted..." Let this be a second chapter in a primer on Southern thinking.[19]

McGill spoke frankly about newspapers and their role in society. In 1947 he talked to the Hoosier Press Association at Indianapolis. Two years later he was on a forum sponsored annually by the *Philadelphia Bulletin*. The North Carolina Press Association invited McGill to speak in 1956. In Japan in 1962 he discussed the "Press and Politics in the United States." On July 12, 1956, McGill told the North Carolina Press Association that "there are some newspapers which are not doing well. I have run my own poll on them in the form of close examination and study and they are, without exception, newspapers which are either so reactionary as to be far behind the times save for a steadily decreasing type of readership, or daily present to the readers a tasteless, monotonous paraphrase of a Biblical truth, 'the same yesterday, today and tomorrow.'"[20]

Much of McGill's speaking in government circles came in the form of committee meetings; however, in 1954 he spoke to the Air Defense Command in Colorado Springs. He addressed a "United Nations group" in Detroit in 1960, and as early as 1948, was asked to testify before the Foreign Relations Committee on the European Relief Plan.

In 1962 McGill spoke in Japan about "Press Leadership in Provincial Areas." The following year he went to Africa on a fact-finding trip for President Kennedy, making several talks and answering questions. Back on July 25, 1943, McGill made what must have been an interesting address, using the facilities of the British Broadcasting Corporation. Although the BBC reported that this speech was not recorded, *The New York Times* carried an Associated

Press summary: "Ralph McGill...praised the British today, saying that they were able to fight the war and at the same time plan to be a better nation when peace comes... He noted in particular plans already made for revision of the educational system to insure wider schooling for all classes and a program for the rebuilding of London."[21]

McGill was often invited to speak for special occasions. On June 3, 1958 he spoke in Little Rock in honor of the *Arkansas Gazette's* Pulitzer winners. On May 29, 1959, he gave the Pulitzer Memorial Address at Columbia University. McGill presented the Lincoln Day Address on February 12, 1960 at Cooper Union, New York. That same year he delivered an oration on the occasion of the Lovejoy Convocation, Colby College. Among McGill's many commencement speeches were those at Duke University, Cranbrook School, University of North Carolina, Oberlin College, Wellesley College, DePaul University, University of Miami, and Butler University.

McGill, then, was an active communicator, both as writer and speaker. McGill claimed "in no sense" to be "an orator," and that he worried about each speech. The night before he was to deliver the commencement address at The University of Miami he "kept waking up thinking about it. Once, at three o'clock" he "got up and cut the speech by four paragraphs."[22] After participating on the Town Hall broadcast in New York, McGill "walked for a half hour to get rid of the tension and excitement of debate."[23] McGill described his personal involvement in "an interracial forum" at Spelman College in Atlanta, the occasion that saw the two young Negroes question McGill after his talk:

I go to these highly controversial programs feeling like a sacrifical lamb. Sometimes I get my throat cut and barbecued. At other times I manage to come out of it intact... I go wearily home, tiptoe in not to awaken the sleeping, and think it over while drinking a glass of milk or so in the kitchen to settle the jangling nerves. Unfortunately, the good Lord gave me no share of omniscience... I accept invitations to appear at these things because it seems to me someone ought to do so. There is a sense of duty...which seems to me to demand it. So I go and talk and go home with my bruises, drink my milk and resolve "never again," as nerves jangle and sleep is delayed. But, always there seems another time...[24]

Reluctant to "reveal personal emotions" of his own, McGill is a reserved speaker,[25] preferring to "discuss with" an audience as opposed to "speaking to" them.[26] Standing five feet ten-and-three-quarter inches tall and weighing one hundred and eighty-five pounds (in 1966),[27] McGill's bodily activity while reflected his dislike for "podium prancers." McGill "never thought of gestures," he said, "and I don't make many. If so, it certainly is a natural one that I'm quite unconscious of."[28] This was certainly the case when this writer saw McGill's address before the National Education Association in 1966. He remained immediately behind the large rostrum, leaning slightly forward as if someone had just reminded him to "speak right into the microphone," his brown "astigmatic" eyes aimed directly to his front. Once or twice he looked to his right, a few times he extended one or both arms toward the audience with his "massive fingers" stretched toward the ceiling as if holding a softball, but for about thirty minutes he was welded into one position. One should note that McGill's weight has varied from one hundred and fifty-two pounds while in college to more than two hundred and thirty pounds in 1947. [29]

Persons usually were impressed by McGill's voice quality. At best McGill's voice was pleasant, but there were times when it was grating, harsh, and unpleasant. It certainly was "different." In 1916 at the age of eighteen he was advised against an acting career because his voice was too "husky"[30] and lacked the "dramatic range" for "real dramatics."[31] Celestine Sibley described McGill's voice as one "which is known to radio, television and lecture audiences and which has the gusty, raspy timbre of a barn door swinging in a high wind."[32] Eleven persons who heard McGill speak at Emory University on May 7, 1965 (and several had heard him on other occasions) chose the following terms in describing his voice quality: "low and raspy," "easy to listen to," "raspy," "awful-thin and rather high," "not attractive to me——it is too husky," "not 'pretty' to listen to [but] not irritating," "a little gravely," "unique and individualistic," "good quality, but cleared throat often," "hoorish-sqeaky," "a high pitched voice of poor quality which grates on my nerves."[3]

McGill said that he wrote his own speeches. His secretary, Grace Lundy, insisted that no one had written one word for Mr. McGill. "Miss Lundy," however, maintained McGill, "is a great help in research. We both sort of work at it together or divide up any area of necessary research. She will find books or articles and I'll find some, and then I'll set in to read and make notes and so forth." When writing a speech manuscript McGill "will do a rough draft of it, sometimes in longhand, sometimes typed, and then" he will "turn it immediately over to" Miss Lundy "before" he "reads it" even, and she will "find any errors, tyopgraphical or grammatical, or any loose construction. I don't think a person is too good at reading his own copy," continued McGill, "at least I'm not. Then when she does that, I will then take it and correct those, indicate the corrections or make them, and then I usually find this gives me an idea to eliminate something or add something. So we'll work it over until it's a pretty-marked-up manuscript, and then she'll do the real draft of it."

Miss Lundy discussed McGill's more typical approach to speech writing. First she stated, because of McGill's unusual ability to recall exact materials needed in research, she does much less work in this area than most secretaries whose bosses speak in public. Also, she advised that the thorough approach to speech preparation described by McGill above had been used on only a few occasions, such as the Cooper Union address and the Harvard Day oration.[34] With most speeches, because of a lack of time, McGill would dash off a first draft, then, Miss Lundy, using that rough copy, typed the final text, asking McGill about obvious errors or "dropped phrases."

When McGill told this writer that his speeches were designed to "supplement" his work in the press, he meant just that. In fact his *Constitution* column often served as a reservoir for speech topics. For example, McGill advocated open public schools in his column on November 19, 1958, repeated the same arguments before the Rotary Club in Augusta, Georgia on February 3, 1959, and, one week later, presented a revised version for the Blazer Lecture series at The University of Kentucky.[35]

Constitution Column
11/19/58

Apparent determination of four or five Southern states to abolish their public schools in the segregation controversy is the more incredible if one reviews the South's long struggle to have education. As the Twentieth Century began in 1900, Southern education suffered from a greater lag than any other public institution in the region.

The report of the U.S. Commissioner on education for the year 1900-1901 showed Southern schools to be wholly inadequate, poorly attended and poorly taught. The amount spent on public education was about a third of the national average. Then, as now, there was a greater proportion of children to adults than in the North. In addition to this, about eighty percent of the Southern population was rural and sparsely settled. School terms were confined to a few winter months. In 1901 Charles W. Dabney of the University of Tennessee, said...

Poverty lay heavily on the South. But nowhere was it as burdensome as on the farms——especially the many small ones. The wan man in the faded denim, his sun-bonneted wife, and his pinched but eager children had already shown their resentment in the Populist revolution. Injustice made what bread they had more bitter. Walter Hines Page described them in a great speech for free education as "the forgotten man."...

Now, in the last half of the Twentieth Century, can it really be true that the political leadership of four or five Southern states is going to close the door to the future in the face of another generation of children?

Augusta Speech
2/3/59

At the time the editor [Henry W. Grady] addressed his New England audience a handful of Southern leaders were well into what was to be a long and arduous struggle for public education.

The report of the U.S. Commissioner on education for the year 1900-1901 showed Southern schools to be wholly inadequate, poorly attended and poorly taught. The amount spent on public education was about a third of the national average. Then, as now, there was a greater proportion of children to adults than in the North. In addition to this, about eighty percent of the Southern

105

population was rural and sparsely settled. School terms in agricultural areas were confined to a few winter months. In 1901 Charles W. Dabney of the University of Tennessee, said...

Poverty lay heavily on the South. But nowhere was it as burdensome as on the farms——especially the many small ones. The wan man in the faded demin, his sun-bonneted wife, and his pinched but eager children had already shown their resentment in the Populist revolution. Injustice made what bread they had more bitter. Walter Hines Page described them in a great speech for free education as "the forgotten man."...

There are already minds and schools closed in the South. There will be more. But I firmly believe those who take this action are trampling out the vintage where the grapes of wrath are stored. I mean no irreverence when I say that while public education may be crucified on a cross of willful decision to end it, it will rise again out of the wreckage. But a whole generation of children will suffer grievous and lasting discrimination. I do not, and have not, advanced a policy of integration. Nor do I have such a policy. My only policy has been one of proceeding by lawful processes.

Kentucky Speech
2/10/59

Some of you will do the job of recreating the domestic equilibrium of our region and our country. I hope we do not leave you too much to do. We must agree with Sophocles that the day can be evaluated only after dusk, that it is through death that one judges life. There is quite a job to do—— In education, for example...

The report of the U.S. Commissioner on education for the year 1900-1901 showed Southern schools to be wholly inadequate, poorly attended and poorly taught. The amount spent on public education was about a third of the national average. Then, as now, there was a greater proportion of children to adults than in the North. In addition to this, about eighty percent of the Southern population was rural and sparsely settled. School terms in agricultural areas were confined to a few months. In 1901 Charles W. Dabney, of the University of Tennessee, said...

Poverty lay heavily on the South. But nowhere was it as burdensome as on the farms——especially the many small ones. The wan man in the faded denim, his sun-bonneted wife, and his pinched but eager children had already shown their resentment in the Populist revolution. Injustice made what bread they had more bitter. Walter Hines Page described them in a great speech for free education as "the forgotten man."...

There are already minds and schools closed in the South. There will be more. But I firmly believe those who take this action are trampling out the vintage where the grapes of wrath are stored. I mean no irreverence when I say that while public education may be crucified on a cross of willful decision to end it, it will rise again out of the wreckage. Kentucky, North Carolina, Tennessee and West Virginia have somehow escaped this ugly compulsion to close schools. One naturally asks——Why? There is one immediate answer. It is leadership.

McGill often met a pressing deadline by revising a used speech for a new occasion. His secretary demonstrated this procedure with a text written for the Birmingham Rotary Club on May 17, 1961 and revised for a later speech at Georgia Institute of Technology on December 7, 1962. She placed the two manuscripts on her desk, turning the pages simultaneously to show how the second speech was based on the first.

Miss Lundy pointed to remarks McGill had made to inform her of desired changes: "1," "Insert 2," "Insert 3," "Delete and Insert 4." After that came: "delete," "Insert," "Ole Miss," "Cuba now," "Mention Ga. Tech." Miss Lundy pointed to a comment which she said she had written on the old text: "Is this up to date?" She related that it was her practice to check statistics and other data to determine if they were appropriate for the new occasion.[20] Quotations from the Birmingham and Georgia Tech speeches illustrate how McGill revised an old text for a new audience:

Birmingham Rotary
1960

You and your fathers *have been the makers of productive and technological revolution. This* city is the site of a *major* Southern *research institution* which spends its time *developing new techniques and materials which will accelerate the changes in our region and in our lives.*

Georgia Tech
1962

Graduates of this institution *have been the makers of productive and technological revolution. This* school carries on *major research* and experiment in developing *new techniques and materials which will accelerate the changes in our region and in our lives.*

Out of a total of three hundred and twenty-one typed lines in the Birmingham text, two hundred and fifty-three were unchanged for Georgia Tech, and five lines received only minor alternations. McGill deleted sixty-three typed lines from the Brimingham text when preparing the Georgia Tech speech, and added only two typed lines within the original three hundred and twenty-one lines of the old manuscript. He attached three pages at the end of the old manuscript when writing the Georgia Tech oration. While deleting all references to the Birmingham area, McGill added no material specifically pertaining to Georgia Tech. There were at least three possible reasons for this. The original Birmingham address discussed education, so the thesis would have been appropriate at Georgia Tech. Indeed, this probably was the reason McGill selected the Birmingham speech as the one to be revised. Second, McGill may have added comments about Georgia Tech after he arrived on the scene, a practice very common to his speaking. Third, McGill could simply have failed to make adequate adjustments when hurriedly revising an old speech for a new situation.

While speaking McGill was able to "take in a pretty good paragraph" of the manuscript by "just looking" down at it; he did not "have to read a line of the manuscript," but could "follow it almost exactly without seeming to be reading it." "I think in almost every speech," McGill concluded, "you depart from a manuscript in some instances. I can't recall, oh maybe once or twice...that I followed it absolutely. Most of the time you depart from a manuscript. Something happens after you get there or you meet someone or there will be some local subject come up that you learn the audience is interested in, and you work in something about that."[36] "I was making a commencement talk the other day," McGill recalled, "and I was trying to talk plain... I had started with a line from Walt Whitman... I was having a difficult time with Whitman vs. spring and the end of school... When I switched from Whitman to [Jack] Dempsey I knocked spring right out of the hall."[37] In his Lincoln Day Address at Cooper Union, however McGill knew almost nothing about his audience so he "stuck to the manuscript except for one or two little departures."

McGill preferred to speak extemporaneously, and was reluctant to accept speaking engagements which required a manuscript. Since he never rehearsed an oration, McGill relied largely on his selection of topic, his excellent memory, and his habit of taking notes wherever he went. Once in 1965 McGill was to speak at an Episcopal church in Marietta, Georgia. As he drove to the church, McGill asked the Reverend Albert Hatch, "What do you want me to talk about?" Hatch reported that this gave him "quite a scare."[38] Writing about a talk he gave in 1950 to one thousand 4-H club members, McGill stated: "In the moments before the young man had risen to introduce me...I was deep in...thought... 'I cannot in conscience offer you a challenge," was all I could muster as a beginning... Words, whether spoken or written, come hard with me."[39]

McGill's secretary said that audiences "expect" McGill to talk about "Southern" issues, causing him to repeat similar messages to different audiences and making it easier to speak with little immediate preparation. On January 26, 1966, Dr. Morton S. Notarious, chairman of the forum committee at Temple Beth Am in Miami, invited McGill to speak "on aspects of the South other than Civil Rights."[40] What did he treat? Notarious wrote that McGill "spoke mostly about civil rights, which was not the requested topic."[41]

McGill's good memory permitted his somewhat casual approach to extemporaneous speaking. When asked if he had found what *Newsweek* called his "prodigious"[42] memory to be useful in speaking, McGill replied, "Yes, it has been very helpful." He described a talk made from "the bed of a truck" to members of the Gordon County Farm Bureau in Calhoun, Georgia, showing how his extemporaneous speeches often consisted of several personal experiences loosely put together for a particular audience: "So I stood there on the truck and talked about how I had seen the countries of Europe and the East where soil erosion has created deserts... I meant to tell the story about looking down into Boaz's valley where occurred the prettiest story in the Bible...of Ruth and Naomi... I forgot that one. But I told others."[43]

McGill's speaking also benefited from his practice of recording his personal experiences, whether in south Georgia or Europe. For example, he often headlined a column with such phrases as, "From an Editor's Notebook: At DePauw University,"[44] "Some Notes Made on an Envelope at New Haven,"[45] "From Notes Made at the Chicago Meeting of American Sociological Association."[46] In 1954 McGill wrote, "Always when strapped in my seat, I help the aircraft to become airborne... And with a typewriter or a writing pad on my knees, I like to put down something of how it seems."[47]

McGill liked to speak extemporaneously even on formal occasions. For these speeches, however, he committed their "facts, opinions and coherence to memory."[48] This writer saw McGill speak to more than six thousand delegates at the National Education Association convention in 1966 without a single note. Notice, however, how he relied on common ideas and language at that convention which he had used one year earlier at Emory University (both texts taken from taped recordings):

Emory University
1965

I suppose only grey heads or semi-grey heads like mine will *remember the boll weevil...* The boll weevil hit, roughly around 1920...to destroy a crop, to destroy a *way of life.* It was then, in the late 20's when the *tenant cabins* began to be *emptied,* their *doors sagging,* their *wooden* shuttered *windows sagging,* stones falling off the old *chimney*...we began to see truck *loads and train loads of people* being *recruited* to go up North and work... I remember...seeing the sometimes pathetic efforts to contend with *the boll weevil*...the *wife and* the *husband and* the *children* carrying *buckets of poison syrup with a stick* and *a rag* tied on the end, and going down the rows of *cotton touching a* leaf on *each plant* with some of the *poison syrup*... I'm sure some of you maybe saw in the 20's...how the *labor recruiters* were here in our area, taking people North to work...

...the great *migrations* were those of the First World *War*, and they were small compared with those which began well before the Japanese attacked us at Pearl Harbor... Probably the single most dramatic *phenomenon* of the American *people* as a whole is their *mobility*. We are a *people* that *move...* And you travel America and you see *trailer camps by the* hundreds and *thousands* and you see *people on the move...*

...as someone said, and I wish that I might have thought of it myself, they took with them *hands* that *were curved to fit plow handles* and *hoe handles*, and little else. They could repair tractors...*farm* machinery, but here they went.

No, I'm very proud, as you are, to be in *the South*. I, *born* just over the line *in Tennessee*, I've never lived or worked anywhere else except *Tennessee* and *Georgia*...*but I* ask you to keep in mind that *we...have...far to go*, and we're going and we're making *progress...*

National Education Association
1966

I can remember the boll weevil decade... I can remember how the cotton sharecropper and *tenant cabins emptied*, some of them burned, leaving the *chimneys* there like silent sentinels representing something gone...their *wooden windows...sagging*, the *doors sagging*... And out of the South in that decade, there moved over one-hundred thousand persons, because their *way of life* was gone... I remember people trying to *poison cotton* for *the boll weevil*, and seeing in the fields, grandmothers and grandfathers and *wives and husbands* and little *children* even, with a *bucket of poison syrup*, and *a stick* with *a rag* on it, *touching a* drop of this syrup to *each plant*... I remember watching the *labor recruiters* get their crowds together in country towns and in cities, and seeing whole train loads and bus loads of people move out...

And when the great tragedy of December 7, 1941, came and it became necessary for this nation to build...ships of all kinds...never have I witnessed such a *migration* I suppose when historians look back at this nation they will say that one of the great *phenemenon* of it was its *mobility*, the *mobility* of its *people*. And we got used to *trailer camps*, and we got used to *people on the move*, in *thousands by thousands*...

I remember one of our writers watching train loads of people leave...he wrote of them that they left, and he seemed to see that their *hands were* still *curved to fit* a *plow handle* or a *hoe handle*, and that he felt like weeping because all they were taking with them was a small skill of a small *farm*...

Now, certainly, as a Southerner, *born in Tennessee*, in Atlanta, *Georgia* for thirty-seven, almost thirty-seven years now, I've known nothing else, in so far as birthright is concerned, but *the South*. I have a great respect for what it——its *progress, but I* must most earnestly say, that *we have far to go, far to go*...

Opinions varied concerning McGill's effectiveness as a speaker. For example a law student at Emory University, concluded that "Ralph McGill, to my mind, is one of the giant intellects of the South of today... I have heard McGill speak on several occasions... My reactions have not changed since the first time. McGill is a writer, not a speaker. The oratory that flows so easily from some people is almost totally lacking in him. He does not seem to have the 'presence' necessary to the truly effective public speakers. The spoken word simply does not allow the presentation of complicated ideas; the reader can stop and think, and gather ideas into a cohesive whole. The listener is denied this. His speaking is directed to a reading audience, not a listening one. His thoughts seem to encompass the whole of society and to be too large for a short talk."[49]

At the other extreme was the view reported by the editor of the student newspaper at Washington and Lee University:

Mr. McGill is not the first speaker we have had here this year, but by a very comfortable margin he is the best... Why?...we would answer such a question by saying that he spoke "straight from the shoulder." To us it seemed that he was thinking first of informing his audience——and not at all of impressing them... Students on the verge of plunging into the whirlpool of life want——and need——considerably more than beautiful oratory, untried political theory, and moral didacticism. They want facts; and it was facts which Mr. McGill gave his audience Monday night.[50]

McGill's speaking effectiveness probably would have to be determined on the basis of a particular speech designed for a certain audience and occasion; however, his performance probably fell between the opinions of the law student and college editor. Certainly one basing his judgment upon a loquacious platform personality would have been disappointed in the oratory of Ralph McGill. This publisher usually gave little thought to sartorial smartness; "he looked real *everyday*——like a storekeeper."[51] He rebelled against "podium prancers"[52] and talkers "who put that phony excitement in their voices."[53] McGill's goal appeared to be that of leading his audience in an informal "discussion" of important and timely issues. Whether he accomplished that objective probably should be decided in relation to individual addresses.

To measure the impressions of one of McGill's audiences, this writer distributed five hundred postcard questionnaires immediately following his address to the National Education Association convention in 1966. Since the respondents were not chosen randomly, and because it is difficult to determine whether the questions measured the information sought or the audience's attitude toward McGill, no statistical inferences can be drawn concerning the more than six thousand delegates. However, it is interesting to note the reaction of the one hundred and forty-six persons who did respond:

1. On the basis of *this speech*, how would you rate Ralph McGill as a speaker? Circle one:

poor - fair - adequate - good - superior

poor	fair	adequate	good	superior	
7	6	22	78	33	Total (146)

2. Were McGill's ideas presented so as to be clearly understood?

3	7	12	60	64

113

3. How conclusively did McGill prove his point(s)?

8 8 21 57 52

What was McGill's evaluation of his own speaking? Both he and his secretary, Miss Grace Lundy, insist that he "does not consider himself a speaker."[54] One can learn more about what McGill really thought by going to what apparently was the most detailed account McGill recorded pertaining to his own speaking. Notice how he contrasted the "talker" (his own manner of speaking) with the "speech-maker":

I am not a speech-maker. Oratory is not one of my assets. But I am willing. I can stand on my feet and talk without any knocking of knees or tightening of the solar plexus nerves. But, unfortunately, this is not speech-making and it is not easy. If one is not a speech-maker and it is not easy. If one is not a speech-maker with at least a half-dozen portable trapezes which one may set up and perform upon in any sort of hall or upon any open platform, then one is forced to have something to say. This is dangerous. It also annoys the audience. If one has something to say there are always those in the audience who disagree. They are forced to sit there gritting their teeth and growing red about the gills, their civic club luncheon, always a digestive shock, all the more lethal as it delightedly sabotages the digestive juices and curdles the cheerful little aminoacids. The honest speaker, in such a situation, must always say that what he is expressing is his own opinion and that it may be wrong, but that it is what he thinks, based on experience, observations and study. But this never appeases the dissenters. This sort of thing is never a success.... The speech-makers are different. They have at least three or four speeches tailored to any occasion. They begin with the polite little jokes, which fit any community. They toss out a bouquet to any or two local celebrities who sit beaming in the audience. They then proceed to the introductory paragraphs of their "message," move powerfully into the meat of it, and bring it to a ringing conclusion. The old-fashioned virtues, God, Mother, soil conservation...blend richly to produce a warming, satisfactory result which makes every one happy and inserts no grains of irritating thoughts into the oyster of the mind. I seriously envy these gentlemen. Of course, I think some of them carry it too far. One I know, who makes a modest charge, sends out photographs of himself on slick paper. Beneath it are listed his subjects. Then follows the praises of critics. For a fee he will come and set up his trapezes and swing back and forth on them with the greatest of ease... He does it well. He startles no one... The talker, as opposed to the speech-maker, invariably is persuaded to accept invitations when he has nothing to say, a fate which has been my lot on several occasions. Lacking a speech to pull out of the file, the talker stumbles around, and ends up angry with himself and in agreement with the audience that it was a dull affair. I am almost persuaded the field is best left to the speech-maker.[55]

Finally, persons who concurred with McGill's concern for human rights demonstrated great trust in this world-known Southerner from Atlanta. For example, twenty-eight of thirty-six persons responding to an inquiry relating to McGill's speech at Emory University on May 7, 1965 expressed their reaction with such comments as:

I think Mr. McGill is outstanding as a clear thinker on social issues. His perspective of background information about the South is unmatched...

Fairly complete agreement [with McGill]. It is hard to see how anyone with a sense of fair play, morality, and Christian ethics could feel any other way.

He has shown more "Guts" than practically all Bible-belt preachers put together. He has been a leader of thought in an intellectual desert.

Research, then, revealed this Southerner to be a man of integrity, good will, intelligence, courage, and purpose. Both his speeches and writings served as tools of justice in behalf of men exploited by man. Persons who shared McGill's hope for equal citizenship for all often found encouragement and strength in his *oral and written instruction.*

EIGHT

1   *Newsweek*, LIII (April 13, 1959), 102.
2   All of above taken from taped interview, December 29, 1965, Atlanta.
3   *Atlanta Constitution*, October 25, 1948, p. 6.
4   Typed statement given this writer by Grace Lundy, December 29, 1965, Atlanta.
5   *Atlanta Constitution*, February 7, 1947, p. 10.
6   *Atlanta Constitution*, October 8, 1947, p. 10.
7   McGill, *South and the Southerner*, pp. 232-233.
8   Typed statement provided by Lundy, December 29, 1965.
9   *The New York Times*, June 15, 1961, p. 14.
10   *The New York Times*, August 17, 1961, p. 15.
11   *The New York Times*, December 2, 1963, p. 46.
12   *Atlanta Constitution*, March 29, 1946, p. 1.
13   *Atlanta Constitution*, May 14, 1946, p. 6 (AP).
14   *Atlanta Constitution*, August 19, 1947, p. 12.
15   Open Forum speech at Daytona Beach, Florida, January 3, 1954; manuscript provided by McGill.
16   *Atlanta Constitution*, February 28, 1948, p. 11.
17   *Atlanta Constitution*, March 1, 1948, p. 6.
18   *Atlanta Constitution*, March 1, 1948, p. 6.
19   *Atlanta Constitution*, March 5, 1948, p. 10.
20   Manuscript provided by McGill.
21   *The New York Times*, July 26, 1943, p. 7 (AP).
22   *Atlanta Constitution* June 9, 1949, p. 14.
23   *Atlanta Constitution*, May 19, 1947, p. 6.
24   *Atlanta Constitution*, February 29, 1949, p. 2D.
25   *Atlanta Constitution*, May 20, 1946, p. 6.
26   Letter to this writer from Grace Lundy, July 27, 1966, Atlanta.
27   Letter to this writer from Grace Lundy, October 11, 1966, Atlanta. She noted that McGill had brown hair and wears a 7 3/8 hat.
28   Taped interview, December 29, 1965, Atlanta.
29   See *Atlanta Constitution*, October 15, 1950, p. 1; *Nashville Tennessean Magazine*, November 5, 1961, p. 10.
30   *Atlanta Constitution*, August 6, 1947, p. 6.

31 *Atlanta Constitution*, November 8, 1949, p. 10.

32 *Saturday Evening Post*, 231 (December 27, 1958), 52.

33 Responses to an inquiry by this writer. Addresses of audience members obtained from Emory University.

34 "A View From a Tight Small Compartment," June 14, 1961, Harvard University; "The Meaning of Lincoln Today," Cooper Union for the Advancement of Science and Art, February 12, 1960.

35 Manuscripts provided by McGill. That McGill generally followed his text was confirmed in the *Augusta Chronicle*, February 4, 1959; and *Louisville Courier-Journal*, February 11, 1959.

36 Taped interview with McGill, December 29, 1965.

37 *Atlanta Constitution*, June 8, 1950, p. 1.

38 Interview with Miss Lundy, December 29, 1965, Atlanta.

39 *Atlanta Constitution*, August 25, 1950, p. 1.

40 Information sent by Notarius, March 29, 1966, Miami, Florida.

41 Information sent by Notarius, February 2, 1966.

42 *Newsweek*, LIII (April 13, 1969), 102.

43 *Atlanta Constitution*, August 28, 1948, p. 4.

44 *Atlanta Constitution*, April 24, 1958, p. 1.

45 *Atlanta Constitution*, February 14, 1961, p. 1.

46 *Atlanta Constitution*, September 9, 1965, p. 1.

47 *Atlanta Constitution*, February 10, 1954, p. 1.

48 *Atlanta Constitution*, January 27, 1948, p. 4.

49 Letter to this writer, July 2, 1966, Atlanta.

50 *Ringtum Phi*, February 21, 1947.

51 *The Nashville Tennessean Magazine*, November 5, 1961, p. 10.

52 *Atlanta Constitution*, July 31, 1949, p. 18A.

53 *Atlanta Constitution*, October 6, 1948, p. 6.

54 McGill in taped interview; Lundy in letter to this writer on July 27, 1966, Atlanta.

55 *Atlanta Constitution*, May 25, 1949, p. 12.

NINE

RALPH McGILL SPEAKS

Although McGill tackled many important topics, he usually was identified with human rights: jobs, the vote, housing, public accommodations, etc. In no area, however, did he demonstrate more interest than in the entire field of education. For forty years McGill revealed a keen concern for the nation's public schools. He was motivated by the belief that "the public school is the foundation of America and of the country we have built. It could not have been built save by the secular public school."[1] As early as 1937, McGill traveled to Scandinavia where he "visited and spent time in the rural schools."[2] When he published his findings in *A Comparison of Education for Democracy in Northern Europe and Georgia*, McGill concluded: "An educated man with at least some idea of how to rationalize himself with the world about him is better prepared for making his lot a better one and for making his community an improved one."[3] It was this premise which prompted McGill's concern and campaign for the public schools.

As early as December 3, 1946, McGill wrote in his *Constitution* column that "to point out that the Negro has been standing at the end of the line in housing, justice, schooling, and ability to work for

118

what he is worth, is just plain common sense." After the Supreme Court desegregation ruling in 1954, there came a great movement to close the public schools in the South, McGill began a personal campaign to see to it that the schools stayed open. Week after week he wrote and spoke of the "evil harvest" of segregation and of the great need for open public schools.

McGill considered one of the chief causes of the school crises to be the failure of the leadership. Southern political leaders, stated McGill, "have repeatedly told the people that the Supreme Court violated the Constitution and that the Constitution, therefore, is not the law. Still others have been so untruthful as to tell the people their state Constitutions provide state sovereignty in conflict with the federal... The Constitution is the basic law. And the answers to change lie through the executive and legislative branches...not defiance or deceit in telling the people the Constitution is not valid."[4]

By the early 1960's McGill believed that, though the threat to schools was far from over, "there is evidence that the people of the South slowly are beginning to think for themselves... Little Rock, Birmingham, Montgomery, New Orleans——all these suggest to us to think and evaluate... The wages of violence, like those of sin, is a sort of death. Something dies in a city or a community when there is an explosion of hatred. Changes in the law have opened the way for a slow, orderly process of desegregation in schools, and in all public aspects of our daily life where American citizenship rights must be the same. This will continue. Corrupt governors, promising violence, will not stop it."[5]

For his personal campaign to save the public schools, McGill was given the Sidney Hillman Award, The American Education Award for 1969 was awarded posthumously to McGill for his "outstanding contirbution to the field of education" in his role as "courageous journalist." McGill recalled that "it was not easy to be patient in 1938 on leaving a wretched rural-slum school, or in 1954 when so much of the leadership began to urge the closing of schools."[6]

To understand forces which were working when the speeches printed below were given, one must piece together events which led in the 1950's to the precarious position of public education in the South, and to racially integrated public schools in the 1960's. Prior to the Supreme Court's ruling against segregated schools on May 17,

1954, the South was relatively calm with its separate but unequal school systems. Indeed it was this silence before the social storm which concerned McGill. Torn between fear and hope he tried to prepare his reading and listening audiences for the social revolution of the 1950's and 1960's. In his University of Arkansas commencement address, just four months before the Supreme Court ruling, he stated: "Now we face, presumably sometime in the spring, another decision which will test all Americans.... It is not what we personally would prefer. It is that segregation by color based on law simply does not fit concepts of our world today, neither political nor Christian."

The South's reaction to the idea of racially integrated public schools was decisive. *The New York Times* reported that within the first year after the court's ruling the South has "witnessed considerable confusion, much indecision, more uneasiness and a few bold experiments."[7] Legal opposition began three days after the 1954 decision when "Governor Thomas B. Stanley of Virginia...invited Southern governors to meet in Richmond early in June for exploratory talks on the school segregation question."[8] When those states met on June 10, 1954, "governors and other officials" from twelve of fifteen states attending agreed "to seek legal means of circumventing the" ruling.[9]

Legal logistics took many forms. On January 10, 1956, the *Atlanta Constitution* reported that "the first of a series of bills to strengthen segregation in Georgia will begin moving through the State Senate."[10] Virginia voters, on January 9, 1956, "by a margin of more than 2-1...directed the General Assembly to call a convention to amend the state constitution so state money" could "be used for tuition grants in private nonsectarian schools,"[11] Virginia's palliative proposals were struck down by the courts; on October 21, 1957, the Supreme Court refused "to review a decision holding unconstitutional the state's 1956 Pupil Placement Act,"[12] and on January 20, 1959, "Virginia's legal barriers against racial integration, under which nine white schools" had "been shuttered since September, toppled...in the State Supreme Court."[13] Alabama probably was least imaginative in its legal opposition to school integration. The Associated Press reported January 19, 1956 that "the Alabama Senate...shouted its approval of a House-passed 'nullification' resolution declaring the U.S. Supreme Court

120

antisegregation rulings 'of no effect' in Alabama."[14] In 1958 the state legislature of Mississippi authorized its governor to close the public schools if needed and, until 1962, Florida law required total segregation of public schools.[15] During the late 1950's McGill spoke to the Augusta Rotary Club, the University of Kentucky Blazer Lecture forum, Emory University, and on several other occasions in his personal campaign to save the South's public schools.

Many leaders used personal persuasion to defy the courts. On June 6, 1954 Governor "Herman Talmadge of Georgia...called the U.S. Supreme Court's ban on segregation in public schools a 'judicial brainwashing' and said, 'We do not recognize it as a legal decision.'"[16] This kind of response angered McGill most and caused him to say in his Harvard Law School address and on many other occasions that "what we have needed...from public leadership generally has been a continuing defense of the integrity of the Federal judiciary. Had the people been told by Bar associations that court orders require compliance, we would, I believe, have escaped some of the trouble caused by the deliberate deceit of the people by political leaders who invariably were loudly assured by a 'leading constitutional authority' that they could, and would, defy the courts."

Denial by the church often came in the form of silence. Meeting in Harrisburg, Pennsylvania on October 17, 1956, for example, the "United Lutherans, in a stormy session...defeated a proposed statement specifically endorsing the Supreme Court decision against segregation in the schools" by a vote of three hundred and forty to one hundred and fifty nine.[17] On May 17, 1955, the *New York Times* summarized reaction heard from the South:

There are thirteen Southern and border states that constitute the traditional "Southland." The "official" attitude of this grouping since last May 17 breaks down as follows: South Carolina, Georgia, Mississippi and Lousiana have declared that they will maintain segregated schools regardless of the Supreme Court's directives. Kentucky, Tennessee, Virginia, North Carolina, Florida, Alabama, Texas, Arkansas, and Oklahoma have adopted a "wait-and-see" policy. Each state has its own distinct "climate" of opinion on the extent to which school integration is possible in certain areas. The principal characteristic of the "wait-and-see" states is that in the main they have counties with widely varying population ratios of Negroes and whites.[18]

Court decisions were also met with open violence. On February 6, 1956, Autherine Lucy was "barred from classes" at the University of Alabama "as a safety measure."[19] In September of that year "bayonet-armed National Guardsmen wearing gas masks moved into position in front of the Anderson County courthouse" at Clinton, Tennessee "to break up a new mob which had gathered boisterously...on the scene of previous anti-integration demonstrations."[20] On September 7, 1956, "mob pressure...blocked efforts of three Negroes to register at the Texarkana, Texas Junior College."[21] In Little Rock, Arkansas on September 24, 1957, violence finally caused President Dwight D. Eisenhower to send one thousand soldiers "equipped with live ammunition" "to back a federal court integration order with force."[22] Violence returned to Clinton, Tennessee on October 5, 1958 when "three explosions rocked integrated Clinton High School...and the FBI immediately launched an investigation into the bombings."[23] By February 5, 1959, just a few days prior to McGill's "Crisis in Schools" speech at Emory University, social disorder had become so wide spread that President Eisenhower "asked a divided Congress...to make it a federal crime to use force or mob violence to block integration of schools under court orders...[and for] more authority for the FBI in dealing with schools and church bombings, and to authorize federal funds and advice to help states make the change to desegregated schools."[24]

One can see, then, that between 1954 and 1959, response to the desegration decision from legal opposition to open violence. McGill, as he revealed in his Hogate Lecture at DePauw University, did not challenge one's right to oppose the ruling. He stated, rather, that "there could be full disagreement. There could be organization and efforts to have legislation enacted to change the effect of the decision. There could be a decision to close the schools and some have enacted enabling legislation to this end. All these were legitimate." What McGill did dislike were "the campaigns of outright defiance and" the "programs of villification of the Supreme Court and any who accepted its findings as the legal constitutional interpretation."

The battle for equality spread from the court room to the halls of Congress and finally out into the streets. Reaction between 1959 and the late 1960's varied with the attitude and goal of the participants. In Atlanta on December 12, 1960 "a shattering explosion...damaged a Negro school and a dozen homes along Pelham Street, NW, and started intensive...investigation."[25] On May 21, 1961 in Montgomery, Alabama, "an angry mob of club-swinging, rock-throwing white youths stormed a cordon of U.S. Marshals and state troopers at the Negro Baptist Church."[27] On September 30, 1962 "bloody rioting among University of Mississippi students and adults from off campus protesting the arrival of Negro James H. Meredith resulted in one death and numerous injuries Sunday night before troops arrived on the scene. By midnight one newsman had been shot dead and a U.S. Marshal was reported dying with a wound in the throat."[28] In Birmingham, Alabama on September 15, 1963, while this writer worshiped just a few blocks away in Trinity Methodist Church, a package of ten to thirteen sticks of dynamite was set off at a Negro church...killing four children in Sunday School and injuring at least twenty other persons. Negroes, angered by the outrage, retaliated by hurling stones and bottles at policemen and white motorists [including this writer, his wife, and three-year old son as they returned from church] all day Sunday. Two Negro boys were shot to death in other racial incidents...and a Negro man and a white man were wounded by gunfire.[29] On August 6, 1964, "four Athens, Georgia men identified by investigators as Ku Klux Klansmen were arrested...in connection with the pre-dawn highway slaying of Lemuel A. Penn, a Washington, D.C., Negro educator."[30] In October 1965 violence broke out in Crawfordville, Georgia when Negroes "mounted a daily campaign to board the public school buses that carry white children to nearby communities... The daily scrimmage had aroused one of Georgia's worst racial flare-ups in years."[31]

Racial integration brought demonstrations, as civil rights marchers invaded the rural communities and urban centers during the 1960's. On March 15, 1960 "nearly two hundred Negro college students staged sit-down demonstrations in ten white eating establishments in Atlanta...at lunchtime."[32] In Birmingham on May 2, 1963 "an estimated seven hundred Negroes were jailed...in a massive onslaught of anti-segregation demonstrations as pupils skipped classes to stage marches."[33] Two days later in that iron city "snarling police dogs

123

chased away crowds of Negroes and fire hoses flattened youthful demonstrators...as hundreds of Negroes tried to stage anti-segregation marches."[34] Speaking at Wellesley College in 1963, McGill analyzed some of the causes of Alabama's social problems:

The state elected a governor committed to defiance of court orders in education. There was no commitment. There was no leadership. There was no assumption of responsibility by businessmen, the clergy, or the newspapers. So the police dogs and fire hoses were loosed on women and children and the jails were filled. And still there was abdication of responsibility, and then one Sunday morning the children were shattered by dynamite.

As civil rights organizations became more aggressive and better organized, demonstrations took new form. On August 28, 1963, in Washington, D.C., "an estimated two hundred thousand 'freedom marchers'——most of the Negroes——demanded of Congress...that it pass an 'effective civil rights bill now.' "[35] Dr. Martin Luther King, Jr. was one of the most influential leaders. On February 1, 1965, Dr. King "was arrested with two hundred and fifty-six other Negroes" in Selma, Alabama "during a right-to-vote protest."[36] On March 21, 1965 King "led four thousand civil rights demonstrators, guarded by carbine-carrying soldiers, to a cow pasture campground eight miles from Selma...on the first leg of their historic 'freedom march' to Montgomery."[37] In June, 1966, a few days before McGill's address to the National Education Association at Miami Beach, James H. Meredith, first known Negro to enter the University of Mississippi, attempted to lead a similar march along U.S. Highway 51 from Memphis, Tennessee to Jackson, Mississippi. Just "two miles beyond Hernando, Mississippi, Meredith was plodding doggedly up a small hill when a white man popped up from the brush along the highway... A sixteen guage shotgun roared once, and a spray of bird shot blasted into Meredith's right side... Twice more the gunman fired... Meredith...suffered from "multiple superficial abrasions."[38]

The week before McGill's speech to the National Education Association, a heated debate raged among civil rights workers as to acceptable and effective means of protest. *Time* reported that "many militant ideologues are impatient with what they consider the glacial pace of progress in civil rights. They espouse instead a racist philosophy that could ultimately perpetuate the very separatism against which Negroes have fought so successfully. Oddly, they are not white men but black, and their slogan is 'Black Power.' "[39]

Non-violent opposition to racial desegration ranges from blockades to bombasts during the 1960's. On December 18, 1962, McGill's hometown made what he called a "mistake that can be photographed": "The city of Atlanta erected barricades across Peyton and Harlan Roads...prompting the second court action in two days against an ordianace creating a racial buffer zone and setting off a "selective buying campaign" by Negroes against merchants they said supported the ordinance."[40] Alabama Governor George C. Wallace attracted world attention when he carried out his campaign promise of "standing in the school house door" to block integration of Alabama's public schools. Although he was later able to get his wife Lurleen elected governor of Alabama, Wallace was unable to match the soldiers sent by the President: "Still claiming victory, Gov. George C. Wallace retreated from the campus of the University of Alabama Tuesday afternoon and two Negro students whom he had vowed to keep out were enrolled for the summer quarter. Wallace agreed to leave only after President John F. Kennedy federalized eighteen thousand Alabama National Guardsmen and an estimated six hundred of them began arriving on the Alabama campus."[41]

Three months later "twenty Negro children entered white schools in three Alabama cities...in a historic move that came only after another showdown between President John F. Kennedy and Governor George C. Wallace. Kennedy put the seventeen thousand Alabama National Guardsmen into federal service, thereby removing them from the control of Wallace, who had ordered some units on active duty a few hours earlier."[42]

Some leaders voiced their opposition to what they called "forced integration." On April 25, 1965 for example, "an estimated crowd of more than one thousand flag-waving, sign-carrying whites ignored occasional showers to stage a protest march to downtown Atlanta...and listen to a fiery oration by segregationist Lester Maddox."[43] Maddox personified the mood of the South in his successful campaign for Governor of Georgia in 1967. The dialogue of the 1960's continued until in 1965 "a group of Southern governors" planned to "meet with Governor Carl Sanders in Atlanta...to discuss a federal ruling that at least four grades in all schools must be desegregated by "the fall."[44]

Slowly a few cities in the South decided to chance compliance to court decisions. In 1964 "Atlanta schools opened quietly for the most part...despite sharply increased desegregation."[45] There was surprising progress in a few of the states bordering the deep South. After several noisy incidents in a few isolated communities, Kentucky passed a far-reaching civil rights bill in 1966. It went "further toward banning discrimination in public accommodations and hiring than the 1964 federal law. It opens to Negroes all public facilities except barbershops, beauty shops and private clubs, guarantees fair employment standards to the ninety per cent of the labor force that works for businesses employing eight or more persons."[46]

On January 7, 1966, looking back at the events of the past twelve years, McGill wrote, "there is no question but that had the top political and public leadership of the South given support to the processes of law in 1954 when the U.S. Supreme Court school decision was handed down, the South——and nation——would have avoided the bitter and disgraceful harvest of hate, the murders, the bombings, and the burnings that have been so much a part of the years since 1954."[47] During that dangerous period, McGill provided a lonely but decisive voice of reason which many said contributed to the relative calm in Atlanta and, in some measure, throughout Georgia and the South.

The speeches presented below are representative of the many addresses McGill gave during his personal campaign to save the public schools in the South, and to convince the public that "the greatest tradition we have in America is that of peaceful social change. There is room for us all to live in peace."[48] It should be remembered that these speeches were written for a particular period and with certain problems in mind, and were not carefully conceived essays necessarily having universal appeal. Indeed four of the talks were taken verbatim from taped recordings. The speeches are presented here to reveal McGill at work with issues important to the welfare of the nation, and should be understood within the context in which they were given.

126

NINE

1 *Atlanta Constitution*, October 12, 1950, p. 1.
2 *Atlanta Constitution*, June 9, 1948, p. 8.
3 Ralph McGill and Thomas C. Davis (Atlanta: State Department of Education, 1938), p. 12.
4 *Atlanta Constitution*, September 27, 1957, p. 1.
5 *Atlanta Constitution*, August 31, 1962, p. 1.
6 Ralph McGill, *The South and the Southerner* (Boston: Little, Brown and Company, 1963), pp. 260-261.
7 *The New York Times*, May 17, 1955, p. 1.
8 *Atlanta Constitution*, May 21, 1954, p. 1.
9 *Atlanta Constitution*, June 11, 1954, p. 1.
10 *Atlanta Constitution*, January 10, 1956, p. 1.
11 *Atlanta Constitution*, January 10, 1956, p. 1 (AP).
12 *Atlanta Constitution*, October 22, 1957, p. 1 (AP).
13 *Atlanta Constitution*, January 20, 1959, p. 1 (AP).
14 *Atlanta Constitution*, January 20, 1956, p. 1 (AP).
15 Richard Barnett and Joseph Garai, *Where the States Stand on Civil Rights* (New York: Sterling Publishing Company, 1962), pp. 12, 13.
16 *Atlanta Constitution*, June 7, 1954, p. 1 (AP).
17 *Atlanta Constitution*, October 18, 1956, p. 1 (AP).
18 *The New York Times*, May 17, 1955, p. 18.
19 *Atlanta Constitution*, February 7, 1956, p. 1 (AP).
20 *Atlanta Constitution*, September 3, 1956, p. 1.
21 *Atlanta Constitution*, September 8, 1956, p. 1 (AP).
22 *Atlanta Constitution*, September 25, 1957, p. 1 (AP).
23 *Atlanta Constitution*, October 6, 1958, p. 1 (UPI).
24 *Atlanta Constitution*, February 6, 1959, p. 1 (AP).
25 *Atlanta Constitution*, December 13, 1960, p. 1.
26 *Atlanta Constitution*, May 22, 1961, p. 1.
27 *Atlanta Constitution*, September 10, 1962, p. 1.
28 *Atlanta Constitution*, October 1, 1962, p. 1.
29 *Atlanta Constitution*, September 16, 1963, p. 1 (AP).
30 *Atlanta Constitution*, August 7, 1964, p. 1.
31 *Time*, (October 15, 1965), 31.

[32] *Atlanta Constitution*, March 16, 1960, p. 1.

[33] *Atlanta Constitution*, May 3, 1963, p. 1 (AP).

[34] *Atlanta Constitution*, May 5, 1963, p. 1 (AP).

[35] *Atlanta Constitution*, August 29, 1963, p. 1.

[36] *Atlanta Constitution*, February 2, 1965, p. 1 (AP).

[37] *Atlanta Constitution*, March 22, 1965, p. 1 (UPI).

[38] *Time*, 87 (June 17, 1966), 26.

[39] *Time*, 88 (July 1, 1966), 11.

[40] *Atlanta Constitution*, December 19, 1962, p. 1.

[41] *Atlanta Constitution*, June 12, 1963, p. 1.

[42] *Atlanta Constitution*, September 11, 1963, p. 1 (AP).

[43] *Atlanta Constitution*, April 26, 1965, p. 1.

[44] *Atlanta Constitution*, May 7, 1965, p. 1.

[45] *Atlanta Constitution*, September 1, 1964, p. 1.

[46] *Time*, 87 (February 4, 1966), 27.

[47] *Atlanta Constitution*, January 7, 1966, p. 1.

[48] *Atlanta Constitution*, August 31, 1962, p. 1.

SPEECHES

129

UNIVERSITY OF ARKANSAS COMMENCEMENT ADDRESS
Fayetteville, January 30, 1954

Less than four months before the Supreme Court's historic desegregation ruling, McGill "told an unsegregated graduation class at the University of Arkansas" that "the outcome of the battle for segregation was no longer in doubt." President John Tyler Caldwell introduced McGill to six hundred and twenty-five midwinter graduates, including "several Negroes" assembled in Razorback Field House on the University campus.

After discussing what he considered an ideal educational experience, McGill took a strong stand against the wrong done the Negro in the South. He accurately predicted that "we face presumably sometime in the spring another decision which will test all Americans... It is not a debate on whether segregation is right or wrong or beneficial... It is that segregation by color based on law simply does not fit the concepts of our world today, neither political nor Christian."

I am, of course, happy and honored to be here in Arkansas, and at this University with its fine traditions and history. Nonetheless, I have been a bit hesitant about such a gambit since a visit some years ago to South Carolina. When I mentioned my pleasure at being present in that state a voice from the audience said, with great complacency, "Well, I reckon so."

Also, I come with a certain hesitancy to the business of a commencement address. I am not sure but what it would be a better idea to have at commencement exercises music by some great artists; brief readings from some of the philosophers, and a prayer. Then the president would rise and say, "Ladies and gentlemen, there are no convenient answers to what lies ahead. There never has been, there never will be. But history seems to show that those who have at college obtained the best working tools, and those who will go ahead with courage and ideals, very often find some of the answers and in the finding enjoy a satisfactory and useful life."

But, we have the established ritual and I am honored, as I said before, to have been invited.

130

A short time ago we had a Vanderbilt University alumni meeting in Atlanta and the Vice Chancellor, in addressing it, recalled the days at the university immediately after the first world war. "That was, as you know," he said, "the era of flaming youth." He then proceeded to name some of the alumni of that generation and to my dismay I heard my own name prominent among them. I felt like a cinder looking back at the flame. It had not occurred to me I was of a generation already acquiring the aura of ancientness.

Therefore, I stand here today with very real humility. Thomas A. Kempis, one of the great men of the early church, left us many priceless verbal legacies, but none, I think, better than this:

"Be not angry that ye cannot make others as ye wish them to be, since ye cannot make thyself as ye wish to be."

I think of that when I go anywhere to make a talk——especially a commencement address. Being unable to make of myself what I would wish to be, I assuredly have no "message."

I am well aware that some of us who come as college speakers are so egocentric that we speak with great assurance and give dogmatic advice on what to expect when one leaves the allegedly cloistered confines of a school or university. Yet, I very much doubt if any of the graybeards or nervous editors who stand before college audiences this year can honestly say that in his youth he saw the future clearly and walked with confident step toward the fulfillment of a plan.

I cannot come to you with dogma. Yet I can say with a certain dogmatic confidence that I believe that from you and from other college groups like you will come enough young minds which will be restlessly impatient; which will not be blunted by the ideas and the standards established by the more complacent in our society who live on, for and by an inflexible set of ideas which they will not change. Too many of us live by a familiar and comfortable set of ideas. We hear new ones, but even though they sound logical, most of us reject the new to keep the old.

You who attend this university, which I believe will give you a questioning, testing mind, will be eager to go out and put that sort of mind to work. I urge you to hold such a mind and not lose it, even though disappointment and the conformists join in pressure against it.

I know a very good editor who has framed above his desk this motto:

"Lord, give me this day my daily idea and forgive me the one I had yesterday."

It is not a bad motto. In this day when many of the things we know as truths are being revealed as not true, when we see how close about us has been the horizon of knowledge about our own minds, instincts and behavior; when science is busy producing a new energy which is sure to change even more some of the truths in the books of physics, chemistry, and to shake at least some of the foundation stones of our most ancient concepts of life——that motto is not a bad one to keep in mind.

As parents, relatives and friends sit with their sons and daughters at graduation, it seems to me certain inevitable thoughts must come. Some would think of the sacrifices made to provide educational opportunity and rejoice they had been made. Others would be thinking of the future and what their sons and daughters will do with what they have learned. There would be many thoughts. But, I am sure there will be one which should come to all of us. It is this...

"Education is a part and parcel of life's experience. It does not begin with school. It should not end with graduation." That is a trite observation, but a true one because whether we like it or not education begins in the cradle and ends with the grave. Have you ever thought of what a tremendous amount of learning a child has attained at the age of six or seven years? It is phenomenal. It is quite likely there is crowded into the brain of a child between six and seven as much or more than that child will absorb from that time on. Everything we do in work and play has a molding influence on the sort of person we are. That continues right on until the last breath comes.

The part that formal education plays——that which we learn in school——is, I suspect, merely a supplement to what we learn by experience. An astonishing and frightening number of things can be learned only by experience.

So, if I were asked to say what education is, I would say it is that combination of formal instruction and experience which enables a person to rationalize himself——to explain and understand himself or herself——in terms of the life and culture in which one lives. That is about all education, formal and experience, can do.

Formal education of whatever kind——academic, professional or technical, deals with subject matter which has been collected and analyzed and classified from the accumulated experience of the human race. Millions of persons, through several thousands of years, perhaps five thousand years, have contributed to that formal education. Recently I was in India and saw there things written on clay which were about three thousand years old and which recounted events which had happened two and three thousand years before. There were records of cities, streets, buildings of several stories, and of a civilization of substance. In medicine, mathematics, science, astronomy, philosophy, the arts, literature and so on, part of what we study and learn today was old five thousand years ago. Yet it is necessary to us today.

The dawn of what we call recorded history could perhaps be said to begin roughly at the time of the building of the great pyramid at Gizeh in Egypt——where thousands of slaves labored across a long span of years to erect that great pile of stone which was to guard a king's body, since the king believed that he would some day have to come back to it as a spirit and reoccupy it for another life.

Five thousand years is not a long time in history. It isn't with us. A great aunt of mine would be one hundred and forty years old if she were living today. Yet I recall her quite well. I can see her yet about her house, can recall the pats on the head she used to give me, and the war stories she told. She had a relative who had lived to be old and who, as a boy, had shaken hands with George Washington. So, in a sense, by way of a great aunt I am in touch with George Washington, the father of our country. There are roughly three generations to a century. Most any person here of fifty can, through knowledge of some old person, reach back a shockingly long time. Take one of these students here today. They see in me a man whose great aunt knew and talked with a man who had known George Washington. That in itself is meaningless save for one thing. In all those years man himself has remained about the same. It is wise not to expect too much from the individual biological animal called man, even though his creator gave him a soul.

But, the human race has been changing all the time because of what it has learned from the collections of formal knowledge in schools and from experience. There have been great political, moral and technical changes, even revolution.

Those who built the pyramids had already domesticated most of the animals and vegetables we know. They had a written language. They had skilled craftsmen in metals. Their women used beauty preparations and paid great attention to hair-dos. They were good mechanics and did pretty well with agriculture.

Time, and experience, steadily have added to, changed and refined much of what they knew. Experience keeps adding to the great reservoir of human knowledge. I don't know how many courses are offered here. But I would assume that if one set out to take everything offered, and did so at the regular number of hours per week, it would require one perhaps twenty-five years to do it. A professor at Harvard told me some years ago that if a man set out to master all they had in their many colleges and schools, more than three hundred years would be required. And, even then, such a person would not know all of knowledge. In the time he had been studying the past the intervening years of experience would have added up as much again.

That is why the most learned of men and women are

sometimes the most ignorant of much of life's experience. We can't expect too much of individual man. We can only be pleased when some of the individuals do rise to great heights of achievement, dignity and spirituality. The race changes because ideas change. What we call democracy is, because of two great wars fought in its behalf and the new aggression of a totalitarian ideology, almost something new. Democracy is, as I see it, something rather simple. It is free men working together——or free peoples working together. Democracy might take one turn in one country and still another when some other peoples try to fit it to their freedom. We can't think of democracy in terms of the United States representing perfection. It suits us. But there are many things here which are not democratic, though we are striving to eliminate them. We can't seek to make all people just like us——their experience is not the same. We can only try to keep each other free and to work together. Man by nature is somewhat primitive. As the race improves through education and experience, we are all moved forward. But we do this step by step. Never by leaps.

Formal education can do much in this picture. It presents to mankind the best that has been said, thought and accomplished through the thousands of years man has recorded his thinking and his achievement.

I think we are making progress——slowly——in politics and in the knowledge of living. It interests me that in two years the Woolworth stores reportedly have sold more than five hundred thousand framed reproductions of famous paintings by Van Gogh, Renoir, Monet, and others; that cheap paper-bound copies of Homer's Odyssey have sold almost a million copies; that four of Faulkner's titles in this cheap edition have sold over a million each and three othes have sold more than four hundred thousand. At a time when we are supposed to be interested only in the cheap and the superficial, the best seller books indicate a more serious frame of mind.

I am encouraged by the fact that the professional politician is no longer the accurate source of information he

135

once was. The independent vote is growing larger each year in this country. Mass thought is enlarged and improving——slowly. Man progresses by inches.

It is a good thing we are progressing.

We are up against the atomic and hydrogen bombs—— and all the family of new weapons and forces.

And we have no experience to cope with them. We must gain it slowly and with great pain, praying only that we do not learn it in war. We have launched an atomic submarine. We are already building five small atomic engines, and another type to power aircraft is in the late design stages. Atomic energy can already compete with fifteen dollars a ton coal in commercial productions. Now RCA has announced the discovery of a direct method in transferring atomic power. They predict a matchbox amount of power will, within a few years, light our houses, run our refrigerators and so on. And it was only nine years ago the first bomb was exploded.

So, we are entering an era which will demand more formal education and more experience than ever before. And parents, contemplating children today, must feel a sense of guilt that they, the parents, have not themselves kept on learning and employing formal knowledge and experience in community and public affairs.

Five thousand years from now the great reservoir of human knowledge is going to be twice what it is now. Formal knowledge must refine it. Today a chemical or physical formula can be taught in ten minutes which likely required the work and thought of many generations to bring it into being.

Today we are just beginning to understand what democracy means——free peoples working together.

Adult education classes are springing up everywhere as grown men and women say, "There is so much new going on, I must learn something about it."

That is hopeful.

But, as we gather here tonight——parents looking with pride on their sons and daughters who are themselves dealing with the great stockpile of knowledge which thousands of men and women have accumulated through the years——let us all keep in mind that before we came to formal education the mind was receiving knowledge, perhaps the most important of all our lives. And that when we leave school that process goes on to the grave.

"I am a part of all that I have met," said a poet.

It is true.

Therefore, how important it is to be sure that we meet along the way enough of good music, books, conversation, experiences, hours for thought and meditation, and work so that we keep learning and are thereby able to go forward and grapple with what life gives us.

To my way of thinking, the one working tool more valuable than all the others is the ability to read, understand and express what one reads. A stubborn, inquiring mind, able to read and understand, able to hear and analyze, provides the one real freedom there is. Upon not merely freedom of inquiry, but on the will and ability to seek the answer to the word "Why?" rest all the four freedoms of which we have heard so much. All freedom, of whatever kind, stems from a mind free and able to doubt, inquire and test.

So, my chief advice is to go out with a doubting, inquiring mind, taking what I and the graybeard sages you will encounter say to you, but testing it all. When a man's youth is past, he too often rests upon the past and sees it as the promise of the future. Two cynics have expressed it well.

Bernard Shaw said that youth was such a wonderful thing it was a shame to waste it on young people.

And some anonymous philosopher recalled that:

King David and King Solomon led merry, merry lives,
With many, many lady friends and many, many wives.
But, when old age came upon them, with many, many qualms,
King Solomon wrote the Proverbs and King David wrote the Psalms.

I do not at all attempt to tell you what to choose. You properly would pay little attention to me if I did. You must find out for yourselves. But I will urge this. Study the basic concepts of this country. Disavow the spell-binders who will try to tell you that freedom and culture and security are a political gift which may be handed down to you by the state. That I most profoundly believe a lie. We are now engaged in a great struggle and your living concept of it has been that of an emergency. Most of you were born at the beginning of that emergency, the end of the era following the first world war, the great depression, and the developments leading to, and through the second world war. It is important, I believe, to know something of our beginnings; to know what the writers of the Declaration of Independence and of the Constitution had in mind when they selected, after long argument, the phrases employed. What are the elements of our national character? What is the American? Are we a mechanism set in motion by the Declaration of Independence? Our cities have created problems which have made it popular to sneer at individualism and say that it can no longer solve the social and economic problems. Perhaps it can't. But, think twice before you give up your individualism for conformity. It seems to me we can solve certain problems created by the continuing growth of our cities through government and yet at the same time encourage individualism as the only real safety valve our system possesses.

The individualist, be it a university or a person, is more and more suspect. Society becomes more and more mechanized. The communists get control of labor unions and organizations because they always show up for meetings and serve on committees. The democrats prefer to take their evenings off. While the little "d" democrat is out in his boat fishing, going to a ball game, reading a book, or listening to the record player, the authoritarians are holding committee meetings. The individualist, for liberty's sake, may have to give up some of his liberties. We have got to go on counting heads to avoid breaking them.

I hope that as many of you as can will stay in the South

138

and that all of you will, in one manner or another, learn about politics and participate at least as a voter.

Each of us is in politics, since our taxes, our government, schools, police and fire protection, are all a matter of politics.

The South, and especially Southern politics, needs some men and women with tough, inquiring minds.

Like you, I get weary of the moral lectures read the South by the Northern moralists, who have a beam in their own eye, and I resent much of the stupid abuse which the Northern demagogues use in articles and public speeches. Like you, I know the race issue is not a special problem of the South, but the most dangerous symptom of a special sickness which affects the whole country and which can be cured by planning, applied to each phase of our economic and civic life.

The old political structure of the South is beginning to fall apart——and there are many hands already stretching to pick up the pieces.

The big question is "Who will pick them up?"

I hope many of you——and others like you in our schools, universities and in the ranks of citizens, will try.

Perhaps enough has been said, perhaps not, to indicate my perception of the background of a great problem. Certainly all of us must think seriously on it.

In the nation's solemn temple of justice final argument has been made in the case of segregation.

Now the nation waits.

And waiting, it must surely plan to avoid folly.

North, South, East and West, there must be those who, perhaps for the first time, see by way of warning, that what happened when the North "at the moment of opportunity," threw away the policy of reasonableness of the dead Lincoln and the living Johnson, was folly.

Then and there the destiny of both the South and the Negro was delivered into the hands of a few desperate, designing politicians who used the party lash to bring on the cruel and dismal years of reconstruction.

At all times, before and during the Civil War Between

the States, there was a strong union sentiment in the South. In most Southern states support of secession had been given reluctantly, sorrowfully. Only the hotheads urged it.

There were many in the North who, like Lincoln, knew this fact and wanted to use it. But, they too were swept aside by their own hotheads who wanted war, and had it.

And to this good day there are but few histories which adequately tell the story of that tragic, awful period when reasonableness was abandoned.

Lincoln had urged the North to share the cost of emancipation since it had shared both in the responsibility for, and profit from, slavery. After Lincoln's murder the North was persuaded by a few vindictive radicals to ignore a policy of reasonableness for a "conquered-province-in-chains."

Yet, Old Whig traditions in the South were by no means dead. This was proved years later when the Old Whigs, in the Democratic Party, helped Northern Republicans steal a recount election for Rutherford B. Hayes. There was enough Old Whig and Union sentiment strength remaining on which a powerful and respected following could have been built to support the new nation.

Instead, the radicals in the Congress, ranting before the mute corpse of Lincoln, trampled his policy under foot, occupied the South and put their regime into the hands of Northern carpetbaggers and Southern scalawags. Instead of reasonableness there was armed occupation, brazen and flaunting dishonesty of federal officials, election frauds, crooked government devices to enrich the politically favored, disfranchisement of the people, profiteering in stolen cotton and land, preposterous political manipulation of the Negro and cruel, corrupt uses of the military courts of the occupying armies.

All people are a product of their history and economy. Yet, Southerners do not even now realize that the wounds which throb today, the cult of "supremacy" and other "traditions" came not from the war itself, but from the tragedy of reconstruction abuses. It was this cruel folly which solidified resentment against the Negro, produced the theory of White Supremacy, and which drove every person of whatever previous political faith into the Democratic Party and made the word "Republican" an epithet. The spirit of the South was not defeated. It was magnificent. But abuses warped and distorted it.

Now, we face, presumably sometime in the spring, another decision which will test all Americans. Even a person who sincerely believes in segregation sees about him today, in a world torn by communism's battle to destroy the freedom and dignity of man, ample evidence that it is no longer a local, or even a national issue, but a world-wide one. It is not a debate on whether segregation is right or wrong or beneficial. It is not what we personally would prefer. It is that segregation by color based on law simply does not fit the concepts of our world today, neither political nor Christian. Indeed, the Christian is the most heavily beset of all.

So, as we wait, history now cries out to us to have a policy of reasonableness which, when the decision comes, will not deliver us into the hands of a few political radicals who will lead the nation again into the folly and tragedy of destroying public education and of violence.

Who are the Southern leaders who say that we in the South are so bankrupt in ideas and character that we cannot work out this problem save with violence and by pulling down the pillars of public education?

Indulge me but a moment more.

Certainly we must also see that if we add racial hatred and fear to the already existing hatreds and neurotic fears created by what has come to be called McCarthyism, it might be more than the fabric of our society safely could endure.

Recently, Archibald MacLeish talked on this subject, and I would like to give you some of it:

"There is a poem of William Butler Yeats called 'The Stare's Next by My Window'——'stare' being west-of-Ireland for starling——which ends with these lines:

'We had fed the heart on fantasies,

141

The heart's grown brutal from the fare;
More substance in our enmities
Than in our love; O honey-bees,
Come build in the empty house of the stare.'

"Yeats was thinking of another country and another time——Ireland and the Civil Wars of the 'Twenties'——but there is not an understanding man or woman in America today who will not read these words as though they were written of us. We share the same guilt and we know it. With us in this country also the heart has been fed on fantasies——the most degrading of all fantasies——the fantasies of hatred. With us too the heart's grown brutal with the fare. And it is our tragedy, as it was the tragedy of those of whom Yeats wrote, that hatred is more real with us than devotion. The true indictment of our generation is precisely the terrible indictment of the great Irish poet: 'More substance in our enmities than in our love.' "

I believe we will all have to agree that... We must respect the fact of honest differences. But, all of us must be careful never to accept the support of, or give aid and comfort to, the crackpots, the fanatics of the lunatic fringe and those who, filled with maliciousness and hate, have only the substance of enmity.

You have honored me greatly.

May God go with you——and with all of us.

EDITORS VIEW THE SOUTH
Emory University, Fall Quarter, 1957

This speech came during an eight-week night course at Emory University called "Editors View the South." Eight prominent Southern editors discussed the region's problems with emphasis upon race relations. Among the editors participating were Harry Ashmore, Pulitzer prize-winning Little Rock newspaperman, and McGill. Although the exact date of McGill's address was not known by Emory University and could not be found in press coverage, McGill talked to approximately one hundred adults who had registered for the series sponsored by the office of Community Education during the Fall Quarter, 1957. At the time, Ashmore commented that he knew of no other such forum being conducted in the South. Tempers across the South were high and emotions boiled concerning possible desegregation of the public schools.

McGill attempted to explain the South's situation by tracing some of the history of that region. Near the end of his talk, he became more specific and when he stated, "I will say that they've sold us a false bill of goods, namely that integration would mean amalgamation," a voice from the audience stated, "It always has!" The same topic was brought up during the question and answer period; thus, even on the Emory University campus one could find signs of the great concern over the possibility of desegregating the public schools. (Manuscript taken from taped recording.)

Thank you Mr. Griffin:

Ladies and Gentlemen, I am delighted to be here because I'm one of the persons who believes the more discussion there is about a subject, the better. I always approach one of these or any speaking with some trepidation because of the matter of semantics. And because, while you may know very well what you intend to convey, your weakness with words doesn't always allow you to do it to the satisfaction of those who listen and sometimes not to your own. But I am happy to have a try at talking a little about it.

I don't mean to take a text but I remember when I was about ten years old, my father, who was a great admirer of

143

Henry Waterson, the then famous editor of the *Louisville Courier Journal,* took me on an excursion. I don't know if any of you are old enough to remember excursion trains but you could travel very far very cheaply. And he got in to see Waterson despite the fact that he had no engagement, and he did most of the talking. I will always remember though, a motto which Waterson had on his desk which went like this, "Lord, give me this day my daily idea, and forgive me the one I had yesterday." (laughter) Now in a time when what today seems so sure, tomorrow doesn't always seem quite so sure and the day after sometimes has proved to have been quite erroneous, that isn't too bad a motto and it's an especially good one I think for anyone who has the temerity to write for a newspaper and to offer opinions daily. And so with that in mind, we'll proceed. I am often wrong. I don't know the answers to things. I stand a little bit in awe of those persons who are so sure they know the answers to things. And at times I envy them and because they seem to feel that they have been touched with a sort of omniscience. But, if you don't mind, I suppose that all of us here tonight could be classified as seekers after answers. And answers are all usually elusive.

I thought I might, not having had the privilege of hearing the others [speakers] but having read the reports about them and especially the excellent job done by the Marietta paper, carrying them more fully than others, I thought I might go a little bit into background, not of why we act like Southerners but to try to understand a little bit of what happened to us and why attitudes developed. I have the feeling that attitudes or mores or whatever you want to call them sort of grow in a certain climate of waters, much as coral demands a certain type of warm seawater with a constant temperature the year round to develop a slow, growing but very hard fixed stone against which swimmers can be gashed and ships can be wrecked. So do I feel that attitudes and customs and traditions and mores sort of grow out of a sea or a climate of opinion or events.

It was just about seventy years from the invention of the cotton gin to the war between the states. That is not too long a lifetime, one man's lifetime. In 1820 the South, which was about the time of the cotton gin, the South produced by the very hardest about a hundred thousand bales of very poor grade cotton. In 1859 that production was almost five million bales. You might very well say that from 1840——I didn't mean 1820 was the invention of the cotton gin, it came a little earlier——but beginning in 1820 when cotton production began, a hundred thousand bales to nearly five million in 1859. You might readily say too that from 1840 to 1860, which was just twenty years, saw the greatest acceleration of the cotton economy and it saw too the greatest acceleration of differences and the growing intensity of recrimination and accusations between the two regions. But at any rate, taking seventy years before the war between the states, the invention of the cotton gin, the lifetime of a man or a woman, this whole thing happened to make us "Southern."

In 1820 there was really no region, regional feeling in the United States. In that year, 1820, Monroe was President. He had eight cabinet members of which four were Southerners. Crawford of Georgia was one, Calhoun of South Carolina was the other and Clay of Kentucky. But two were from the Deep South. There was only one political party in 1820, the Republican Party. This did not mean of course the same as today's Republican Party. But there was a feeling then not of regionalism a'tall but of nationalism, the one country; the War of the Revolution, the War of 1812 were not too far behind. And in 1820 there was not even a feeling of being from the South, or the Southwest, from the North, East or West. Indeed in 1820 the population was rather thin. The frontier reached into almost a little wedge; it began at Lake Erie and you could trace it down——it ran a little wedge into Oklahoma, I mean not Oklahoma, Ohio. It came back down around on down into Georgia. It hadn't reached to Texas even then in any great amount, just a little bit. 1820 to 1860, a mere forty years; so what happened?

145

Well, in the South cotton happened and I suppose that if we had to pick one thing which made us a region it would be cotton. If you had to pick another it would be, of course, the climate, the weather which made cotton possible. If you had to pick another, you would pick, of course, slavery and a slave economy. Keeping in mind a hundred thousand bales in 1820. Then some seed were brought in from the Bahamas; upland cotton began to grow from these; a gin was enabling cotton to be manufactured or produced rather cheaply. Slavery, which had been pretty well on the way out up to about 1820, suddenly became enormously profitable again, because with a gin you could produce a great deal of cotton and so it became profitable to open up new lands and so, without really seeking it but having it almost thrust upon us, this region of ours found itself set apart as no other region in the United States.

We were a different region, the South was different. It was different because of its weather; it was different because of its economy. New England, you might say, was different too in that it was a commercial shipping center. But pretty soon that spread all the way down to Philadelphia, this industrial commercial development. And it didn't confine itself to a region. And certainly the Midwest area or the West at that time was essentially a farming area. It produced wheat and it produced corn. It produced a great many other diversifed crops. But here in our part of the world we had——tobacco had ceased to be a slave crop in general although a few slaves worked at it, relatively few. But cotton and to some extent rice, along the South Carolina coast the rice growers probably were the real aristocracy of that time. But that demanded a great deal of slave labor. But at any rate all of these things set us apart. And in very truth there was not another region in the United States which a'tall resembled us.

So as inevitably happens as the nation began to grow and this peculiar region of ours with these peculiar attributes are rather peculiar in that they differed from the other regions of the United States, it became necessary to

146

establish, to defend, and to continue that system. So the people thought, so any people would feel. And so it became necessary to rationalize the situation wherever it seemed to clash with conscience or with morality. And an interesting fact of that time is that up to about 1840 when the regions had pretty well developed, separated themselves, up to about 1840 there was a substantial sentiment in the South to somehow bring about emancipation. It was so strong in Virginia, for example, that the planters of Virginia hired a certain Professor Dew, his first name escapes me now, to write a defense, an analysis, a rationalization of the Southern civilization, a defense of slavery. And he did; it became a classic. It was published six or eight times; in six or eight editions. Other states had it published. Others began to spring up and to silence this sort of voice. Professor Dew had been appointed to the university largely because of his views. His two predecessors had held emancipation views. Even in Georgia there were two of our Congressmen who made speeches in the Congress suggesting that slavery ought to be ended and so forth.

Now what I am trying to say is that as late as 1840 there was this diversity of voice in our region. But by that time something had begun to happen, about 1840, certainly by 1843 the extremists on both sides had become very clamorous. The abolitionist voices grew louder and louder and more accusing. The Southern defense of what it came to call a peculiar institution, being peculiar to the South because of these things I have enumerated, climate, the cotton economy. Keep in mind that this had another effect. There was not much farming done in the South. They didn't grow the food crops in any great amount, except sort of to sustain the farm or the plantation. We were not a wheat growing section, we didn't grow any great amount except maybe to just have enough for home use. Cotton, it was cotton and the slave labor, of course, did another thing. It caused us to not develop in the South any craftsman's class or any class of skilled artisans. And there was a great shortage of that. There's no accusation in

147

this, it was a perfectly natural thing that everything had to be subordinated more or less to this one economy of the whole region. We didn't have much transportation except by rivers and by the forties we had begun to complain about that. The railroads were being built in the East and the North; the North slowly was becoming more prosperous. It was carrying on a great industrial business; it was mostly Northern owned and English owned ships that called at Southern ports to take the cotton. And so if you will read the history of the time, you will begin to read, in the South a tremendous discontent; things weren't going too well. Not many of the cotton planters by 1850 were making very much money. Most of it seemed to be flowing up North. You will find that a greater protest against the wealth of the South flowing eastward to the eastern banks and manufacturers, than you would have found in the thirties when we began to really feel the pinch of what might be called a colonial sort of economy which was imposed on us during the reconstruction period.

At any rate, during the forties to the sixties——there are several books which give this very well, the almost incredible hatred that grew up between the two regions. The most inflammatory speeches, the most inflammatory editorials. It grieves me, as a newspaperman to read the very sorry part the newspapers, north and south, played in that period. It was an incredible performance.

So pretty soon the sentiment began to grow for secession. You began to hear about 1843 the first talk of states' rights. The people began to argue seriously in the papers and in lectures, "What did the Constitution mean?," "We the people of these United States." Did it mean the people of the United States or did it mean the people of the states? A tremendous argument, "What did the Constitution mean? What did it mean?" It hadn't been spelled out, "We the people."

And so you began to get the fierce partisans who said "Well, the state is sovereign. The state is sovereign." And you had others equally positive saying, "That's ridiculous. We had the old Confederation and it failed because of states' rights." In the old Confederation they even set up tariff, custom houses, one against the other and prevented trade and the Confederation just was failing because each one was sovereign, and so by great effort they managed to get the Constitution adopted. But still the framers of it didn't spell it out and it was a little ambiguous to some people and not at all ambiguous to others, what did it mean? At any rate, states' rights began to be born or were born in that period. And they became almost a passion with people. They became almost a religion with people.

Now all of these things, I've dwelled a little bit too long on them, books have been written about a great many of just these things I have mentioned, the impact of cotton which solidified us, slavery, our weather, our devotion to three basic crops. But especially two, or especially one really in cotton, but then of course, rice and tobacco. But a whole lot of things set us apart; we were different. So it was perfectly inevitable that our thinking should be a little different, that out of all these pressures should come a different sort of approach to problems. That out of all this life should come certain attitudes which are, of course, different.

Then, of course, the war which we won't go into but keep in mind that when the war came, most of the leaders thought there really wouldn't be a war. And when they founded the Confederacy at Montgomery they were very careful to keep out the people who had really brought the war on. The extremists such as Rhett and Yancey, to name two of the greatest ones perhaps, they wouldn't give them any part in the government. Both of these men were embittered by it, thought they should have had high office. But the people who really made the Confederacy were in the main, conservative and thought "Well if we get out of the Union, then we can get what we want perhaps as a price of getting back into the Union."

All the while, of course, the great fight had finally culminated on the extension of slavery, the South feeling it was losing out anyhow. The North was getting more prosperous and it was. The North was developing industries, greater wealth. The per capita income was greater and the feeling that somehow they were imposing on the South because they handled all the money end of it. That led to the fight about the extension of slavery into the new states and territories and while it is not true that slavery per se caused the war, it didn't start out certainly to free the slaves, but slavery indirectly caused it because the great fight was about the extension of slavery.

Now all of those things had an impact on us. They have an impact on you and me today, those of us who are from the South and indirectly they have an impact on the rest of the United States.

Now what lost the Civil War? Well I wouldn't——I brought along a book and I'm glad to bring it along because I think Georgia has a great historian. He is so recognized by the historians, the better known ones in the greater universities. Dr. E. Merton Coulter of the University of Georgia is really a very good historian and has a very excellent reputation, a national reputation as historian. This book, *The Confederate States of America*, by E. Merton Coulter, it's Volume 7 of *The History of the South* published by the Louisiana State University Press and the Littlefield Fund for Southern History of the University of Texas. I'll read just a little. Ben Hill was one of the great leaders before, during and after the war in our state and Hill had advanced a program of cooperative action by the slave states in an effort to stay in the Union. But it was lost. And Coulter says, saying that this was the greatest hope of avoiding secession, the voice of fifteen states and a united cooperative demand would have sobered opinion far beyond the weak voice of each state offered separately. And then Coulter says "If the south had left the Union by the cooperation plan instead of by individual state action, the new government might have avoided the withering effects of the dissensions that came from the states' rights dogma which were so powerful in destroying the Confederacy." I wanted to read this rather than to offer it as an opinion of my own——you will find this in several other books——but again, Coulter——this whole thick book is about the four years. "States' rights was the Southerners deepest political passion. It had provoked secession might it not have brought victory. If the Confederacy was to win at all" (this is in the chapter on Internal Dissensions) "if the Confederacy was to win at all it could not be through greater military resources. It must be through superior morale. Whatever destroyed this morale would make victory impossible. Irrespective of how logical it was to place power in the central government. If the confederate administration had recognized the rights of the states by taking the governors into its council, the states might have been satisfied with such theoretical recognition, but the editor of the *Richmond Examiner* simplified the whole purpose of the war in these few words. 'The principle now in contest between the North and the South is simply that of state sovereignty.' And another Virginian declared that there were now no people in the South but only states of the South."

Now it is an incredible thing how this very, this almost religious fervor, a sort of holy war for states' rights began to develop in the forties and continued on through the war and after. Again, "it is easy to argue in circles" (this again is Coulter) "why the Confederacy did not win. It must be remembered that there were the seeds of destruction, states' rights, which were implanted at its birth, destined to sprout and flourish, tended and watered by such expert gardeners as Governor Brown, Vice President Stephens and others." All through the war we had states which refused to obey orders of the central government. Joe Brown of Georgia actually took his Georgia troops out of the Confederate Army before the Battle of Atlanta. When the ships were running the blockade runners the central government passed a law saying that at least a third or half the cargo space had to be given over to space for goods for the Confederate government, shoes, ammunition, uniforms, woolens, cloth, medicine, and the states absolutely rebelled. They said, No, they were operating the blockade and the government couldn't give them orders, and so it ran.

Now when the war was over and——Stephens went up in 1865 to try to make peace and he couldn't, because the government had said that he had to obtain recognition of the independence of the Confederacy. He went up and had a talk with Lincoln, this committee did. I often wonder, history is so peculiar, fascinating a thing, I often wonder what might have happened. Lincoln, without any question, was ready to make peace, he was ready to idemnify the South for slavery. He said I will introduce it in the Congress and we'll get it worked through. But he said he had to have union. Henry Waterson once told me that Stephens told him, and you've heard this said, that Lincoln said, "that if you will write Union in it, Alex, I will let you fill in the rest." Now I don't know whether it was literally that or not. But at any rate that was about it maybe. At any rate he was willing to have the war stopped——work out——to introduce legislation to indemnify the South for its losses. But it couldn't be done. Now I often wonder what would have happened if it could, I certainly doubt that Lincoln would have been assassinated. Certainly, Lincoln had a plan for bringing the South back in, in honor and without any punishment. But he was, of course, killed and the radical Congress took over.

I don't know any more——I can go back to Cromwell in Ireland, you can go to other extremes in history, but I don't know any more melancholy ruthless, sad, cruel period than the reconstruction period, nothing more withering to this country and to——more erosive of human spirit and so forth. And, of course, it was during that period that the thirteenth, fourteenth, and fifteenth amendments were passed.

Now I'm sorta coming down to today in a hurry. I suppose that one of the great heroes of Georgia certainly is Ben Hill. And I don't know a more worthy one——Ben Hill——[couple of sentences missing here on tape]. "These amendments mean more," said Hill, "They mean on closer examination that the United States government has become national not federal, for jurisdiction over the civil and political status of all races in all the states will be held

152

who have been transferred by these amendments from the states severally to the general federal government." And said Hill, "These powers being conferred, it will be difficult to determine what power has not been conferred." I don't know a truer prophecy made in 1870. Hill was denounced up and down the state as a traitor, as having sold out his people, as having gone over to the enemy, but he kept on despite the bitter resentment; newspapers denounced him. I won't go on, it's taking too long but Hill——*The Augusta Constitutionalist* announced that it would print the letter of December 8 from Hill only as an act of courtesy to a once distinguished gentleman. They called him some very vile language. I won't go on, but Hill was making it very plain. "I hold that the fourteenth amendment has not changed the right of the state to regulate its civil affairs save only to quality its exercise by saying that you must not discriminate on account of color. I hold that the fifteenth amendment..." Speech after speech which is so reminiscent of today when you hear arguments about the fourteenth amendment.

Now I don't know the answers, as I said, but certainly I think that today we ought not to deceive ourselves and we ought not to lie to ourselves. Certainly the fourteenth amendment was adopted coercively, there isn't any argument about it. It was adopted in a most brutal pragmatic fashion, "you either adopt this or you don't get back into the Union." So you can argue all you want that something adopted under coercion is not legal. But let's don't deceive ourselves. As Hill was trying to say shortly after it was adopted——of course it's there, it's in the Constitution——it isn't going to be taken out——actually as it stands today in times of change you and I wouldn't want it out. It's a very necessary sort of amendment if you will read it. So that however we may say the brutality that brought it into being is not to be excused and not to be condoned and I certainly don't. There's no more brutal chapter in anybody's history than that. But the fourteenth amendment is in there and it isn't coming out and it is valid.

153

Then I think that the Constitution is vague, the tenth amendment which says about all other rights not reserved to the government shall belong to the states or to the people. What does that mean? Well I don't know. But somebody has got to interpret it finally. You can interpret it one way to your satisfaction——I may——but again I say let's don't lie to ourselves and say that the Supreme Court has violated the Constitution. The Supreme Court has not violated the Constitution because it can't. The Supreme Court is created to interpret the Constitution. Now you may argue and truthfully so that the Supreme Court certainly reversed former procedures, that the Supreme Court reversed a former court.

There isn't time here to go into another reason of why we are, and yet, it would be perfectly possible to prove, I think, that a speech made in Atlanta, Georgia at a time of great emotional crisis in 1885 at the old Cotton States Exposition by Booker T. Washington became known all over the South and all over the nation as the "Atlanta Compromise," when Booker T. Washington stood here in Atlanta and made the speech in which he said that the Negro——that up to then, of course, the Negro had been allowed to vote very generally. You had had the great populist movement in which the Negro had been part of the executive committee of the populist parties in this state. When Tom Watson had gone up and down Georgia saying to the farmers, the commercial democrats are separating you, the Negro and the poor white farmer, so that you may be fleeced separately. Negroes used to come up and try to touch Watson's clothes and go home and tell their families, "I touched him." They looked on him almost as a god. Then you had the change. By 1885 violence, lynchings were pretty common. Washington made this speech in which he said that the Negro didn't need to vote. In fact that's what he said——that's the time when most of the laws were passed to disfranchise the Negro, property ownership, poll tax, the grandfather clause, and so on. Washington is an enigma to this day, one of the great neglected figures in the history of the South.

He was the one who said that the Negro just wanted a job, an opportunity, and of course that's about all the Negro could get then and maybe Washington did him a great favor but still he set a pattern and he reminded industrialists speaking all around that the Negro was not a strike-breaker, that he was a faithful, loyal worker; you wouldn't have labor troubles if you had Negro workers. He made those speeches in Birmingham, he made them in Atlanta, subsequent to the other. I think it very significant that one year later the Supreme Court had the Plessy-Ferguson——"separate but equal." I think it very significant that two years later union labor began effectively then to exclude or put the Negro in separate compartments. This speech, coming at a very critical time set a pattern, became known, as I said, all over as "The Atlanta Compromise."

So many things in our history have affected us and reached down to us today but at any rate certainly the Supreme Court did reverse the Plessy——, separate but equal and certainly reversed it very fundamentally and certainly it brought in some extraneous things and as I said a while ago it changed, it violated form of procedure or it had reversed them if it hadn't violated them. It brought in things no other court had brought in to aid it in its interpretation. Now whether we approve of that or not, I'm very much afraid that doesn't really matter because the court——the Constitution doesn't say how the, it doesn't lay down rules, it simply charges the Supreme Court with interpreting the Constitution. So let's don't delude ourselves. We can still keep on disagreeing with it. We can hope that the Supreme Court some other day may change its mind and reverse itself again, some court years from now, or we may try to get legislation which will somehow change the function of the court. There are a lot of things we can do but let's don't delude ourselves and listen to people who say that the Supreme Court has violated the Constitution. That just isn't true.

Now, I don't know what we're up against today any more than you. I don't know the answer to what we're up against any more than you today. Certainly we can see very plainly that the old cotton South feels differently from Maryland, Delaware, Missouri, Oklahoma. Desegregation is practically completed in Oklahoma. It is completed in Missouri without a single incident——part of Missouri is further south than Paducah, Kentucky, part of Ohio is further south than Paducah, Kentucky——at any rate——Indiana——I mean, not Ohio——you get all of the changes in those states. You come down to North Carolina, Tennessee have made a token beginning in desegregation which is certainly within the meaning of the Supreme Court's deliberate speed and an act of faith. Arkansas had made even further advance until the Little Rock crisis came on, so that Arkansas, Tennessee, North Carolina made beginnings, but the Deep South hadn't.

I have tried to reach whatever people I could with the idea that this difference is here and must be recognized in a matter of approach. I know I've heard every...[Few words missing here on tape.] figure in Georgia government——the present, past, say privately, that one day it will come but not as long as I live or not as long as I have anything to do with it. You get that attitude in the deep cotton South but just north of us in the upper tier you get another attitude. Why? Because of our past history. That's why. Because of attitudes which grew out of certain climates. They aren't different people from us really.

Well now what can we do? I think it very tragic but I would rather see Georgia which needs education as much or more than any other state; I would nonetheless rather see Georgia close its schools than to go into a period of violence and mob actions. I am confident that they will close the schools if it comes to that. And if it comes to that I hope that they may close them without any violence. I am hopeful that before that comes if we can avoid in the Deep South the filing of a suit about a school, say for two or three more years and if the process in which it's begun in Arkansas, North Carolina, Tennessee, could be allowed to progress——I happen to know that some of the cities in North Carolina are making plans for next fall

156

and they are going ahead and desegregation is moving fairly fast in Texas which has a law which requires a vote and if the people vote for it then they may have it. I know that in some of the North Carolina towns they are going to change back their high schools to segregate them on the basis of sex, a boy's high school and a girl's high school, to thereby avoid the initial shock which is a shock to so many people of mixing the two races.

There are a number of things which people can do and are doing except here in the Deep South where there is simply complete defiance. I think the tragedy is that in the Deep South that local school boards haven't been allowed to do what they would like to do. I cannot name him here but I have a good friend who is a county commissioner in a north Georgia county. Two months ago——three months ago he was talking to me, he said "You, know," I'll quote him as exactly as I can, he said "You know we haven't got but three nigger kids that'll go to school in our county, just three. And we all know them, know their folks, they ain't bad niggers and we can just sit them kids over in a corner in the schoolroom and nobody will care." Well, they can't do it. Most of the schools in Chicago high schools, I do not know about the others, and until recently most of them in New York, were either nearly all white or nearly all colored. Why? Because of the geographical facts of population. Schools are where the people live. Savannah, Georgia where they have had very little trouble desegregating, just a little trouble in two or three schools. Atlanta, Georgia would have very little trouble because most of them would continue to be just what they are, white schools or colored schools. You would have a few where you have a little trouble. Then if the local school board had the authority such as Louisville had to allow transfers to people who weren't willing——if you would allow common sense to function, you could get a lot done. But here in the Deep South we aren't——common sense isn't allowed to function nor is local school board authority allowed to function and you and I know why it isn't and it isn't just because of the present government. I

157

fully subscribe to the fact that all people everywhere and anywhere are pretty much a product of their history. So, we aren't going to allow common sense to function, we aren't going to allow democracy or local school board authority to function. Now, I would very much hope——I don't care——this isn't worth recording or quoting to anybody, but I have been to certain persons in Washington. I have got word, I hope, to certain attorneys outside the government. And my theory being that if you could allow precept and example to work in North Carolina, Tennessee, Arkansas, for two or three years that you might have a change. These governments might say we'd better go——these five or six Deep South cotton states might say——another administration——might say we'd better go to the North Carolina system which is the only one that's had a test by its district court so far. Time works changes. Nothing was ever lost, I don't think, much in a situation like this by taking time. If we could delay suits in the Deep South for two or three years at least, I think a lot of things might happen. I don't know what——I don't know that they would. I just have a faith in human beings that it would. I just don't know any other out for it.

Now, I don't think that private schools, now, I'm no lawyer, I've talked to lawyers; some of them will tell you that private school systems such as Georgia has is fine. I don't much think so. Anything that's a subterfuge isn't legal and if a state is supplying money to keep children separated, compulsory separated, separations then private schools set up by state money, indirectly by state money——a number of awful good lawyers have said they haven't got a chance. It has been knocked out in Virginia already, and has been knocked out in two or three other states.

So we're up against it here and we ought not to delude ourselves into thinking that forever we can keep it up. Something else, now I'm talking much too long, that annoys me and I've worried about this. It seems to me that the greatest falsehood has been imposed on us, on a lot of people and I'm sure that I must be wrong about it because I just can't see where it makes any sense. But it seems to me that a very phony bill of goods has been sold, namely that integration——I don't know anybody that's demanding integration——a person would be a fool to demand integration now in the Deep South. That would be foolish. But I still say that they've sold us a false bill of goods, namely that integration would mean amalgamation. I just think a little bit too much of the white race and the colored race to believe that only a law prevents them from rushing to the marriage courts. (laughter) That's ridiculous in my opinion. And yet it's the *overpowering* one sentiment in this that it would mean mongrelization or amalgamation——(From audience——"It always has.") All right sir. All the statistics——there has been desegregation in the North, Northern schools to a degree since the Civil War. The only statistics I have is that while the population figures are up that percentage-wise, the number of intermarriages in the North are down, certainly there is less miscegenation now than ever before, the police court records demonstrate that. It seems to me that both races are developing a greater pride and so I think there has been a bill of goods sold us that needn't have been done. My personal opinion is that certainly integration does not mean amalgamation. You may differ, I may be wrong. But at any rate I hope I've made it clear that I'm——I don't know anyone who is demanding integration, certainly it would not be acceptable, there's no chance of it, a person would be a fool to demand it. But I think we will be greater fools if we don't commit ourselves to a process, a mental process of determining that whatever we do, we will stand by the law.

Mr. Griffin, I've talked too long, I guess. [There now began a brief question and answer period.]

Griffin: You've given us a very different approach from other approaches we've had in this class where we have had emphasis on what North Carolina is doing, we've had emphasis on what Georgia may do and we've had emphasis on a sort of moral emphasis, I think, out of the talk last week. You've given us a very fine historical background to talk about. Let's have some comments and some questions in terms of what Mr. McGill has had to say tonight.

Question: Hasn't there always been amalgamation in other countries where the races have been thrown together?

McGill: Pretty thoroughly in all of those countries, entirely a different situation, they were literally thrown together from the very beginning. We have a different racial background——a different approach——from the very beginning the Spanish approach was amalgamation where they set out to bring that about in the very beginning as quickly as they could beginning even with the Indians so you would have a pretty thorough amalgamation. You never had the differences such as the cast differences such as this country had as you might argue sir that——the British have had colonies a great many years but the British people in those colonies where they had been thrown together have not amalgamated. There has been almost eighty percent amalgamation in the countries you mentioned sir, as I understand it.

Question: The British colonies maintain strict segregation I understand.

McGill: Well, they did up till about twenty, thirty, varying, forty years ago depending on where they were; there was no overall pattern——yes they did and so did we and that's why I say it won't happen here because you've developed two racial prides. Certainly in the eastern schools there haven't been any intermarriages in the high schools and they've been at it for about——they have been going to school up there for about, well since the war.

[Question was not audible.]

McGill: Well, I don't know sir, that's the enormously frustrating aspect of it. I think discussions such as this will be helpful even though you might say this is a small number but people are talking. I think it's significant that more and more ministers are speaking out. If we aren't careful we are going to allow——I've heard some people who have been speaking and writing saying, Well all this

160

bunk about brotherhood and loving your neighbor as yourself and so forth, that's all Communism." Well, it'll be a
sad day in this country if we ever attribute to Communism
all of the things that we've been taught for Christianity. I
have hoped sir, that the Deep South can avoid any suits for
some time and that our leadership, national leadership,
which I hope and believe certainly will see the necessity
for speaking more and more to the people, offering more
leadership. I think it very helpful that Mr. Brownell has
resigned. He was a very rigid man, an austere man and he
lost the ability to operate in this business of politics. The
new man, I don't know, I've never met, but by all accounts
he is a man able to get along with people and understand
their problems and that's part of the essence of government is understanding the other man's problems. I don't
know sir——there isn't much hope except just to hold on
and try.

Question: What was your attitude and the attitude of
the *Constitution* concerning the sending of federal troops
to Little Rock, Arkansas?

McGill: No, sir——if we——I think we abhorred the
necessity for sending them in——I hoped we phrased it that
way. The *Constitution*, I hope did. (laughter) I don't mean
that critically but I was trying to think of what we had
done. I don't think the President had any other choice
than to send them in. And when the situation had reached
the point it did——I don't know how——I know a lawyer
over there who is a good friend of Governor Faubus'. This
is open for quotation isn't it so I can't tell this
story——[From audience, "This is off the record."]
(laughter) oh——this is, oh——(laughter). He said Orville
had been listening to some fellows who said, "Go
ahead——bluff him, bluff him, bluff him. Ike always runs
away from decisions. He'll never do it, so just go ahead and
bluff him." So we reached the unhappy point where it was
Governor Faubus who was trying to ram something down
the President's throat so to speak. Now, we all watched the
President take his inauguration oath to defend that district
court and let's say it doesn't matter whether we think the

court was right or wrong——maybe the court was wrong and maybe it was right but still the government of the United States can't abandon its courts, then you would have anarchy. I think we might have regretted and I think it was tragic that troops had to be sent in. I think the commander was a fool for allowing them to put bayonets on the rifles. There were a number of errors there, certainly that was a horrible error, the bayonets, unnecessary, but still in all it had reached the point where in my opinion that there was nothing for the President to do but to send in the troops.

Question: [A question was asked about McGill's attitude toward the law.]

McGill: Well, it might——but what I'm about to say sounds so corny that I apologize (laughter) for it. But I feel a certain majesty about the law——I really do. And this sounds even cornier but I learned some years ago and it took a little doing, I some years ago made up my mind that I wasn't going to——if a national issue came up——I was going to try to approach it as an American citizen and not as a regional citizen. If we try to decide everything regionally we pretty soon won't have much of a country left. No sir, I don't know——I have a feeling that there's a great majesty about the law——I know its corrupted at times. I know bad things——

Question: What I mean is wouldn't that make a lot of responsible citizens feel as you do?

McGill: Well, I don't know. I think it took the bombing in Nashville to do it——took another think in Nashville. The police department got angry in Nashville. The crowd up there was cursing the police and calling them nigger lovers and so forth and finally they lost their temper and they just moved in and they acted pretty rough. And they got it settled down, then the bombing came which shocked the public conscience a great deal. The law end of it is something, well I don't know, I just feel that if we, this year, next year were to have an issue at a school——I would rather see it shut down than to have mobs and fighting and people being clubbed and hit with stones, brick, etc.

162

MINISTERS WEEK
Emory University, January 21, 1959

Approximately nine hundred Methodist ministers from the Southeast, many of whom were alumni of Candler School of Theology, Emory University, gathered in Glenn Memorial Auditorium on that campus to hear McGill speak at 11 a.m. Discretely and with considerable caution McGill analyzed why the Deep South now confronted racial problems, and recommended that communities hold "calm" and "reasoned" discussions concerning the possibility of integrated public schools. Reading this speech even in the 1960's, one is tempted to question McGill's reluctance to advocate a more decisive position; however, when viewed in the extreme tenseness of the social situation in which given, this speech is further indication that McGill was indeed a mover (however slowly) of change. (Manuscript taken from taped recording.)

Ladies and Gentlemen,

Thank you very much for that gracious introduction and for your welcome. I come to you today very sincerely in a state of some trepidation and concern because I don't know the answers to things. I don't know that anyone does know the answer or answers to what is one of the great complex and agonizing problems of our time. And nor is it true, as some have charged, that I have a program or that I advocate a program. I can't quite explain to you myself why I feel so earnestly that there is a need for rational observation of this problem. It may be that, like many of you, perhaps all of you and I am inclined to think that the status of any person today of any sensitive heart and mind must of necessity be something like that of Martin Luther and his famous statement, *"Ich kann nicht anders,"* "I can't do anything else; I must be concerned with this." But as for a program I have none. If asked, I might try to formulate one. I have not advocated any policy or program because I'm not sure what one could be. It would be necessary, I think, to do a lot of work to establish a sort of policy or program.

I don't know how much theology I have about this. I've

thought about that a lot. I heard a sermon some years ago that was based on the great commandments, the second of which is like unto the first——"thou shall love thy neighbor as thyself," in which this minister said something which was not original——which I'm sure each of you has said in many sermons, but this is the first man I heard to say it. And he said that this commandment, "to love thy neighbor as thyself," and its symbolism and in its actual meaning, was of course something that man couldn't will to do. Just man by himself can't will himself to do this. It takes another power and he said it took, in his opinion, the grace and strength of God to enable a man to do it and I find myself believing that. And so I suppose that is the chief theology I have about this question if you would call it that.

Now I envy persons, a great many of them in my business——television or radio or newspapers——who seem themselves to be touched with a sort of omniscience and who know all the answers and who speak with great dogmatic finality. And this I can't do. I envy sometimes those men and sometimes I'm irritated with them. (laughter) I remember——my text, and I use this text very often. When I was a boy of about eleven, living then in Chattanooga, Tennessee, my father who was a great admirer of Henry Waterson, the then great editor of the *Louisville Courier Journal*——determined that he would take me to see Waterson because he said he always wanted me to remember that I had seen him. So we took an excursion train——you could go very far very cheap on an excursion train in those days——and we went to Louisville and we got in to see Waterson and I remember how he looked in the old dark room and the desk——the office and desk, and hearing my father ask a few questions and talk. But I've remembered most a motto which Waterson had framed on his desk and it read like this, "Lord, give me this day my daily idea, and forgive me the one I had yesterday." (laughter)

Now, in a time when just late last year the first physics books which were up to date began to come off the presses and which in some instances already are a little bit obsolete, and in a time when any person who is willing to look around can almost feel the great forces loose in the world which are working tremendous change. When our missionaries, when our state department people and when our visitors all bear eloquent witness of the fact that these forces are at work, it's a dangerous idea, I think, to have a fixed opinion which isn't subject to change. I rather like Abraham Lincoln's idea. When the editors and delegations called on him early in the war and demanded to know what his policy was, and he said, "My policy is to have no policy." Now, I don't go quite that far, nor did Lincoln, of course, but what I'm getting at is that I believe in this time we must have not merely an open mind but we must understand that no generality will fit any phase of this problem. I was sorry I didn't hear Dr. Carmichael yesterday. I've read his book. I'm familiar with his precepts and with his formula which will in general fit and they do and they have great validity but they demonstrate exactly what I'm trying to say now. Namely that in at least four states——we——you and I——as a people are in what might be called a straight jacket. Each of us, inescapably, is a part of the past. We are a part of our homelife; we are a part of our religious life; we are a part of what we've met with. One of the great poets, as I recall, has a line which says "I am a part of all that I have met." And that's true I believe, not merely of individuals but of nations and of even areas and regions. Certainly in this great United States that is true. We know it to be true in the great complex country of India, for example. And it's true everywhere. We are a part of all that we have met. And we have met with quite a lot.

If you wanted to examine into it, and I give this as a sort of background to the problem as I see it——and I could be wrong, but this is how it seems to me. There are only four states in the whole nation where the business, the matter of race has been consistently and rather emotionally, even violently, exploited for political ends——only four. Now, I'm not here to blame somebody for this. Perhaps it grew out of certain inevitabilities, out of pressures. It grew out of the fact that at the proper time the wrong sort of leadership arose, but there are just four. They are the same four states who have produced almost a hundred percent of all those persons, who for one reason or another have earned the name of having been demagogic in the field of race. Many of these men made excellent contributions on the very positive asset side. But none-theless, in this particular field, they exploited it demagogically. And this has been true for almost ninety years. We forget, for example, that in another generation one of these men, Tillman of South Carolina toured the Chautauqua Circuits and was in great demand over the whole South preaching a doctrine that the Negro was not really a human being. This might startle us now but this was exactly and literally his position. He expressed doubts whether he had a soul, he was something of an animal. At best, he conceded him to be probably the missing link, the halfway creation between man and animals, at best that. Sometimes we forget how far we have come in Christian influence and in civilized thinking. But at any rate I men-tioned just the one. Almost one hundred percent of the names familiar to history and the sociological studies who have been explosively and violently demagogic in the field of race are from four states. And they are Georgia, Alabama, Mississippi, and South Carolina. Now, as I said, I couldn't blame anyone for that, nor could you, nor should we. And that is not my intent and purpose. I'm not shaking a finger in anybody's face. I'm thinking purely in the sociological terms that we are a part of all that we have met.

Now it so happens that if you study the situation you will find another interesting thing. These same four states are the ones which have the largest percentage of Negro population. They are the states also which have the largest carryover of the old plantation type economy, demanding a considerable amount of hand labor, requiring large amounts of farm labor. They are the four states which were and are today last in the acquisition of industry, to take up jobs, to provide jobs for people being released by the land in this swift agricultural revolution which is going on simultaneously with the other great changes. And so, an honest person looking at his region must say to himself, These things are true. They help explain the depth of our dilemma. They assist us in understanding why the agony of our situation is perhaps greater. Actually, of course there isn't any great difference between a citizen of Mississippi or Georgia or Alabama or South Carolina than one in North Carolina or Kentucky or Tennessee. We are all essentially basically the same sort of people. We all have basically the old Anglo-Saxon stock so to speak. Most of our forebears, those in Tennessee, North Carolina and Kentucky, came through the Mountain passes and pushed on into the other states. And so there isn't really any basic difference between a Tennessean, a North Carolinian, a Kentuckian than one from the other states of the South.

Why then the difference? Well I think that what I've said is one of the facts. Secondly is that of leadership. Now these same factors you may argue properly, although not completely, produced the sort of leadership which we have had. But nonetheless, what I'm trying to say is that no generality will apply. You can't write a formula and say because the people in much of the South are in a straight jacket. Now I'm sure that any person willing honestly to discuss this problem would agree. I am one of those who admires extravagantly what Dr. Carmichael has done. And I understand that he said that his formula would not fit here. But certainly he is absolutely correct in saying that the final solution must come out of each community. And that is what I think is so wicked on the part of those state governments which have refused to allow communities to work with this problem on the basis of what it is in their community. They can't write a formula for it any more than you and I can. Inescapably it must come out of the people themselves. But when the people are given no opportunity to allow it to come then we have a state of paralysis and we have a condition of enormous frustration of all that is best in us. Every goodwill instinct, every

167

honest wish to get on with the job, every sincere concern to apply Christian principles and civilized thought to this problem; it is frustrated, nullified, it is barred off, it can't go to work because it isn't permitted.

And so those of us who live in this situation, there is no need to curse the past and to face the future with lack of hope; there's every reason I think to understand the past, to be aware of it, to know how it affects us, to know why it paralyzes us but allows a North Carolinian or Kentuckian or a Tennessean to make some beginning and some progress without violence and without destructive chaos. These things we must understand and we must, we must be reasonable and we must proceed, as I see it, with unrelenting determination as best we can. I think it important that we stand up when we can and when we do we do so calmly and as reasonably as we can. I have the feeling, and this is a feeling and it may be wrong, but I have the feeling that within the past eight or ten months, the people are thinking more and are beginning to distrust the extremist leadership which permits of no application of civilized principles, or of Christian thought, for that matter, to this problem. I hope I'm right and it may be wishful thinking, but I sense that and I hope very much that it is true. At any rate, I think the role not merely of the Christian minister but the role of the Christian laymen——this isn't the minister's problem anymore than it's the layman's problem, except that the minister does have a pulpit and I'm not suggesting that every minister speak out. Every minister has a problem, I know that. (laughter) His community differs, his community has had a history which may be different from the one fifty miles away or a hundred miles away. I'm aware of all that. I feel that editors too have a pulpit. And I think they're in a better shape to do it, to speak, than a minister. Some of them are, at least. But it's the job of the layman every-where, I feel, within the limits of what he can do to resist the extremist doctrines which have always been wrong all through history. They've been wrong in every aspect of history. The extremists doctrine has been wrong and it's wrong now. It's wrong in this situation.

Well, what's going to happen? I don't know, but we can theorize. It seems to me, and again this is an opinion and I could be wrong about it——it seems to me that the Virginia decision was, insofar as the meaning of it and the ultimate effect of it is concerned is the most important one since the first [1954] one. I must have had in the past year twenty men pretty well up in political leadership say to me, "Well, of course I know that this is inevitable. But my political future depends on me fighting and I know that in the end it's going to prevail but I'm going to do everything I can to delay it." Now the morality of that sort of position may not appeal to you, but then you and I are not in politics. It still doesn't appeal to me, but that sort of thinking is going on, but the Virginia decision, it seemed to me, was important for this reason. It is the first court, state court, to rule. Now whether others would prefer to rule as did Virginia or whether they would be politically fearful and would rule with the state legislative enactments, rule them legal and then prefer to be reversed by the Supreme Court of the United States, I don't know, but I prefer to believe in the integrity of courts because, I don't know why, but I've had all my life, maybe because of a family influence, I've had a great what amounts almost to a reverence for law and courts. I don't mean that I haven't violated laws. I don't say that——but for the grace of God go I, many times, but I nonetheless have the feeling about the need for law in our sort of country or any sort of country, but in a country which is based on——from the lowest position up to the highest, the President of the United States——on the free elective choice. If there isn't the anchor of law and respect for it I think we would be lost. So I wouldn't presume to think that the courts of the Southern states aren't equally strong in integrity as is Virginia. At any rate, Virginia's court has wiped out every one of Virginia's laws dealing with the problem of school——integration in the schools. There isn't any law left. Eventually that same thing is going to happen in all of the states. When? I don't know. How many years, one

169

year, two years, three, four? I don't know. But eventually that's going to happen.

There will be new ideas conceived and there will be new legislative enactments but in time they will all come down to a choice between the pupil placement law and no public school systems at all. Now it may come quicker than we think. It may take longer. I haven't the vaguest idea. If asked to guess I just wouldn't do it. But eventually, unless we break down our system of law, which I don't believe this nation will, finally it's going to come. All of the state laws which are evasive actions will be unconstitutional and so-declared as has happened in Virginia. Virginia will probably enact some more. This while it is annoying at times because it looks so absolutely ridiculous at times to keep on when you know the answer, rather than turning to active planning and some sort of constructive way to meet it and to make the best of it.

The pupil placement law which is in operation in North Carolina will permit what amounts to, a very token sort of integration in the schools, a handful. It permits transfers out of the schools if you don't want your child to stay there. I think they've had something like six hundred transfers and they've had no incidents or trouble. The pupil placement law allows you to look into the moral background of the children involved. It will permit you to look into of course the scholastic ability and background. It absolutely removed that fear. It gives to each community an active and legitimate and constitutional mechanism to proceed with deliberate speed, that is with great slowness. (laughter) For a long time, for a good number of years——does it make sense not to start working in that direction rather than proceeding in one which can be productive only of sorrow and disrupting of the educational process at a time when we all know that we need more education, not less, at a time when we are going through some very critical changes in the school system; when we are making all sorts of examinations of our methods and procedures; when we are determining that we must toughen-up some aspects of our teaching; when we are

170

trying through various measures to produce more teachers, more qualified teachers; I don't——this region will lose next September a great many of its younger, more ambitious teachers; those who have been teaching for a long time with a vested interest in retirement and pensions and of an age where it is not easy to move will stay I assume. But we are going to lose many, many of our best teachers and we are already short of them. Someone has said that today there is a shortage of even poor teachers. (laughter) Factitious as that may sound it is true.

There are great things stirring in education. The federal education bill which makes available for the next four years over seven hundred million dollars; this is a lot of money but when spread across forty-nine states is not as much as it sounds. That bill is a very complex bill reflecting the complexity of the American education problem but it's interesting to read it. It's long and tedious, but surprisingly the chief emphasis in this bill is really not on science and mathematics as it seemed at the time we remembered the debate about it last August when the bill was passed. The chief emphasis in this bill is to encourage people to go into teaching. In the loan aspect of it, for example, if you are an undergraduate and you get one of these loans, you are eligible and you are awarded one, you can get a thousand dollars a year for five years. And you pay it back at three percent interest beginning one year after you are out of school, one calendar year, at three percent. But if you go into teaching you don't have to pay back but fifty percent of your loan, two thousand five hundred dollars. And still other aspects of the bill, there is encouragement to teach, to produce new teachers. Next Tuesday I hope you will look for a report by Dr. Conant the former president of Harvard College who for twenty years has been a leading advocate and supporter of the public school system saying that in our sort of country, that of course there is a place for private schools, there is a place for schools run by churches if the churches see to it that they have adequate education. Some people want their children to go to a private school, to have small

171

classes, to have emphasis on certain subjects perhaps, to be able to have personal attention from the teacher because they think the child may need that. Others want them to go to a church school because they are willing to pay for that because they want their children to have emphasis on religious instruction, and to be taught the Bible, and to have other aspects of religion made available to them. There is a place for those schools. Dr. Conant has been saying for twenty years, but in our sort of country and especially now when we are seeing the tremendous burgeoning cities grow, when to drive from Atlanta to Marietta is like one city and to go from Boston to New York is like one city and from New York to Washington is like one city and from Washington to Baltimore is like one city. When we are having these increasing concentrations of people, there isn't any other answer for our kind of country, a free elective country, but a public school system. And Dr. Conant for two years now, has been heading up a well staffed committee which has done research into the American high schools. That report is coming out next Tuesday. I commend your attention to it. I hope the newspapers will print an adequate amount of it so that we may be well informed.

The office of education, in addition to administering this new federal aid bill of seven hundred millions to be spent across the next four years is planning a four year study of the high school curriculums, the effect of it on students. This too, will be announced in the next few days. And I say this to point out that we literally are in the midst of a great new ferment of change in education and determination to support it. And that we should be confronting a withdrawal from education, an interruption of it, a chaotic period for a long time, is to me unworthy of us.

But I've talked too long. What the role is, what can I do? Well, I think each man and woman must examine his own heart and conscience. He must not waste himself or herself, but wherever we are, and to the best that we are I think we owe it to ourselves to reflect and whatever possible degree we can, it will be effective. Perhaps a little bit here, perhaps a great bit somewhere else; we must somehow stand quietly and calmly but as forthrightly as we can against this sort of thing which is destructive to all that's best in our lives. But when you are in a straight jacket there isn't too much you can do. And that's where we are. But there are things that can be done and it is being done. I have a great admiration for the Christian churches. One of the great differences in my mind, as I read and study history which is sort of a hobby of mine——one of the great differences and one of the great hopes, as between 1857 and 1957 and 1959 is that the position of the Christian church is the exact opposite from what it was in '57, 1857, the exact opposite. And I think that the real hope lies in that. I think that if you wanted an evidence of the effect of Christianity you could see it in evidence in the communities and in the hearts and minds of people who are worried about this and the increasing number who are beginning to try to do something about it. I think it's the effect of your preaching and your predecessors' preaching who illustrate what I have said before, "I am a part of all that we have met, that I have met." And you are too and this generation and the one before it has met with a great deal more that was different than it was those generations had met up to 1857.

I'm not at all without hope. Most of the time it is a day-to-day frustration but certainly there is a real opportunity ahead of us because when the thing collapses and the rebuilding starts, then the great burden and responsibility will really be upon you and others who are willing to work to rebuild because there will have to be rebuilding when this is done. So I certainly think that we should continue. It needs your prayers, it needs your hopes, and it needs as I've said before for each of us——I remember the old, little song of Sunday School days when I was a child, "Brighten the Corner Where You Are." And one small candle's light can help in a time like this. Thank you very much. (applause) [A question and answer period followed.]

Moderator: We are not going to let our man go just yet, so you can save some of the applause for a little bit later. Right now we have a few minutes which we can have for your questions to be directed to Mr. McGill. And I will ask you if you have a question, to stand so that you can be recognized and state your question and I will make an effort to restate it to the group. Are there questions at this time?

Question from audience: Mr. McGill what do you think of the possibility of the leadership, educational and political, at this time going ahead with the kind of study and proposal that might be made when the Court does strike down [what we now have]?

McGill: I think there is every reason to go ahead in any community where there are people willing to discuss it. I don't know who the gentlemen was who said that you'd had only one side of the question. I'm not really interested but the point is, I think it's obvious that whoever he was he was wrong because a debate goes on and you can't debate unless you have contending views, and certainly there is a growing debate and I would think that if you are in a community where there are interested people, you may have to meet quietly, you may be able to bring in some of your political leadership. If so that certainly is all to the good. But carefully and quietly evaluating your own community. I think it very wise that you do have some sort of committee, some sort of thinking, and some sort of at least preliminary planning to try to cope with the situations ahead. I don't think we can expect it from a state level. It will have to be community and that's where it ought to be. It ought to come from the state level but when it doesn't, then it must come from the community. You may have to be almost secretive about it in some places.

Question: [McGill repeats question below.]

McGill: I don't know if you heard the question——it was——"Do I think that integration compelled by the courts would be possible in the states mentioned without civil war?" I don't think it could be compelled generally

174

without violence and tremendous resistance. I do think there are areas where it could be. I think and I certainly do not say this out of any talks with Atlanta educational people. I do not want you to think I'm quoting them. I'm not. But on the basis of what little I know about it, I think it would be possible sir, in Atlanta. I think it would be possible in Macon. I think it would be possible in Columbus, if it were permitted and if it were not agitated all the while you were trying to do it. Now, let's face it. The eastern cities have a great many schools which are segregated without law but they are segregated simply by the fact of geography of population. We have been lucky in that we have built schools where the population is. And in these cities I mentioned people who ought to know have told me that there would be relatively little integration required because most schools would be all white or all Negro. There would be one or two where you would have a problem. I think that could be handled. But I think that if it were tried generally in all the districts, sir, there would be a great deal of violence. But I think, I don't see why our people can't make a beginning as North Carolina has done if they are given an opportunity to do it. Or as Tennessee has done. There isn't that much difference between us. The difference lies in the background, in the things that have happened. I'll tell you a story——this is a true story, I won't name the county and this man was one of the most violently opposed to integration you ever saw. He was from a North Georgia county and he was a county commissioner. Now I'll quote him as exactly as I can remember. He said, not for quotation, of course, but he said "if they will just let us handle it——(he was talking from the community viewpoint) we wouldn't have any trouble a'tall." He said "We haven't got but three Negro children in the county that we would have to deal with. We know their people——their parents——they all work for us and we've known them all their lives and we wouldn't mind sitting those three nigra kids in a corner in the schoolroom and we could get along alright." Well, I don't know whether he could now or not. But I think we all live,

175

we all think, in the terms of images and the image of integration in these states where the large Negro population is that of a great engulfment of the schools by Negro children, and the fact that the pupil placement law would enable you maybe to put one in a school, or three or four and they would be distributed is completely ignored. I don't know if that answered you or not.

Question: Mr. McGill what about the possibility in our state of Georgia of a movement without the legislature, petitioning the legislature to give us an opportunity to referendum to repeal the amendment that gave the governor the power to close schools?

McGill: I think that is much preferable to having the Supreme Court rule it out. But I must in candor say to you that I don't think that is now possible. I think there has been such an excitement of the problem, I think that the people have been so deceived, that might not be the right word, but they have not been well informed on it. I don't know if you could get enough people to sign such a petition now. But I think, the gentlemen over here who asked——I think the beginning ought to be made at the community level, then after some time has passed you might be able to have such a petition. I like the idea; I don't think it's now politically possible. I think the majority of the people——the heavy majority of the people support the present political position. I wanted to make that clear, that I understand that.

Question: As a Christian layman do you think that the church schools should have the right to do as they want too? Should they begin themselves as a pilot [project to racially integrate the schools]? Do you think this is the responsibility of the church?

McGill: Again I wouldn't... I don't like to talk in generalities. I have this feeling about church schools. I have interested myself in education and on a lot of committees I worked at it and I picked up just enough information to be ignorant about it. But, here's the trouble about starting a church school. And this, I have from reports on those. In the first place you haven't got the money. You would have to try to get up money. In the second place if you got up money you wouldn't be able to pay, except in rare instances of a very wealthy church or a wealthy benefactor or so--—you wouldn't be able to pay the going wage for teachers. Therefore you would be almost dependent on hiring retired teachers or people who had had a little teaching experience. As always there would be a great--— and this is good--—I don't think the effect's good but I understand this as a Christian charity sort of thing. There will always be some people around, "Well we ought to give so and so a job in this because he or she needs it so badly." And we wouldn't take into account their real qualifications. So unless you are very careful, a church which moves without careful evaluation and planning and thinking this whole thing through, I think we would make a grave mistake to hurry into setting up a school. I don't know if that answers. Maybe I misunderstood the whole question.

Moderator: I believe as I understood your question you were talking in terms of a church school that is already established, in the sense of a church related college. Whether they should take it upon themselves at the present time to be a pilot project in the matter of breaking down the segregation pattern in the schools in Georgia and other states of the South.

McGill: I wouldn't say that a'tall sir, because again I think you can do only what you can do, and if you are going to destroy a school or disrupt it, then I wouldn't do it. But if you can by careful planning and, I guess Dr. Carmichael told you, they spent a year a half, almost two years preparing the people of Louisville for what they did. I think if a church school was in a community where it thought it could start out and do this legitimately after a period of time, X months or so on then they might well do it. But again, I wouldn't try to speak generally. A curious thing is happening--—we all think in terms of images. We are all used to seeing some sort of colored people in our schools now. I can remember twenty years ago when a Japanese or a Chinese was not welcome and that's not true now. I'm a great man against generalities. I don't like to generalize.

Question: Shouldn't we look for better ways to communicate different views on social problems?

McGill: Well, if I understood you sir, you were speaking of communicating with people. It always embarrasses me, being in the business of communications, that we have done such a poor job. I would say sir, that anytime a Christian church or leader or community can carry out by discussion, information programs, all to the good. I think that if you can get them out of the process of debate you will do better. Unhappily, a lot of people don't want to hear the truth. They don't want to hear the facts, they don't want to hear the other side. But if you could have somebody who could project the real dilemma or have just a discussion, have both sides but let it be talked, the important thing is that it will be discussed. I think we have been in a position where we have been almost afraid to discuss this until the last few months. It was a subject that was taboo, let's don't talk about it. Now people are beginning to talk about it and a debate is beginning and I think that will be healthy.

Question: I, like you, think the people of Georgia support the present political leadership, but do you think the people of Georgia realize that they might have their schools closed? Do you not feel that the leadership has made them believe that somehow or other we will go on like we have been? Do you believe that if all the schools are closed in Georgia that the people in this state will say that's perfectly all right?

McGill: No, I do not. I quite agree with you. I think that the people somehow feel, "Oh well, they'll work it out somehow." Well, I don't think so, I wish I did. In other words, I wouldn't like to be a young and ambitious politician who was strongly on record today because I think that not too many years ahead that politician will have been proved so wrong that he will be out of politics. The time to be right when you have just been elected to office——the time to be right is not now but four years from now when your term is up. (laughter) That's the time to be right——not now——four years from now.

The Reverend Mr. Long [with an apparently impromptu statement]: Mr. McGill I don't have another question but I would like to make a statement sir. The people of Atlanta and Georgia have appreciated you. You have been the one single voice it seems to me in the state [offering] leadership. I think you ought to know that the people of this state love and appreciate you for the stand you have taken. (loud applause from audience)

McGill: Thank you sir, I appreciate that more than I can tell you.

Moderator: I believe there is nothing further for me to add to what The Reverend Mr. Long has spoken so eloquently in terms of our gratitude to Mr. McGill, not only for his service here today but for his continuing service in this community.

CRISIS IN SCHOOLS
Emory University, February 16, 1959

Tension was so great in the South that Harry Ashmore, after participating on a panel at Emory University concerning "Editors View the South" (see speech above McGill gave during that program), predicted that Emory University would be unable to have an adult program concerning the "Crisis in the Schools." In the fall of 1958, however, Emory University sponsored what likely was the only forum available in the South concerning desegregation of schools. Approximately ninety-seven adults registered for the evening non-credit course sponsored by the Office of Community Education. The program was continued in the winter quarter and McGill spoke on February 16, 1959.

The Emory Alumnus described the course and told how it "won nationwide attention. *The New York Times*, for example, staff-covered several of its sessions. It was one of the rare open forums——and perhaps the only one——where one could speak out freely and openly on such things as integration, segregation and the prospective closing of Georgia's public schools. In their political and social views the guest speakers and the regular members of the class ranged from one extreme to the other. Participants during the fall quarter included Dr. John A. Griffin of Emory who in an objective lecture laid the background for sessions that were to follow."

"Ed Ball, executive director of the neutral and fact-finding Southern Education Reporting Service, presented facts and statistics on the progress of desegregation in Southern schools. James M. Dabbs, Mayesville, South Carolina writer, farmer and former college teacher, expressed the viewpoint of a lifelong Deep South resident who had come to believe in the propriety of integrating the races. Former Florida Governor Millard F. Caldwell, a militant segregationist, presented the South's 'case' against the U.S. Supreme Court. Georgia's U.S. Senator Richard B. Russell, a strong segregationist was scheduled to speak, but he withdrew with the explanation 'it would not be proper for me to appear on the program at this time.' Georgia Governor Marvin Griffin, a firm segregationist, vigorously condemned the Supreme Court's decisions on matters he said were outside its authority and called on Georgians to stand firm on segregation."

"The Emory class, whose ninety-seven members paid ten dollars each tuition fee, could hardly be called a typical group of Americans for all but five had been to college and all but twenty-two had college degrees. Forty had had one or more years of graduate work beyond the college level. As to occupations most were educators (nineteen), housewives (eighteen), and secretaries (ten). There were also physicians, nurses, lawyers, bankers, businessmen, accountants, salesmen, geneologist, army officer, research analyst, city planner, an employee of the German consulate, journalists, social worker——and an agent for the Georgia Bureau of Investigation. Sixty-three were women, thirty-four men. Such a group, disparate in their beliefs, made for intelligent questioning and lively discussion" following each speaker.

McGill's speech was representative of the moderates' view concerning race relations and emphasized the need for *open* public schools in the Deep South.[1]

This speech was taken from a taped recording. Some of the material in the speech McGill first wrote in his column on November 19, 1958; several pages are identical with the text he prepared for the Augusta Rotary Club Speech (Georgia), February 3, 1959, and the Blazer Lecture, February 10, 1959, at the University of Kentucky.

Dr. John Griffin: Our speaker this evening appeared in the first series of this course in the fall, a year ago when we called the class, "Editors View the South." We had lined up Mr. McGill and Mr. Ashmore, two other liberal southern editors, and four conservative ones, including Mr. Waring who appeared on the Chett Huntley show the other night. And I asked him to come back this time because of the particular relevance of his understanding of the Georgia situation and his intimate knowledge of what is happening in Georgia. But more than that, he is an astute observer of the Southern scene and a particularly qualified person to talk to us about the changing patterns of race relations. In case you don't know some of the biographical facts about Mr. McGill, let me point out that he is a native of Tennessee, that he went to the McCallie School in Chattanooga, to Vanderbilt University, took time off to

181

serve in the Marine Corps in World War I, that he worked on the *Nashville Banner* as reporter and sports editor and it was in this role that he first came to Atlanta, as sports editor of the *Atlanta Constitution*. His interests were so wide and his mind so active that the sports desk didn't contain him long and he was soon moving toward the editorial side, moving to the position of Editor-in-Chief of the *Atlanta Constitution*. Many honors have come his way along the road such as a Rosenwald fellowship, such as membership on the Board of the Fund for the Advancement of Education, perhaps the most distinguished educational body in this country and various other honors. Mr. Ralph McGill, it's a great pleasure to have you at this class. (applause)

McGill: Mr. Griffin, ladies and gentlemen, I'm honored to be back again. I have followed at a distance and through reports and friends I think most of what has gone on here, I hope all, and I thought that tonight I might try to get it down in a manuscript form. I had some notes and I got them put together, with a little bit of interpolation here and there as we go along with your indulgence.

I thought it might be profitable to take a look at not so much the changing race relations of which you have had some discussion, but probably to take a look back and to have a little background because I'm one of those persons who is always convinced that the past, either whether we are an individual or whether we're a region or a country, that our past history determines in great part what we are and why we are what we are.

Seventy years ago in the winter of 1899, Henry Woodson Grady, editor of the *Atlanta Constitution*, spoke in Boston to the Merchant's Association. The dominant, industrial, commercial, educational and cultural position of the New England states of which this city of Boston was and is a spiritual and material capital inspired at that time both envy and emulation. Grady envisioned a new industrial South in this winter seventy years ago, almost exactly. And he spoke to the Boston audience in a spirit of hopeful, prophetic challenge, and I quote, "Far to the

South, Mr. President," he said, "lies the fairest and richest domain of this earth. It is the home of a brave and hospitable people. There is centered all that can please and prosper human kind. A perfect climate above its fertile soil yields to the husbandman every product of the temperate zone. There by night the cotton whitens beneath the stars and by day the wheat locks the sunshine in its bearded sheath. In the same field the clover steals the fragrance of the wind and the tobacco catches the quick aroma of the rain. There are mountains stored with exhaustless treasure, forests, vast and primeval and rivers that bumbling or loitering, run wanton to the sea. Of the three essential items of all industries——cotton, iron, and wood——that region has easy control. In cotton, a fixed monopoly; in iron, proven supremacy; in timber, a reserve supply for the Republic. From this assured and permanent advantage against which artificial conditions cannot much longer prevail has grown an amazing system of industries. Not maintained by human contrivance of tariff or capital or far off from the fullest and cheapest source of supply, but resting in divine assurance, within touch of field and mine and forest. This system of industries is mounting to a splendor that should dazzle and illumine the world."

I could stop, there are some chairs over here. [pause] I might say for the benefit of those who just entered that I just quoted at the beginning two paragraphs from a speech made in Boston seventy years ago this winter in which he looked at the South as he then saw it and saw a fixed monopoly in cotton and proven supremacy in iron and the supply of timber which would be a reserve for the whole Republic.

Grady spoke in pride, hope and conviction. Discovery of iron ore in Alabama closely beside coal supplies had excited visions of a great steel empire. It was his optimistic belief that an industrial society would, because of the added wealth which would come, automatically enrich its education and culture.

At the time the editor addressed his New England audience, a handful of Southern leaders were well into what was to be a long and arduous struggle for public education. The "Report of the U.S. Commissioner on Education" for the school year of 1900 and 1901 showed Southern schools to be, in his language, "wholly inadequate, poorly attended, and poorly taught," unquote. The amount of money spent in that year, school year 1901, was about a third of the national average. Then, as now, there was a greater proportion of children to adults than in the North. In addition to this, about eighty percent of the Southern population, just as the century turned, was rural and sparsely settled. School terms in agricultural areas were confined literally to the few winter months. In 1901, Charles W. Dabney, President of the University of Tennessee, said in a published report, quote, "in the Southern states, in school houses costing an average of $276 each, under teachers receiving the average salary of twenty-five dollars a month, we are giving the children in actual attendance five cents worth of education a day for eighty-seven days in the year. Such means will never educate the people." You might have seen a few days ago where Dr. Collins, who recently retired as the State Superintendent of Education, recalled that he began teaching in Georgia in about this period of $22.50 per month. In 1900 and 1901, for example, Alabama's Legislature appropriated for the University a total of $10,000. Until 1904, Louisiana had a limit of $15,000 on annual appropriations for Louisiana State University. The total yearly income for the sixty-three colleges and universities of Virginia, North Carolina, South Carolina, Georgia, Alabama, Mississippi, and Arkansas, was $65,843.00 from the states.

We know, looking at history, that the great damage done by the War Between the States in property losses was tremendous. The poverty which followed was harsh, often brutal. But the corrosive damage done the spirit and soul of the South was through lack of education. The children, the grandchildren, and the great grandchildren of the adults of those post War Between the States years did not have a fair chance. I have known many fine men and women who were deprived of any chance at adequate education in those years. My own father was one. But these persons had almost a passion for educational opportunity for their children.

By 1901 the situation was so desperately hopeless that it attracted the attention of Northern philanthropists. George Foster Peabody's name is familiar to all of us. He came-in in that year. John D. Rockefeller, Jr., and his father poured fifty-three millions of dollars into the general education board between 1902 and 1909 to help the Southern educational effort. There was literally a crusade for public education. It was preached at barbecues, in churches, courthouses, schools, fairs, and at camp meetings. There was considerable opposition, some persons of influence in learning did not believe in free public education. Others frankly said they did not want the Negro to have it.

Poverty lay heavily on the South in this period. But nowhere was it as burdensome as on the farms, especially the many, many small farms. It might be interesting to note that today we still have in the Southeast, most of the nation's farms for the simple reason that most of our farms were small units. The wan farmer in faded denim, his sunbonneted wife, and his pinched, but eager children, had already shown their resentment in the populist revolution. In Georgia, Tom Watson was the central figure of those furious populous years. Walter Heinz Page described these people in a great speech for free education as the "forgotten man." Franklin Roosevelt, years later, was to take that phrase out of Page's speech and make it a part of our present day political vocabulary. By 1913 a certain momentum had been attained. Standards of admission and graduation were, which had been widely debased, were tightened and public education could be said to have come to the South about 1913.

In the fifty-eight years that have passed since that 1901 period of which I spoke, education in the South has come a long hard path. Teachers and parents have sacrificed and toiled for it. The despair of the first years of the century are but memories for the old, or stories to be read in books, but it was a great and heroic period of struggle and determination to have it.

What of education in 1959, today, seventy years after Grady spoke in Boston? The compulsive determination of some politicians and many of the people to destroy public education in four or five states is almost incredible even though one lives with it. To speak the phrase, "close the schools," seems to me to mean a previous process of closing the mind has been completed. Certainly the mind must be shut before doors to schools may be shut. In early January of this year, this past January, the Census Bureau of the United States released some figures on education. They were picked up and sent out by the Associated Press and the United Press, and I quote from one of the dispatches sent out from Washington, D.C. on the general newswires last January. I quote, "Arkansas spends less per pupil," now this is just past January, "to educate its children than any of the thirty-one states that finance schools through school districts, the Census Bureau reported today. Arkansas provided $69,636,000.00 for its 388,000 school children, or $154.00 per child, according to the report which covered 1957. The next five low-rankings all went," continued the United Press, quoting the Census Bureau, "to Southern or border states——South Carolina, $165.00 per pupil; Alabama $177; Kentucky, $185; Georgia, $192; and West Virginia, $205.

The obvious question growing out of these school figures for 1957 is, what about the rest of the picture? Southern schools are still, despite the tremendous advances we have made among the lowest in expenditure per pupil. But it must be noted that the amount spent in 1957 was a tremendous increase over that of twenty years ago, and it is a moonshot away from the educational totals of Grady's era. A study of the South's position today reveals a national story of change, shifts, economic, population, and also a pattern of growth and progress. All of what has happened and will happen to education in the South, serves to emphasize the need to look into our public schools wherever we may be living. There is exposed the

186

acute need of evaluation and of long distance planning and support for education. Moreover, there is need for educating the people in the need to be constantly on the alert to realize and keep in mind the necessary complementary power of the schools in our present situation. The South has put more sweat and tears into education than any other area. Yet today the political power pattern plans to close them in four or five states. Grady spoke in 1887, of an economic trinity of cotton, iron, and timber. Today cotton is no longer the major crop. It is important, but the South does not expect it to sustain the future. Indeed, hybrid corn scientists say that in the future and by that future they do not mean the next ten or twelve years, but they're looking ahead so they say, to about forty or fifty years from now. They say that in the future we will plant present cotton fields to food. We will, they say, obtain our fibers from plants which will grow in the hills and from a new development of just two years ago in hybrid corn, a product called amulous corn, which is already being planted in great amounts this year for the first commercial crop. It produces a very fine fiber and it produces a great quantity of starch and the stalks will make feed. The 1887 hope of supremacy in iron which had so excited the South at that time, did not materialize. There was a great development at Birmingham, but the ore proved to be relatively of low-grade and the coal supply was difficult to attain. It was a profitable business but it did not give to the South proven supremacy. The harvest of the massive ruthless cutting of the hardwood timber of those years and also the great pines, is one which has produced books about the rafts which darkened the Altamaha and the Savannah Rivers. But today the South, as we know, grows pine as a commercial crop for paper mills and it is a greater asset than the hardwood and the tall pines would have been. The coastal areas of the South which have oil, gas, sulfur, and water are already building and well into a very considerable chemical industry. The remainder of the South is still in the process of breaking away from the agricultural bonds in order to enter more fully into the industrial revolution. I think we could well say that the symbol of the New South that is ahead is a test-tube rather than a cotton field.

Certainly, this South of ours has grown, changed, and progressed. But so have the other regions. And it is important, I think, to know what the picture is, otherwise, we will not know what the job is that we must do. The progress story as revealed by carefully checked Department of Commerce figures is a spectacular one in Texas and Florida. But because the South started in the Industrial Revolution without any real manufacturing base, certain paradoxes emerge. Perhaps some of you recall that the University of Georgia Department of Economics at the time, in the early 30's, when it was under the direction of Mr. Malcolm Bryan, now president of the Federal Reserve Bank in Atlanta, concluded a bit of research which revealed that the South's share, percentage share, of the national, of the nation's industry was, in 1930, almost exactly what it was in 1860. We had progressed tremendously and then typically——when we're doing well we forget to notice what the neighbors are doing. So, when we're doing well, we just don't notice it. But at any rate, these paradoxes emerge again today. In personal income gain, for example, and I——these figures are from the Department of Commerce——in personal income figures gained, for example, the South's advance since 1940 is higher than the rest of the nation. Yet we are still last in income per capita. There's another paradox. Percentage retail gains in the South are the second highest in the nation, despite our lowest per capita income. And apparently our wives spend a great deal of money at Davison's and Rich's. According to the Department of Commerce the per capita income for the continental United States for the four years from 1954 through 1957 was $2,027.00; the per capita average income for the United States, which was a gain of fourteen percent for those four years. The per capita income of the twelve Southeastern states in that same period '54, '57, was $1,427.00 as against the national average of $2,027 or exactly six hundred dollars a year or fifty dollars a month less than the national average. Yet, keep in mind, this was a sixteen percent gain for the South, the second highest in the nation. Now these paradoxes, and I apologize for so many statistics. But what they rather dramatically reveal is, that while we have the second highest gain or the first gain and so on, our per capita income remains low testifying again to what a lack of industrial base we had back in the '70's and '80's when we were struggling for education and struggling to bring industry in to provide new jobs to take some of the load off the land.

So here we are after all of this great progress with still a very great deal to do. Not even Florida with all her really spectacular growth——I don't know if you've kept up with Florida. She, she has——well, I've got more statistics about it, but one I haven't got in here. She's building school classrooms today at the rate of seven a day——seven each working day. Her population is estimated by the Bureau of Statistics that by 1970, which is only eleven years away, will be seven million dollars——seven million *persons*. Florida already has passed Missouri in gain. Florida had——and these statistics aren't in here, but Florida has had in the last ten years more newcomers to come in than is the total population of Arkansas or Arizona or Oregon. It's a fantastic state. Not even Florida, however, with her spectacular growth reached the national per capita income figures. Florida's was $1,836. Georgia was second with $1,431 and Mississippi was lowest with $958 against the national average of $2,027, revealing again what happens to a state which has not kept some sort of pace in the industrial revolution.

Continuing with these statistics for which again I ask your indulgence——for the past ten years up through 1956 we find these interesting results. In employment the South is fifth in percentage increase with twenty-four percent. If employment is an indication of industrial development, we have here a clear and rather interesting picture. Where is the greatest growth in the United States? The Pacific states have, by this yardstick, an employment percentage gain of sixty-seven percent. The midwest is up forty-one percent. New England which was so dominant at the time of Grady's speech, has declined——a steady decline, I might say and a consistent one, showing but a one percent gain. The mid-Atlantic states of New Jersey, Pennsylvania, New York, long heavily industrialized, are just about holding their own. The west central states are up forty-one percent. But it is the astonishing state of Texas where employment is up seventy-eight percent which brings up that average. Here in the South our average is up twenty-four percent in great part because of Florida which has out-done even Texas in percentage employment gain, showing a whopping eighty-one percent in ten years, testifying certainly that the Florida economy is rather soundly based and is simply not orange juice and tourists and beaches. So we have an answer to the question, "Where is the really great growth?" And it is unmistakingly in the far west, in Texas and Florida, the really great growth. The results of employment in industry is what economists call added value. In value added by manufacture, the South is fourth, a *tremendous* come-up.

We all are familiar with the fact that our cities are growing. The shift is from the fields to the factory. For example, today, only about one out of every ten Negroes is now a farm-hand. The rest are in the cities and not just Southern cities. Migration from the South has not slowed down a great deal. Indeed it might be said that the contrary is true. In the decade from 1910 to 1920 almost ten percent of the population of the South migrated; that was more white than colored. In the decade from 1920 to 1930 it was almost fifteen percent, about evenly divided it was probably a little more Negro migration because in that period we had the coming of the boll weevil, the destruction of much of the cotton crop and a lessening of the need for hands. That's when we began to see the empty cabins and the chimneys where they had burned. In the last decade ending with the Census in 1950, 18.9% of the South's population left us. It has slowed down some during this period according to tentative figures and we won't know until after '60 what really happened. But at any rate the Negro problem of population annually grows less. There were six cities, just six cities and all cities over the nation gained Negro population, have gained in the last two decades, more especially, in the last ten. But in the past eight years there are six cities alone which gained a million in Negro population. In the years since 1950 through '58, just eight years, there has been a growth in the United States of fifteen percent in population. Only two Southern states have reached the national average. Florida, again with an astonishing 51.9% increase in population, and Virginia with a 15.4%. Now much of this latter population is a spill-over from Washington's great force of government workers. How many of those will be citizens in that they register to vote and so on, it's not yet possible to say. Three Southern states have actually lost population, keeping company with Vermont, the only other state in the Union to lose in that period up through the '50 census. They are West Virginia, Arkansas, and Mississippi.

Recently most Southern papers made page one stories of a release from the Bureau of Census. The next count of the nation's people is 1960, next year. The Bureau estimated that after the 1960 census, when Congress by law proceeds with reapportionment, the seventeen states in the West will gain eleven House seats. The North will lose seven and the South four. Georgia, incidentally, is expected to lose two seats, two House seats. But with Alaska in the Union, the seventeen states of the West now have thirty-six of the ninety-eight senators. This is fourteen more senators than the total in our twelve southern states. When Hawaii comes in this session, as she commonly is expected to do, the count will rise to a majority of sixteen more senators. Now this certainly causes us to know that population shifts have a rather profound political effect. Southern senators have been very frank to say since the 1958 election that the South's long years of political veto, the veto power, are near an end if not actually ended. In the last election in November, Southern democrats gained only one member in the

191

House, a Kentuckian who is by no means committed to the Deep South position. The fifteen new democratic senators all came from states completely outside the South. We've already seen Rule twenty-two materially amended. The Congressional——the months ahead with the Senator, with Senator Lyndon Johnson's Civil Rights bill and that of the President, plus some more, shall we say, extreme legislation introduced individually by eastern senators will certainly give us a lot of activity in the months ahead. But at any rate, no one, I would believe, would think that the fourteenth or fifteenth amendments are likely to be repealed or amended.

This is, I hope, in not too much detail, some of the background of economics and population and also of the dramatic change which has touched us all stopping at every door, passing over none. Now for all of our deep earnest, sincere struggle and great considerable progress, our needs in education have remained considerably unmet. Now, we're not alone in this; it is a national problem but as we look at the South today with all of her progress, we can see that really with Florida coming as she has and with the rest of us coming not nearly so fast, but still coming——we can see that as New England declines, as the great long industrial states are showing——just about holding their own, certainly it is, it is no stretch of the imagination to say that the South is right on the verge of a breakthrough into this industrial future.

Now that we should at this time be willing to destroy the advances made in education when today we see that the educated person is a greater need than is the raw material of bauxite, or cotton, or iron or whatnot; the educated person today is the greatest asset any country or region has, an absolute necessity. When we consider this, it is almost too fantastic to be believed that we should have at this time a serious consideration for the destruction of the public school system and an attempt to substitute some sort of private, unplanned really, private system to take its place, a hodgepodge in which the state cannot participate. It is my opinion that any politicians and public

192

leaders who agree and urge and who finally bring about such action are tramping out the vintage where the grapes of political wrath are stored. I mean no irreverance when I say that prejudice and——if prejudice in a sort of mob spirit should crucify public education on a cross of willful defiance and determination so to do, that I believe it will rise out of the wreckage because the people will will it. But a whole generation of children will suffer grievous and lasting discrimination. And history I believe will write that the bitter-enders and irrational persons who closed the schools were the worst enemies of the South. And I do not see how it would be possible for any one of these to emerge as the hero of a lost cause. One thing, it seems to me, must be plain——we must all defend public education as the necessary foundation of our form of government and our place in the industrial revolution. In the past there have been some who, thinking narrowly, in my opinion, viewed the private and parochial schools of Catholic, Episcopal, and other churches as somehow being in competition with public education. This, it seems to me, was never true. It also seems to me to be a dangerous thought. Those persons who send children to parochial schools do so because they wish to pay for something extra that they want them to have in a way of emphasis on religious instruction. Those who choose the private schools do so only because they want smaller classes or because they have children whom they believe demand more individual instruction and a tighter curriculum. It would be most unwise and thoughtless, I believe, for any person believing in our system of representative free government who, sending his children to a private or parochial school, and not at the same time wholeheartedly support the public school system. It seems to me obvious, that no system of private education can possibly do more than educate a fraction of the great and growing population of children. The birthrate, the children already born, has caused us to hear, not the patter, but the thunder of little feet.

I think one of the most eloquent tributes paid to public education was by Senator Talmadge, and I want to make it plain that I understand and you understand that Senator Talmadge is strongly against the Supreme Court decision and he feels the court acted out of its scope. But nonetheless, I think it proper to quote what he said in his speech at the time he introduced an amendment to the Constitution proposing that such an amendment would give control of the schools to the state. "The closing," and I quote from the text of his speech, "The closing of any school anywhere is a lamentable occurrence. The closing of a public school system is a terrible tragedy. The destruction of public education in an entire region of our nation would be an unparalled catastrophe. The importance of education hardly can be overstated. With the exception of seeking the salvation of his immortal soul, man has no greater responsibility than seeing that his young are educated to the fullest extent of their abilities and are equipped spiritually and intellectually to achieve mankind's highest destiny. The American concept of universal education, more than any other factor, is responsible for the greatness which this nation has achieved." He goes on; I think it a very eloquent tribute. Later on, and indeed on this same day, Senator Talmadge said that he wanted the people of this state and of the South to understand that whether they liked it or not the decision of the Supreme Court was an accomplished fact. He then offered his amendment to the Constitution. Now I want to read also——I must say that in his speech to the Legislature last week, Senator Talmadge repeated this, but the speech which interested me most, somehow, was that by Senator Richard B. Russell, delivered before the Legislature on this same day, February 11, last Wednesday. Almost all of the speech is devoted to the discussion of the national defense and to the agricultural problem, then on the last three pages, and indeed just almost to the last page, Senator Russell discussed the integration problem and he concludes with this: "As one of your representatives in our national government I wish that I could assure you that Washington would put its own house in order and strike the hand of the Supreme Court from the throats of the Southern states." Then follows to me which is the most honest

194

statement yet to be made to a Southern state. "In all honesty," said Senator Russell, "I must tell you that your representatives in the national Congress simply do not have the strength to put this judicial oligarchy back to its proper place in our scheme of government. We have not only lost the support of many of those from other sections on whom we once relied, but the Representatives and Senators from the eleven states of the Old Confederacy no longer present a solid front. This was painfully evident when only seventeen votes were cast in the Senate against the Civil Rights bill of 1957. There is no longer any solid South in the Congress." There were four other paragraphs and the Senator concludes, "In the final analysis the success or failure of this drive will depend upon the legislature and the governor and upon the willingness of the people to make the sacrifices necessary to preserve our way of life." And of course the sacrifices necessary are the closing of the schools. Now this statement, and that of Senator Talmadge certainly demonstrates that our representatives in the Congress have let us know plainly that there is nothing they can do about it. They have done all they can do, and I think we must say in candor, that they have tried sincerely to do everything they could in this field and none of us would wish to argue against that. But they now say that they can't do anymore and that it is up to us.

It seems to me that we ought to look, properly could look for a little more direction from these sources. Certainly it seems to me a little unjust that the leadership, general leadership in the Deep South, should have been saying, for at least almost five years, "we are winning, we can get around the court by this device and that device," and now to say, "well we are sorry, we have done all we can, it's up to the legislature and the governor and the people." Now I certainly, personally, do not have any policy of integration and have not had; I am sure you have no policy of integration. Any such policy would have to come now from the courts or from our own political leadership. You and I can't have any policy. It would be a little ridiculous of us to try to have it a policy. I am sure that there are many thousands of persons who preferred things to be just as they were but who prefer also that they would take a beginning of integration rather than to lose the public school system for which heaven knows this South has sweated and worked and sacrificed more than any other region in America. That would be my position, certainly. But it seems to me too, that the sources of information, and I don't necessarily mean newspapers, magazines; I sort of think there has been a bad job done all around; certainly you have all heard and know about the Pupil Placement Law. So I would say that the job of information hasn't been as bad as it sometimes seemed. But the point is, if you wanted to approach this from the viewpoint of one who says, I despise what the court has done; I would give anything in the world if it had not happened but I would be willing to have what has come popularly [to be] called token integration, if that would save the schools.

The fact is, that the court by this decision in the Alabama case has in a very real sense taken itself, so to speak, off the hook, which has been set up, so to speak, by those who say the court acted outside its scope, because certainly by saying that a Pupil Placement Law which permits going into the qualifications of the student, the scholastic qualification, which permits going into the personal or moral background of the student and *his family*. This is an astonishing control given to a state never before conceived or imagined by a state and actually what the Supreme Court has done by this decision is to give to the states a very, almost rigid control of who will go to school and where and how. Now, it may be that I am dense, but I can say truthfully that what has puzzled me and troubled me all along has been that whether we like it or not, I do not see how in the last half, especially in the last half of the twentieth century that whatever we may feel about the Fourteenth Amendment and the method of its adoption or whatever we may feel about our prejudices, I do not see how any person can argue that we can

196

discriminate against anyone to whom we grant citizenship. Now this is a personal opinion and another personal opinion is that certainly the Supreme Court has not assumed control of the schools. Any state may have any sort of school it wishes, a poor one or a good one. It may have almost no taxes for it or large taxes. It may pay its teachers poorly or well. It may tell them what to teach and what not to teach. It can have a school term of two months or nine months or twelve months. A state may do just what it will with its school system; it has complete control. What the Court has said is that you cannot discriminate against the children or between the children whom you admit to those——who are qualified to enter those schools. Then later of course came the Pupil Placement Law which I submit to you is an astonishing thing and not really well comprehended in my opinion. And certainly if it was argued that the Court——certainly those who argued that the Court has taken away control of the schools no longer can argue it because by holding a Pupil Placement Law which allows you to dig into the personal life of the child and of his parents and into his scholastic qualifications to determine whether you can enter a school. I submit that that is real state control of education in a manner never before thought of even. An astonishingly strict control. But at any rate, it seems to me too that——to conclude with this manuscript and I'm about through——so it seems to me that ignorance and prejudice and shabbiness of mind and values are leaks in the dikes of any civilization in which man is a free individual. These forces, I believe, must be recognized for what they are and their presence proclaimed and opposed as rationally and as logically as one may.

There are many paragraphs in Boris Pasternak's *Dr. Zhivago* which seem to me to apply not merely to our region, to our country, but to other countries as well, Russia included, of course. And it is this, Dr. Zhivago is talking to his friend: "If the beast who sleeps in man could be held down by threats, any kind of threats, whether of jail or of retribution after death, then the highest emblem of humanity would be the lion tamer in the circus with his whip, not the prophet who sacrificed himself. But don't you see that is just the point. What for centuries raised man above the beast is not the cudle but an inward music, the irresistible power of unarmed truth, the powerful attractions of its example." And it seems to me, that if we who have struggled so long for public education and who have sacrificed so much for it and who by and through its use have advanced our region to the point of a great break-through——it seems to me that if we lose or betray public education, we will lose this inward music and the ability to offer the example of unarmed truth and our region might descend into chaos and bitterness for a period of years, brief or many, which would distress and agonize us all. Thank you very much. (applause) [A question and answer period followed.]

Moderator: Mr. McGill, we have raised questions and comments after each of these talks——

McGill: I'm sorry about this laryngitis but I'll do the best I can. I'm not tired——

Moderator: Would you like a drink?

McGill: Yeah if you would get me a little water it would be all right. (laughter)

Moderator: I said a "drink" (laughter); I meant Coca-Cola. (laughter)

McGill: I'd rather have water. You can go ahead with the questions; we don't have to wait on John.

Question: Mr. McGill, in 1859, Charles Darwin wrote "The Origin of the Species." Do you think that had any bearing in the present case of the Supreme Court?

McGill: I don't see how it would, but——

Question: I don't believe the Supreme Court can serve as the sociological and psychological authority in regards to education. They just made an arbitrary decision.

McGill: Well, there are a lot of people who are very angry with them because they did make a sociological decision and they quoted a number of books and foot-notes to that effect—— You haven't got the drink yet. (laughter)

198

Question: I'm curious, regardless of the law of the land theory, I'm curious——

McGill: Pardon me, the court decision itself is not the law of the land. It becomes a law of the land when a court directs, directs it.

Question: I'm accepting it as an accomplished fact. Regardless of that, now those of us who feel as you do, that our destiny is involved in the way we face this that it's a moral question, it's an economic question, our whole destiny is wrapped up in it. We talk to each other; we come over here to meetings; we write letters to the papers. What else can we do? I feel lost right now. I have no place else to go.

McGill: Well, just keep on doing what you're doing——now this may be wishful thinking on my part but——I don't think it would be fair for me to name the city but there is a considerable city in Deep South Georgia the Rotary Club of which last week took a private anonymous poll. And I think the club had around a hundred members. There were only two who voted that they would prefer to see the schools closed——only two——the others were all for segregation. They preferred segregation, but if it came to a choice between closing the schools and having some school placement integration, they would take that rather than have the schools closed. It is my honest opinion and I hope it isn't wishful thinking that in the cities of the state——and I would say Rome, Macon, Savannah, Thomasville, Valdosta——I don't know this, but it would be my feeling that in the past four months there has been a better understanding of what the issue is. Since Senator Talmadge told them this, since Senator Russell told them, there has been a change. Now people who have been around the legislature, and not just our reporters, tell me that there has been a marked change in their attitudes, especially since Senator Talmadge and Russell told them so plainly that they couldn't do anything.

Question: Well don't you have the experience of Virginia before us?

McGill: Virginia. You will have another interesting

thing in Virginia next Wednesday, where the people in Front Royal have voted to continue the private school. The court has ordered the high school opened; it will be open on Wednesday; the probability is you will have another Virginia story there with——I think there are nineteen Negro children involved——they might show up and no white children, it might be another sort of story. But certainly the Virginia decision was as Governor Vandiver said in an interview on it, was a very severe blow to the segregation position. So that I think those persons who want to try to preserve the public schools should keep on doing what they can, making themselves known and speaking out, writing letters; it seems to be having a little effect. I mean its accumulative, a great many things are happening, a great many things are happening.

Question: I would assume that cities and towns all over the state have been having the kinds of meetings that have been held in all our P.T.A.'s. Unless I'm greatly mistaken, the great majority of P.T.A. membership in the various schools of the city of Atlanta, composed of the mammas and the papas, voted for continuing the public schools open. But then what? Is that having any effect?

McGill: Yes, I think it is. I don't mean to say it will have the effect of keeping the schools open. It's my opinion the situation will worsen. I feel a little sorry in a way for some of the political leadership. After all, you could go into why are the four states——there are only four left——I don't know if that's generally realized in which no start a'tall has been made. It's generally overlooked that in Louisiana, where a few Negroes have been attending L.S.U.'s graduate schools, that this past September they were admitted to the undergraduate division in New Orleans without any incident. Well, I believe there were some signs put up but no real incident. Florida made the start in September with one Negro in the law school and Governor Collins has proposed that Florida, which has a system of graduate schools for Negroes which has been costing around $63,000 per graduate to maintain those schools. He has proposed that those schools be abolished and that the Negro students in the graduate schools be generally admitted in the fall. He also has proposed to his legislature——which is not——I'm not sure a'tall that it will agree to it, but he has proposed that the federal government set up commissions in each state to be appointed by the president with the advice of the local people. And that those committees in each state will then say where integration shall begin and on a basis of the school placement law. Whether or not this will——he has been up to see Senator Lyndon Johnson and has had a discussion with him about it and it may be that Senator Johnson will amend his legislation which provided for a commission, you remember, to broaden it into this, although no action has been taken. At any rate, where we now are is that only Georgia, Alabama, Mississippi, and South Carolina are the only four in the whole South which have made no start at all. If Virginia continues, and certainly North Carolina——I don't know how many of you saw Governor Hodges' statement. People are already moving to take advantage of us. And you can't blame them for that. Governor Hodges announced three weeks ago, and he invited people from all over the South to come up——newspaper people——he wanted to publicize. They announced that they had raised several millions of dollars from North Carolina sources and they are building a research institute in the triangle between North Carolina State, Duke, and University of North Carolina. And Governor Hodges took great pains to say——we're planning to keep our universities open and to use their great resources in this research institute so that it may redound to the benefit of North Carolina. So I think we can expect some more Negro children, a few to be admitted next fall in North Carolina and Tennessee. If Governor Collins succeeds with his plan——I don't know, the pressure will build up, and I just don't believe the people will put up with a closed school system for very long. How long is very long? A year, two years but whatever it is it's too long, if it's just a month or two. Once you close a system and set up a system of a lot of little schools being run for profit, quick profit, I just don't know. It would be a disaster. It was a businessman in Virginia who finally had quite a lot to do about that, if I judge correctly from the statement they issued, over a hundred of them, so I don't know. It's a bitter choice for a great many people. I sympathize with those people. I have no bitterness in my heart toward them but it will be a bitter choice, but I think they will have to make it finally. I just can't imagine closing the schools for long. But if they're once closed, it will be a terrible job getting them back again. When the legislature was rushing through this bill about closing the schools and forbidding the collection of a tax to——the teachers and they refused to put that in and I think, I can't recall——I believe they said that the county and city teachers——there were over five hundred teachers who inquired about it and said if that was true they wanted to be leaving at the end of this year. They reassured them and the governor said that the state would honor the contracts and this has eased the tension. How much it has eased it no one knows. Certainly, I would think——and I hope they don't, but I would think that most of the young teachers must be thinking of going on. I can see where an older teacher who has got a home and a family perhaps, or quite an investment in retirement and so on, it would be very difficult for him or her to leave, but we're likely to be in a very bad shape even if the schools aren't closed this fall from the teacher standpoint. I hope not. But we are likely.

Question: Do you see much hope of avoiding the closing of schools in Georgia?

McGill: Well, I would guess that the one——this is just a guess because you don't know what courts will do——but I would guess that the one which might be closed in September might be the Georgia State College because unless the Court changes its mind——the Court did say that one of the four, I think it was (voice from audience "three") three——one of the three seemed to be qualified, the other two didn't. Now maybe this new Regents qualification will allow postponement of that. The Atlanta situation is that the suit seeks to enjoin the Atlanta Board of Education from operating a segregated system. If the Court holds that——does enjoin them——the Court has said, Judge Hooper has said that it will be heard in time to allow disposal of appeals before the September term. If he does this, and if he should grant the injunction then you would have to, I think, go through——somebody would have to apply to get into the school. So the court decision, the point I am trying to make is, won't close the schools. Somebody will have to say, "I want to go," and then that might prevent them from being closed by September. I was saying that to a man the other day and he said, well look I'd rather get it over with. But I don't know——I think most people would not like to get it over——I mean——hoping that if they can keep them open something will keep them open longer. And that's the way I would feel. I would like to keep those doors open.

Question: Senator Talmadge I believe said that he hoped that we could return to the states the right of decision in regards to schools. Well now, if this right were returned to Georgia under the present situation, would the situation be better or worse?

McGill: I don't think it would be changed at all.

Questioner: In other words, the state, now imposing upon every district——with the opportunities imposed in every district——would then be more of a liability than if the federal government could step in and do something?

McGill: Yes it might, except——I don't presume to know what Senator Talmadge had in mind. He said first, local control. He then, when the legislature almost panicked and a great many people called him up, and he said well he meant by local control——state control. (laughter) But Senator Talmadge and I must say——I mean this——I don't know anything about law except the little I picked up which I often find is in error. But Senator Talmadge seemed to have relied a great deal on the Alaska case and at the time he made his speech, that hadn't been really clarified. When the Congress created the state of Alaska it wrote into the articles creating it that Alaska would have forever, exclusive control over schools. Well

203

before people got a look at the Alaska Constitution that statement looked pretty radical, different; why should Alaska have something nobody else had? But then, it was brought to the attention of one and all that no matter what the Alaska Constitution said about exclusive control of the schools that no state's constitution had priority over the federal constitution. But then the argument continued until finally they published the Alaska Constitution. It's a real different sort of constitution. It spells out very carefully that there shall be no discrimination and that the schools shall be open to all the children. Not only that, but Alaska is a unique state. They haven't got any counties. They just jumped into the future and don't have any counties a'tall. They just have a state government, no counties in Alaska. A very interesting set-up.

Question: Mr. McGill, you mentioned the role that the businessman had played in the Virginia situation. I know you mentioned the Rotary a while ago but do you see any real signs of any active leadership on the part of the businessmen in Atlanta?

McGill: No, not any, not any. I wish I did, but I don't. The economic harm done is difficult to say. Nobody is going to say, "Oh, I didn't come into your state because I didn't like what you were doing." And I think no damage is likely to occur until you yourself damage yourself. Certainly Arkansas was booming along until this happened. Since it happened, in the three years since it happened, Arkansas had almost nothing come into the state and there has been almost no plant expansion of existing plants.

From audience: It came down from $125,000,000.00 to $25,000,000.00.

McGill: Something like that. You might be interested those of you who are interested in the Association of University Women, is that the correct title?--American Association of University Women. Well, the Little Rock chapter of the American Association of University Women completed about three or four weeks ago, a survey. They got busy, the members, and I'm not sure about these exact figures, but roughly they checked eight dry cleaners, they checked eight automobile retail firms and about eight used car firms, they checked six or eight florists, checked retail stores of various types, women's clothing and department stores, and construction business and so on and they came up just on the basis of——and they quoted anonymously——they didn't reveal who they were——but they quoted the people involved——in charge of these businesses. And it's a very interesting little report which you might write for, if anybody is interested. It shows that about all but three or four businesses felt that there had been a very serious impact because of the school situation. I know I talked to one man who did not bring a plant into South Carolina and he——I just accidentally ran into him in New York at a meeting. And he said it was just business with him, with his board of trustees, not him, board of directors, not him. They thought well you invest in a plant and you might have it shut down; you might have it bombed if you hired any Negro labor. You might have a strike, you might just have a lot of trouble so why invest your money in a dubious situation. Now how, whether that will be widespread, I don't know. I would think that——getting a new plant, so the people tell me, is a business of about three years. But when you decide you are going to have a new plant, then you send out people to check the water and the labor supply, and whatever other resources you may be interested in, you check the tax structure, you check the political climate, you check for many, many factors. And then you start pricing the real estate and then you start determining what size plant, and so on. So from the time you decide you are going to have a new plant, it's roughly two or maybe in some cases three years before you actually decide the plant. It isn't as if you say, well, we will build a new plant and we will put it so and so. It's about a two-year period.

Question: Mr. McGill, do you happen to know whether there is any organization of citizens with any degree of support publicly advocating the reopening of the Little Rock schools?

McGill: There is——I don't think it's businessmen, sir,

but there is a group there of citizens. I'm not——I haven't been to Little Rock but once since the closing of the schools and that was at a dinner they gave Harry Ashmore and the *Arkansas Gazette* after the Pulitzer Prize Award. I arrived late one afternoon and went to the dinner and left early the next morning. So I don't know the make up of that group, but there is a group. You might have seen a story the other day by a man who, his name was H-a-r-a-n or something like that. He described himself as a friend of Governor Faubus. And he headed up a committee which had made a report urging that the schools be opened on a basis of segregation of the sexes. So that interested me and I rang up Ashmore and said is this some real friend of the Governor? He said, "Oh they fell out six or eight years ago, I mean six or eight months ago, and don't speak." So apparently it didn't mean anything. But I hadn't heard of his committee before but there is another one over there but it——well I tell you, when a political leader gets so far out they haven't got any room to maneuver and I think sometimes that some of them might wish they had a little room to maneuver. Maybe that's wishful thinking but actually they don't. I don't know what they——how would you, if you were one of four or five Governors——how would you retreat? (laughter)

Question: How will Governor Vandiver retreat?

McGill: I don't know how he can retreat.

Question: Mr. McGill, political leaders say that token integration would open the flood gates and that that is keeping with the facts in other states.

Answer: No sir, and it certainly isn't in keeping with the fact that if you would enact a pupil-placement law.

Question: Eleven people out of a 1,100,000 in North Carolina——

McGill: Yeah. Pardon me, I don't——I've talked too much I'm afraid, but anyhow——the court decision was a very flexible thing. We all live by images, and I can understand this. A fellow living in an area where there are a great many Negroes. His image of integration is a great decision, again in the Little Rock case, specified——spelled it out, that in those areas, I know that the court said in the areas where there was a predominance Negro population, that the court did not intend that they should all be admitted. The court decisions haven't been well read I'm afraid, and they are difficult to read, some of them, long and they are couched in legal language, but certainly neither the decisions——the decisions didn't intend that, and now this pupil-placement law is, I haven't got it——I wish I had it in there, I would like to read it to you but it's a very interesting thing.

Question: In our [Georgia's] Constitution we state that our public schools shall be segregated. Your pupil-placement law would fall down right there.

McGill: Well I say you would have to *enact* a pupil-placement law but of course, when and if somebody files a suit on the basis of that, no state constitution can be in conflict with the federal constitution. And so this provision, not only of Georgia's but of any other state constitution is invalid once a test is made on the basis of the federal constitution. But you are quite right, if you enacted a school placement law it would have to take cognizance of the fact that the federal court has ruled the state constitution unconstitutional and then they would, so in its place we enact the federal——the school placement law.

Question: In effect are you saying to this question that we wouldn't have to wait two years to amend the constitution if there were a federal provision knocking our constitution in the head?

McGill: Yeah, if you could get the federal decision anytime, it would end that. You wouldn't have to wait for the people to do it.

Question: Mr. McGill, has there been any movement on the part of any citizen to file a declaratory judgment or to file a suit seeking a declaratory judgment that would reach the Supreme Court for that purpose?

McGill: No sir, there hasn't been and if there are any lawyers here, maybe they can help me out. I'm told——(From audience: I sent you a copy of a letter I wrote to Charlie Block.) Well, I appreciated that letter too. If I haven't answered it, I will. (laughter) I'm not boasting, but I've been gone so much that I have got really a lot of mail and I try to answer them without just brushing them off and I haven't got around to a lot of them. But I'm told that——maybe you can ask for a declaratory——but I'm told you can't file a suit until you have been hurt, damaged, so to speak. Now is that true? (From audience: That's the theory back of all litigation.) Well——(A second person from audience: Not so in a declaratory judgment though.) But can you ask for a declaratory judgment before you've been hurt? I don't know. (From audience: We are being hurt. I mean that's the foundation of it. I fail to see any reason whatsoever why a suit has not been filed by a group of individuals seeking a declaratory judgment to determine whether or not it is necessary to amend the Constitution or whether or not that clause, requiring, providing for segregation (McGill: separate school systems) between the races in the public schools is not in direct conflict with the United States Constitution.)

McGill: Well, it is of course——I've wondered the same thing, sir, and then somebody told me, well you have to wait until you are damaged before you can file. I don't know.

Question: I want some encouragement. (McGill: So do I. (laughter)) In Atlanta we are having meetings and you know we are concerned, practically everybody. What's going on——I talked with somebody from Augusta and I say what's going on down there and they said nothing is ever mentioned. What's going on over the state? Anything?

McGill: Well, an odd thing——nothing has been mentioned much in Augusta. They had a speaker at the Rotary Club there about two weeks ago [McGill spoke there on February 3, 1959] to discuss this subject and the chairman said that there was absolutely no public discussion of it anywhere in Augusta, that there was considerable objection to the speaker [McGill] being permitted to speak on it to the Rotary Club and that some people said they wouldn't come, and one man called up and said that he was going to stand up and move as soon as the meal was over that they adjourn (laughter). But there was no interruption and the talk was made and it started some discussion in the paper. [The *Augusta Chronicle* covered McGill's speech.] The paper reported it and there have been some letters but again it comes down to a matter of leadership. You know I've often wondered——there is not much difference between we people and Tennesseans, North Carolinians, Kentuckians. We are all basically the same sort of people. In the beginning, all came through the mountain passes and flooded out and settled. That's the old South——but why are we so different? Why can Kentucky——well, you and I know that certain factors of history, economics and plantation versus other type of economy and the fact that Negro population is largest in these states, but still it comes down to a certain sort of leadership. So in some towns you can discuss these things and some you can't. I think there has been a discussion of it in nearly all cities of any size except Augusta. It has begun there now and, and certainly you will never get a discussion in a great many of the counties——Echols County, Baker County, Clinch County, and so on. That's a long way off, but in the urban areas, I think you would.

Question: The rural counties are not going to have "Nigras" and whites going to school?

McGill: That's right——that's what they say.

Question: Mr. McGill, I was interested in a conversation I had with a very close friend and associate of the governor not long ago before he came out with the stand and the legislative act authorizing the closing down of only one school in a system, as whether or not in your opinion that was a giving on the part——a backing away, trying to get off of that limb that the governor is really out on. And taking it a step further, if some interested citizen were to file under the declaratory judgment act if that is possible——I have not researched it for that purpose——and succeeded in it——would that not give the governor a clear out?

McGill: Yes, it would. He would have exactly the same

out as Governor Almand in Virginia. He would say, I've done everything I could and now I have no more laws to go on and so I have to give in.

Question: It was indicated to me that the position of the governor was to back away from his adamant position that all schools were to be closed upon one Negro entering the school system.

McGill: Well as I said a while ago, I feel a sympathy for some politicians and I can't understand you know what they are doing and how——I can't believe that even they really want the school system closed.

Question: Well it was so unnecessary for him to take that position to get elected.

McGill: Yes, it was. Utterly, utterly. The interesting thing to me and I didn't say anything to anyone about it, but the interesting thing to me was Twitty's statement, that it looked like we might have to prepare one day to have a little integration maybe to go along with private schools. And of course that created a panic and he was promptly asked and had to say well he wasn't——but I can't believe that he would make such a statement without conferring with several people.

Question: The feeling that the compulsory education law would ease the thing some——isn't that what they have done in Virginia?

McGill: That and the private funds... Well of course I think that if time goes on, you know over a hundred counties are losing population in Georgia and some of them, about thirty of the Georgia counties are right now in rather desperate shape. And it might be that time would do that——but it will take quite a long time and I'm hoping that somebody will file another suit and the court will act but I don't have much hope.

Moderator: We have got time for about one or two more questions.

Question: Mr. McGill, do you think that any kind of token integration will hold up in the face of this new push on the part of the NAACP to have total integration. They say they aren't satisfied with what they have done in North Carolina or even in New York.

McGill: I saw that, but I apparently haven't made my point clear. This school placement law abolishes this token integration thing. If you've got a school placement law, then you don't have to say, well, we're going to start with token integration. Actually, token integration, wherever it is, is on the basis of a school placement law and the NAACP if it succeeds——If I were——lawyers can check me on this——if I were a state or a city with a suit——I would say sure we are ready to have total segregation, I mean total integration on the basis of the school placement law. That's what North Carolina has done, Tennessee. That's what Arkansas did in Little Rock. Those children, those nine children in Little Rock were probably the most carefully screened that will ever be screened. They had gone into their family background, their family...[tape runs out here].

BIRMINGHAM ROTARY CLUB
Birmingham, Alabama, May 17, 1916

Publisher McGill told Birmingham Rotarians that "minds are more important than Marines in America's future," arguing that "the South can't solve its problems with violence." He reminded the group that desegregation is already underway in a majority of the Southern states and that a "time for decision" is nigh in the others. He stated that "we can't abandon our schools, and defiance of court orders can't be our only answer. We need firm...positive leadership...from three sources,...newspapers and other information media, the clergy,...and business."[1]

Few speeches have been given during a time of such high tension, and few persons have given such badly needed advice, as was the case on this speaking occasion. It was the historic week when "freedom riders" sought to "test the law that Negroes can ride unsegregated in interstate transportation." Three days before McGill's speech, several "men stopped and burned a Greyhound bus outside of Anniston," Alabama. The day before this speech "a traveling integrationist group which found trouble and delay at every turn in Alabama, reached the end of its journey in New Orleans. The seventeen whites and Negroes left Birmingham ground at 10:38 on a shiny airliner—weary, battered, hours behind schedule, but still labeling their mission 'successful.' " The integrationists tried unsuccessfully for eight hours to get out of town. Drivers of Greyhound Bus Lines refused to take out a 3 p.m. bus, on which they had planned to ride to Montgomery. An Eastern Airliner, due to depart at 6:50 p.m. for Montgomery, was finally canceled about 8:30 p.m. after a bomb scare." By May 16, Birmingham police had arrested an Alton man on charges in connection with gang attacks on a group of CORE integrationists at the Trailways Bus Terminal.[2] These events welcomed McGill as he arrived to talk with the Rotarians in Birmingham.

This same basic speech was given on December 7, 1962, at Georgia Institute of Technology, Atlanta. Manuscript provided by McGill. It would be interesting to note to what degree McGill departed, if any from this prepared text. No mention was made of this in the press.

1   The Birmingham News, May 19, 1961, p. 9.
2   The Birmingham News, May 16, 1961, p. 1.

I think it would be well for any speaker addressing the membership of this organization, and perhaps for the membership itself, to understand that it largely is composed of the sons of the industrial revolution.

I am unwilling to believe that those who create the forces which make for revolutionary change will also be those who blindly oppose the effect of the work of their heads and hands. I am sure they will, and I trust not too belatedly, make the further contribution of being leaders in channeling and directing change so that it will advance, and not retard, or corrupt, the processes of it.

All of us recognize there is a new situation in the world. It is not going away. We are, without question, at a momentous pivot of history——and that pivot is control of nuclear weapons. We also are at an equally momentous pivot in human affairs——and this pivot is not merely the steadily developing military and industrial power of Russia, but the progress of Red China. It has been my privilege recently to listen to discussions at a high level in American finance and industry. Participants are concerned. This country, which began with a rapidly growing frontier society and an economy based on scarcity, now has an economy of abundance and the old patterns do not quite fit. We must be able more and more to compete in the world market if this abundance is to continue. There is competition today from Europe, Japan and Russia. The latter is skilled at using her abundance for political advantages. The free world's petroleum industry, for example, already is deeply worried by the latest Soviet economic warfare in which cheap oil is her weapon.

The best thinkers in American industry estimate that Red China is about thirty-five to forty years behind Russia's present capacity. How fast she will catch up depends upon the speed with which she acquires tools and machines.

Therefore, what our leaders ask us to consider is that if competition now is demanding, what will it be in, say twenty-five years from now when a nation of more than a billion people, under the regimented disciplines of totalitarian communism is strongly competing in the world market? Shall this country now plan what it will be able to do a quarter century from now or not? Shall we proceed to make a stronger economy, which can make full use of abundance, or not?

Khrushchev has said that the free American society contains so many competing special interest groups that it can never attain national unity save in the face of immediate and total danger. This, he said, was why he would be able to bury us. He would avoid confronting us with total danger and, he said, the divided elements of our society would therefore continue in pursuit of their own special interests. This would, he said, enable the Communists' system to triumph.

This accounts for the fact there is in the nation a growing awareness that unless our groups can attain some unity on a voluntary basis, we will continue to find ourselves at a disadvantage in the continuing contest with communism. It is no exaggeration to say that our economic system and our nation face a very real danger.

This seems to me to make certain demands upon our minds, our consciences, and equally, upon the cold, pragmatic facts of our economic life and the future of our region.

Certainly we cannot avoid decisions. I, like you, live in a glass house and do not throw stones. I do, however, try very hard not to deceive myself or others. We can make a decision either way. But we cannot escape a choice.

The accelerated automation of the processes of our industrial revolution, with the accompanying increases in urbanization and the many technological changes required by the growing population, all point to the inescapable need for quality education for the total citizenship, both school age and adult. It is quite clear, therefore, that all facilities which contribute to that end be recognized and supported. It is not at all an exaggeration to say that national survival depends on how well we understand this and prepare ourselves for the testing years already at hand.

No region of our nation has more to offer that future

than does the South. No area has so great an opportunity to make a contribution to national unity and strength.

We recognize that in the South desegregated education, which increasingly will expand, already has begun in thirteen of sixteen Southern states within the constitutional framework and pattern, and that the obligation of law and morality require of us that we assist this to take place in a sensible, orderly and constructive manner so that our economic and education progress may not be interrupted.

Our future will depend upon how well we develop our human resources, both spiritually and materially. There must be no lowering of educational standards for any of our young men and women whose backgrounds of opportunity and environment have prevented their attaining an adequate preparation for higher education or superior skills. Rather, we must supply a system flexible enough to offer remedial training in both fields.

In short, it seems to me we must understand these elements of change, which already substantially have altered our world, and make certain that as they continue to take place, we improve, rather than hold back, the opportunity for quality education and training in skills for all our students, to the end that they will be as well prepared to serve their day and generation as are the young men and women of any other region of our nation. God helping us, we can do no less than this.

There is no need, or wish, to belabor familiar statistics. But they remind us that we must make a choice. We in the South have greatly increased our educational spending. Yet, we still spend much less than the national average. The Southern states, for all our progress, have not kept pace.

According to the NEA estimated school receipts per pupil in average daily attendance in thirteen Southern states, for 1960-61, seven states show less than three hundred dollars per pupil against a national average of $445.31. Of these seven, two are below two hundred and fifty dollars. They are Mississippi at $231.85 and Alabama at $236.70.

We speak of educated leadership. In sixteen Southern states the percent of population twenty-five years of age and over with four or more years of college show the four highest with percentages ranging from Delaware's 7.4 percent to Texas with six percent. Four of the sixteen states have percentages here below four percent. They are Kentucky, Mississippi, Alabama and Arkansas. Further pursuing this aspect of educated leadership, in and out of teaching, the table of earned doctorates, in all fields, for sixteen Southern states, for the twenty years span from 1936 to 1956, show a high total of 2,046 in Maryland, 1,994 in North Carolina, 1,993 in Texas, and 1,015 in Tennessee. We then have a precipitous drop to 754 in Virginia, 631 in Louisiana, and 553 in Florida. The four states with the lowest totals are Mississippi with 23, South Carolina with 24, Arkansas with 45 and Alabama with 65.

There has been improvement. The 1957-58 figures, the latest available to me, showed for this one year that Texas had produced the highest number, 264; with Maryland and North Carolina next in order with 186 and 162. The lowest range was Mississippi, 6; West Virginia, 7; Arkansas and Delaware 21 each, and Alabama 27.

Faculty salaries in higher education (as in secondary and elementary schools) are lower in the South. The Southern Regional Education Board, in projecting future problems, said: "The growing enrollment and replacement of faculties will mean a need for about 50,000 new college teachers in the next ten years in the South... The outlook for college presidents trying to hire faculty members, particularly in chemistry, physics, mathematics and other science fields is dismal indeed... Southern salaries are lower than in the rest of the country...though average salaries have risen, the South still lags behind the rest of the United States by from $1,000 to $1,500. We are not catching up..."

These are familiar figures, but they also are facts. If we do not catch up in education can we catch up in anything else?

I for one am weary of those who find excuses for these

discrepancies. I am afraid that while we truly believe in education that not enough of us have the image of what a first class education is. We must, I believe, raise our sights from our own institutions. I wish it were possible for our state legislatures to visit, let us say, the University of California, or Michigan, to name just two excellent institutions. I long for the day when a Southern boy or girl will be on an equal footing with their contemporaries in every other section. I frankly admit to possessing little patience with those who try to hide the facts or explain them away by saying we are the victims of hostile critics. The facts are what they are. I refuse to believe that is what the business leadership of the South wants, or what the people want.

Let us turn to other statistics. Mr. J. Edgar Hoover, of the FBI, gives us some disturbing ones on juvenile crime. Not just delinquency——but crime. Most of it comes from the drop-out group——those unfortunate youngsters who did not, for one reason or another, complete high school or even attain that grade. Our percentage of drop-outs is the highest.

Let us go to the Labor Department statistics. In teen-age unemployment the drop-outs suffer the most. And in all unemployment the Negro is twice as badly off. Again, the South is the most substantial loser.

We must make a decision. We can either join to assist court decisions and orders relating to our schools, or we can defy and encourage the violent to lawlessness. But what Southerner of any sensitiveness is not made sad by the spectacle of a region, which almost desperately needs more education and more economic progress, allowing defiance to do its work?

Businessmen in some areas have learned the hard way that schools are good for business and that closed schools are bad business. We have learned, too, that not until the businessmen, through their Chamber of Commerce, take a firm position of leadership, is it possible to reach agreement. Three cooperating elements are required. They are the newspapers and other information media, the clergy, and business. Without any one progress is not possible. The business leadership is perhaps the most important. But events have demonstrated that if these three groups, and all they represent, so will, they may chart a way out of chaos and deterioration. It is, however, also clear that if everyone waits for someone else to act, the vacuum will be filled by the extremists who defy the processes of law, who riot in front of schools and commit other acts of violence.

A few days ago U.S. Attorney General Robert Kennedy spoke in Georgia, at the University.

He did not make an anti-Southern talk. It was one dedicated to the American promise. Perhaps because of this his Georgia audience stood, when he had finished, and gave him one of the longest ovations ever tendered a visitor to the University.

He did not single out the South for criticism. He said that the problem between white and colored people is one for all sections of the United States. But, he added, the South has a special role to play "in demonstrating America at its greatest——at its full potential of liberty under law."

More and more Southerners know this, including some of its more Promethian-bound governors. They are, however, prisoners of their own excesses. And, being politically chained to the rock of prejudice, they are pecked and shrilled at by the vultures of fanaticism.

"You ask," he said, "if we will enforce the civil rights statues. The answer is: Yes, we will. We can, and we will do no less... I say to you...that if orders of the courts are circumvented the Department of Justice will act. We will not stand by or be aloof."

He praised the state of Georgia and the university officials for their loyalty to American principles in admitting the two Negro students to the university in January..."when Charlayne Hunter and Hamilton Holmes graduate from Georgia it will without question aid and assist the fight against worldwide communism," he said. "And when Negroes start attending the public schools in Atlanta next fall," he said, "it will show the world Americans living by a rule of law."

I believe him to be correct. Why are so many in the South so afraid of the promise of America? Let me tell you a story. Last week I talked with a Negro father whose son was one of three just accepted for admission to Georgia Tech next September. The father himself is a college graduate. He had worked, after graduation, as an elevator boy, a filling station helper, and at various other such jobs. Finally, he and his wife, also a college graduate, took a job as butler-chauffeur and cook. The pay in these jobs was better than in any they had been able to obtain as an educated man and woman. Now the son, an exceptional high school student, will have a chance to become an engineer and, as things change, to be employed in that capacity. The story of this boy somehow makes me proud to be a part of this developing South and proud of my country. We pay a great cost in lost talent in the South, white and colored. Must we forever keep on? Must a nation which has put a man in space still argue about where, and whether, a colored child shall go to school?

Our country's security and our regional future require of us that we be mature enough to end discrimination in education, at the ballot box and in opportunity.

Castro near at hand, and communism in general, make great capital of our racial violence and discrimination. The Christian church is under attack and is vulnerable. The newest Communist anti-Christian propaganda says that Christians preach against injustice, poverty, discrimination and human needs, but [the] Communist acts against them. Castro's pamphlets now say, "The Christians say to pray for daily bread. The socialist state will see that you have it." This is the old story of the wolf in sheep's clothing, but there is truth enough in it to give us pause. Some churches and some ministers *have* been, and are, on the side of the mobs.

The two best books I know on communism are J. Edgar Hoover's "Masters of Deceit" and Harry and Bonaro Overstreet's "What We Must Know About Communism." Let me quote from the latter:

"The arch-enemy (of communism) is not *reaction*,

which by its very resistance to change helps to create a 'revolutionary situation,' but *reformism*, which by alleviating conditions reduces the tensions of the 'class struggle'——thereby rendering more difficult the triumph of communism."

We have mankind's best idea here in America. Why haven't we exported it more successfully?

Even now we have people who say, "Let's send the Marines." This indicates there are still those who think Marines can settle more than minds.

Communism is an ever present threat and challenge. Shall we meet it with Marines or our minds——our beliefs, our faith? (The Christian in Russia.)

We are proud of being a nation of church-going people. We put "In God We Trust" on our coins. We rewrite the pledge to our flag to insert the phrase "under God." Yet ministers have been driven from their pulpits for trying to apply Christian teaching to our most grevious problem. And, just a few days ago, an Episcopal minister in Mississippi was in very real trouble for saying from the pulpit he believed it to have been best for the Civil War to have ended as it did. Can we blame Moscow or Peiping for this divisive problem?

We assert that the family is the basis of our sort of civilization, and it is. Yet, we lead the world in divorce and broken homes. Our statistics of abandoned children and wives is the highest in any advanced society. Is it the fault of communism, or do we do this to ourselves?

We believe in the dignity of the individual. Why are our mental institutions overcrowded, and why do we take more tranquilizers and read more peace of mind books than any other people?

Let me repeat——there is a new situation in the world.

The French learned that guns were not the answer in Indo-China. We know that the Marines can't settle the issue in Laos. Marines could take Cuba, but before they had finished there would be need for them in perhaps a half dozen other Latin countries.

The South cannot solve its problems with violence.

So what will we do about our future?

Can we export an idea of freedom and not practice it at home?

Social reform is the strongest anti-Communist weapon we possess—— Will we use it, or practice reaction?

Recently, I read in the papers, Birmingham sought to stimulate business and civic spirit with a campaign urging the people to quit sitting down. I do not know the content of this campaign, but I assume it included planning to take care of the city's dilemma when, as one day it must, the school problem confronts it. We know enough about our present and future to know that the South's future will be determined within its urban areas. Each urban community must, it seems to me, be making up its mind what it will do. Will the leadership of business, the clergy and information media create a climate which will demand the schools be kept open, and that law enforcement agencies keep order, or will they be silent, or openly join those who say abandon public education?

Our cities may go either way. But it is important to plan in advance.

I am not an optimist. Yet, I dare to believe that eventually the South will give its great strength and character to setting an example of what we mean by the American way of life——that we will show the world by example what we mean by freedom, by opportunity, by practicing what we say in the pledge to the flag——"One nation, under God, indivisible, with liberty and justice for all."

I do not believe our critics are right when they say we will deprive our children of advances in education, that we will further downgrade our public schools and our universities.

I dare to dream this because I know that change can come over night if the proper leadership asserts itself. I refuse to believe that Khrushchev was right when he said that the many divisions of American life cannot agree to act in the national interest save in the face of total danger.

I would like to think that after the therapy of

Commander Alan Shepard's flight through space, this nation will not again allow petty and unworthy values to prevail.

HARVARD UNIVERSITY LAW SCHOOL
ALUMNI ASSOCIATION
June 14, 1961, "A View From a Tight Small Compartment"

This speech came during the university's commencement week activities. Special presidential aid McGeorge Bundy took part in a panel on "Problems of American Policy," there was a discussion of "Some New Frontiers of Science," and also examined was "The Present State of the Drama." Louis M. Lyons, curator of the Nieman Fellows, moderated a panel on "Current Problems in U.S. Journalism." McGill's address took place during the annual luncheon of the Harvard Foundation for Advanced Study and Research and the Harvard Law School Alumni Association, sharing the floor with Dr. Edward Delos Churchill of Massachusetts General Hospital.[1]

In an article for the *Boston Globe*, Charles L. Whipple told how "a crowd of some six hundred alumni and guests braved the rain and the cold" outside in Harkness Quadrangle "at the Harvard Law School Alumni Spread yesterday and heard two important addresses––one on Southern desegregation and the other on the world's medical needs... Light rain began to fall as McGill started his address...but only a few of the audience retreated to the shelter of tents... McGill criticized the leadership of the Southern bar associations... He criticized Southern governors and lawyers and corporations for apparently advising their firms to 'follow local custom in the South, while in the other areas the same company was told to practice no discrimination.' McGill also criticized the regional press... Then he described dramatically the abrupt turn about in Georgia last January when integration came to the state university" and to a Legislature which but a few hours before had been saying, 'Never.'"[2]

The *Boston Globe* editorialized: "The United States, it has been said frequently, is a government of laws not men. But this is a phrase made to emphasize a point. It is a government of laws and men, and

[1] *Boston Globe*, June 14, 1961. (Manuscript provided by McGill.)
[2] *Boston Globe*, June 15, 1961, p. 17. In a letter to this writer on December 27, 1967, Julie Grenier, Associate Editor of the *Harvard Law School Bulletin* remembered that "about fifteen hundred students, alumni, faculty and guests of the Law School and the Graduate School of Arts and Sciences" heard McGill's address.

223

there are times when one or the other is weak. To this abstraction, Ralph McGill, Atlanta's distinguished editor, addressed himself yesterday at Harvard with a particularization. He brought the law profession in the South before the bar of public scrutiny and found it wanting. Its leadership, he said flatly, has not lived up to its responsibility."[3]

Seventy-two years ago, in December of 1889, the editor of *The Atlanta Constitution*, Henry W. Grady, spoke in Boston at the annual dinner of the Merchants Association.

Grady was seeking to bring the South back into the lifestream of the nation. Industrial jobs were necessary to ease the poverty and tensions in his state and region. So, he detailed to his New England audience what then seemed to be the South's assets. And, of course, he sought to reassure his audience about the race problem. The years have proved him a poor prophet in his predicted schedule of industrial development. His image of the Negro's development as a contented man on his own plot of land, jogging his mule down the furrow, also was in error.

But in the great sense, Grady was right––and his words challenge us even now. The problem of race, he said in Boston in the last month of 1889, "is...so bound up in our honorable obligation to the world that we would not disentangle it if we could."

"I would rather see my people render back this question rightly solved," said Grady, "than to see them gather all the spoils over which faction has contended since Cataline conspired and Caesar fought."

Almost three-quarters of a century have passed, since Grady spoke in Boston. The echo of Alabama's mobs and others that preceded them are in our ears and on our conscience. They are not the real face of the South, though our weakness is that we have permitted them to seem to be. It is my privilege to restate the honorable obligation of which Grady spoke and to say that despite

[3] *The Boston Globe*, June 15, 1961, p. 16. Manuscript provided by McGill. The speech is also printed in *Harvard Law School Bulletin* XII (June, 1961), 6-8, 15.

the ugliness and viciousness of mobs, we are nearer the answer than ever before.

We are engaged in a struggle to do by law and the courts what men of free will have not been able, or willing, to do by themselves.

Historians have noted that our revolution, long before the fighting began at Lexington, was engineered by men who knew the law, men whose minds moved not in terms of violence and quick results, but in terms of law and the courts and the reasoned disciplined action that lies behind the law and the courts.

But ours has become an age of specialization, "with every branch of learning, including the law, divided into tight small compartments," which makes it difficult "to retain the whole view of a profession that makes for pride and excitement."

Since the greatest social reform of our time is being implemented by courts, they and the legal profession inescapably are a focus of attention. That we have not been able to retain a whole view is testified to by daily events.

In the past twenty years, but more particularly since the United States Supreme Court decision of May, 1954, the leadership of the Southern Bar has not lived up to its responsibility. It was not until the spring of 1960 that the Georgia Bar Association heard one of its members publicly state the truth about necessary compliance with decisions of the court. Nor was his heart lifted up by the considerable number of fellow members who later came to him to express appreciation and to say they wished they could have said what he did. "My clients do not want to be in controversy," they told him.

To this day, insofar as I can determine, not a single Southern state Bar association has gone on record with a resolution or declaration of court support which would have provided the people with an alternative to the peddlers of defiance. Only one city Bar association in the South, (Atlanta's), has made a public statement affirming the validity of court orders as they apply to schools.

While the Bar associations in the South were silent, individual attorneys, described glowingly by the segregationist press as "Constitutional authorities," were publicly and slanderously denouncing the Federal judiciary and assuring a troubled and indecisive public that the U.S. Supreme Court's school decision was not legal, did not have the force of law, and was Communistically inspired. That this stoked the fires of violence is unquestioned.

One of the saddest aspects of the Southern race problem has been that governors have, by plan, had lawyers join with them in statements which deliberately deceived the people by distorting, and falsifying, the facts and the Constitution. All too often this alliance has been assisted by lawyer-members of the Congress. One reluctantly concludes all concerned know better, because they could hardly have been ignorant of the meaning of Supreme Court decisions. They, however, like the governors, were and are, prisoners of their own excesses, the best illustration I know in our time of Frankenstein and his monster. And some of them, in private, are men deeply ashamed of themselves.

I do not, of course, mean to suggest that Bar associations, or lawyers, should have agreed with the court on the school case, or with other decisions in this field, although, to be candid, I would hope so. But what we have needed, from the Bar, and from public leadership generally, has been a continuing defense of the integrity of the Federal judiciary. Had the people been told by Bar associations that court orders require compliance, we would, I believe, have escaped some of the trouble caused by the deliberate deceit of the people by political leaders who invariably were loudly assured by a "leading constitutional authority" that they could, and would, defy the courts.

Another aspect of this agonizing dilemma requires thoughtful consideration. It concerns corporations doing business nationally. One dislikes to believe lawyers advised companies doing business across the nation, during the moral dilemma of the student sit-ins, to follow local custom in the South, while in other areas the same

226

company was told to practice no discrimination. The sit-ins telescoped time and courts. They were able to do so because even to many of the extremists, it soon became impossible to defend a situation where persons of both races could stand side by side to purchase intimate items of underwear, for example, but were barred by custom, or decision of the management——not law——from being side by side while buying a sandwich or a cup of coffee.

Student boycotts produced desegregation of eating places in about thirty Southern cities in less than a year.

A national public philosophy, including the morality of our problem of race, held in common by American business, would have prevented economic losses, social disorders, and bitterness. In this day of specialization, every branch of learning, including the law, is indeed divided into tight small compartments. This, I think, explains a part of the dilemma of lawyers. One of the tightest compartments is representing business clients and it is perhaps inevitable that lawyers should take on the neutral coloration of their clients and wait to advise about law until the public relations council has determined what the public policy shall be. I know the lawyer technically is not supposed to make moral decisions. We are told that this is the function of management. But, must the lawyer always be the neutralist in representing corporate clients whose scope is national? Is there not something here lost which is necessary to the law, management and society?

The government has a large responsibility but it is certainly true there are large areas left to private choice. In a totalitarian society the state is all pervasive. In our society only a modicum of political moral and economic order is imposed by government. Our kind of national community, therefore, depends partially on law but in a larger measure on the private decisions of millions of people. Our government has a limited authority but within these limits it must be obeyed. Large areas however are left open for private action and choice. If a free society is to reach an established goal, across the board, it must do so to a great extent through individual decisions. This freedom implies a moral responsibility. This responsibility is that of free business, a free press, free labor, free civic groups, *a free Bar*, and free men. If free Americans do not act responsibly, our nation suffers, particularly in comparison with monolithic states where an established policy is quickly translated into practice. The painful fact of this is a nagging feature of our daily life. We cannot equate the moral value of the just deed of a free man with the same deed of a state automaton. If a group in a totalitarian society acts responsibly——there being no moral choice,——there can be no moral credit.

A people who value a free society must act responsibly and strive to adjust their practices to their professions. When the decisions involved are legitimately private, not public, the only compulsion is conscience.

Therefore, failure to act on the part of the Bar associations, of corporations, newspapers, labor, the clergy and other elements of our society, is indeed a disservice to our free society and to the free enterprise system. This is true not only in a moral sense but in the more important one that makes for the viability of the whole society.

I think one additional reason why many of us, lawyers, and others, have not behaved well in this crisis, is the general failure to understand just what a legal decision is. Law, as I comprehend it, always represents——particularly constitutional law——the best considered judgment of men trained in the law, dedicated to principles on which the government rests, and under oath to support the Constitution. In any legal case in which two positions are represented by able counsel, there are, of necessity, at least two points of view, each logical to the litigant and worthy of argument by counsel. In any case, one side is bound to lose, having contended and argued for a different result. Most decisions, it follows, are not acceptable to both sides. One of the main functions of the judicial procedure is to reach a decision which is *final* and which will, and must be, *accepted*, acceptable or not.

The whole system of law would be undermined if decisions unacceptable to one side should not in fact be accepted. The failure to accept a decision and to abide by the result, if widely practiced, would quickly undermine society. If decisions of the highest court, because they were unacceptable to litigants and partisans, were disobeyed, no will, no contract, no pension right, no insurance policy would be safe or secure. Organized society as we know it would be impossible and people would have to come to rely on private force as a final arbiter of legal disputes. This would return society to a state in which might was right, no person was safe, and no right was secure.

I must enter a "mea culpa plea" for my own profession of journalism. Some of the failures of our regional press to offer truthful, honest leadership have been tragic in spirit and in the encouragement of extremists to violent defiance of law. And the business community and its Chambers of Commerce have been even less responsible.

But, I do not wish to belabor these points any further. I would like to tell a story of how exhilarating it is to see the words of the Bill of Rights stand up from the printed page and take on human form——to see law in action. It is the story of how desegregation came to a Deep South state university, and to a legislature which but a few hours before had been saying "Never."

January 6, 1961, in Atlanta, Georgia, was not unlike other days before the annual session of the State's General Assembly. The legislative leaders of Senate and House had been in the city for a week. The governor, questioned early, said he did not believe there would be any new school segregation bill introduced because none was needed. There would be no changes in the laws.

The then circulating issue of the Citizens Council weekly paper, in its usual make-up of bright red headlines, called on the legislators to defy all do-gooders, race-mixers, and those who would mongrelize the Caucasian race. It urged that Georgia continue to show the way in total resistance.

This was the situation at mid-afternoon.

But one hundred miles away, in Macon, Georgia, at precisely 3:18 p.m., a stone was thrown into the calmed waters of the segregation pool. It was in the form of an order by a Federal District Judge directing that Atlanta Negro students, Charlayne Hunter and Hamilton E. Holmes, whose applications had been rejected, be admitted to the University of Georgia, at Athens, on the following Monday morning at nine a.m.

On that Monday, an hour before the somewhat stunned legislature of a Deep South state with an elaborate set of laws, declared by their successful sponsors of but a few years before to be proof against all desegregation, could take their seats, the two students were admitted. The nation's oldest chartered state university was integrated. The trumpets of the U.S. Constitution had blown. The fast moving legal drama which followed had some of the elements of an old movie "chase." Lawyers for the State Board of Regents, knowing things would look better to the Assembly if they made every possible resistance, hurried to Macon's Federal Building with an appeal for a stay so that an appeal could be made. A Negro lawyer raced along the same road and was in court to oppose. The appeal for a stay was granted.

So, back to the highway went the two cars. They drove another one hundred miles to Atlanta's Federal Building where the students' attorney argued the delay was invalid because previous rulings had covered, and denied, the grounds for it. The appeals judge, in a written decision, agreed.

All over the state the meaning of constitutional rights began to come more clearly into focus as a people, fascinated, angry and applauding, looked and listened.

The next morning the students were in classes. University officials, and at least seven thousand of the seven thousand five hundred students, behaved admirably. The evening before some fifty co-eds in the dormitory with Miss Hunter had spontaneously come to her room to make her welcome.

But the rabble-rousers had recovered from shock and

230

were wildly vocal. A Board-of-Regents member, ironically also chief of the Citizens Council, publicly denounced the University President and did not deny published reports he had threatened him. During the day, resistance-minded students were encouraged and financed to action.

That night, after a close basketball game, lost in the last second to the ancient rival Georgia Tech, an incited, well planned riot took place about the girl's dormitory. A ten o'clock call by the Mayor of Athens to the governor for state troopers was withheld from the chief executive for about an hour and a half. At twelve twenty a.m., the riot wore itself out. A few students, and eight men with "a small arsenal" of arms in a car and loaded revolvers, were arrested. Seven of the latter were admitted Klansmen. The governor's executive secretary issued a statement praising the rioting students who did not "submit to judicial tyranny." The two Negro students were suspended and removed from the University as a safety precaution and an aid to maintenance of order. There were immediate public protests that the wrong persons had been suspended.

Lawyers went back to work. Just after dawn the rival attorneys again were on the road to Macon. Those representing the Negro students argued that the constitutional right of a citizen of the United States may not be abrogated because ther is a probability of disorder. Also, the constitutional rights of some may not be denied while others retain them. So it was that within hours the two students went back to classes under the umbrella of the Constitution of the United States. In addition, the court notified the state its laws withholding funds from the University under orders to integrate were unconstitutional and enjoined the state from so doing. Public opinion, therapeutically shocked by the riot and the abuse of the University president by a Regent, experienced a revulsion toward extremists disorders.

Once the original shock was reduced, the legislature had two restive days. The rabble-rousers were shouting at them. But in those days the Assembly members also began to hear from the alumni and parents. Equally important, they heard from the merchants and the power structure of the cities involved. The messages, by phone, wire and letter, all read essentially the same: "We don't like integration, but don't close the schools."

Had a local school board been somewhere involved, it would have been different. The legislature would have been happy to have remained aloof. But it was Georgia's enormous good luck to have the legislature as a whole confronted with the decision to keep open or close the vast State University System. Many were graduates of it. Some had sons or daughters at Athens. A number of these were seniors.

Some of the letters received were touched in their sincerity.

"I hate what has happened. But my wife and I have worked hard and done without to send our boy to Athens. We want him to graduate. Don't send him home..."

"Our two daughters are at the University. It will break their hearts to give it up. Try to hold things down. But don't close the University we all love..."

The House floor leader announced that he had heard the voice of the people. He had received, he said, more than six hundred letters and telegrams in two days and only twelve wanted the University closed.

It seemed, then, all of a sudden, that save for the handful of die-hard extremists who railed furiously at the governor, reminding him that he had pledged "never," everyone knew a turning point had been reached. Governor Ernest Vandiver said Georgia would obey the courts. He brushed aside those who called him traitor and demanded that he initiate defiance. Georgia's Assembly almost quietly abolished the old segregation laws in their entirety.

The anatomy lesson of this kaleidoscopic drama of law and violence is meaningful to the whole segregation picture. It represents a turning point in the Deep South pattern of pledged total defiance. Grounds for delaying maneuver are about gone. The many tests from Arkansas, Virginia and Louisiana have stripped most of the fat off the appeals possibilities. The dismal abyss of no public education today is but a few steps away from any state which takes the course of defiance.

Leadership, which has become perhaps a trite and shopworn word, nonetheless remains the essential ingredient in each Southern state and each locality confronted with a school order.

Permit me to close with a story which illustrates the failure of the past and the hope of the present and the future.

Because of the processes of law three students have been accepted for entry to Georgia's Institute of Technology next September. I am well acquainted with the parents of one of these young men. This father and mother were themselves college graduates. The father of the young man of whom I speak took various jobs, all poor ones. They were all that were open to a Negro. Finally, he got a better one——as a chauffeur and butler. His wife became a cook. Next September their son will enter Georgia Tech, and President Kennedy's recent employment directive in the field of Federal contracts means he will be able to get a job as an engineer.

Is it not an accusation against all of us that we have waited so long to make a beginning?

Is it not well to learn how to accept the unacceptable?

Publisher McGill delivered the third annual Abramowitz Memorial
Lecture at the Massachusetts Institute of Technology at 8:15 p.m. in
Kresge Auditorium. The Lecture, an endowed series, was sponsored
by the Department of Humanities. Following his prepared text
"rather closely," McGill addressed over three hundred M.I.T. under-
graduates, faculty, and guests. On the evening before the lecture,
Louis Lyons held a party for Mr. McGill to which he invited the
Nieman Fellows, together with Francis Wylie from M.I.T., Edward
Weeks, Victor Jones of the *Boston Globe* and other friends of Mr.
McGill who worked with Boston newspapers.[1]

[1] Letters and information sent by Francis E. Wylie, Director,
Office of Public Relations at M.I.T., December 11, 1967; and
Richard M. Douglas, Chairman, Department of Humanities, M.I.T.,
December 13, 1967. Director Wylie added: "Belonging to Ralph's
generation of journalists (but a humble member) I have a special
admiration and affection for him. Two glimpses remain especially
vivid in my mind: 1) On the soggy day of the Eisenhower-Taft trial
run in New Hampshire in March 1952, with the slush six inches deep,
the courtly editor helping a pretty poll wather across a gutter in
Nashua, and 2) Sitting with him for a drink after his speech at the
Harvard Club in honor of Louis Lyons (1963?) in the company of
two offspring of the New Deal whom I'm sure neither of us expected
ever to drink with——Buzzy Roosevelt and Henry Morgenthau, Jr."

In 1901, an editorial in *The Atlantic Monthly* commented acidly on the disfranchisement acts adopted, or
then being enacted, by Southern states. It was a time when
Mr. Kipling had chided the Americans with his poem, "The
White Man's Burden," imposed, as he saw things, by the
acquisition of the Philippines. He bade them take the
burden of the new-caught sullen people, half devil and half
child. The U.S. Congressional Hawaiian Commission,
meanwhile, had recommended property and literacy tests
as voting qualifications in this new territory. Senator John

234

Morgan, of Alabama, as chairman of the Commission, had said the Commission had acted for "One assortment of inferior races." To reject the tests, the Senator said, "would be to turn the legislature over to the masses," and to "deprive the more conservative elements and property owners of effective (sic) representation." Northern political sentiment, in the Congress and business areas, which favored the voting qualifications for the new possessions, was thus prevented from being critical of the ruthless rush of the Southern states totally to disfranchise the Negro. Indeed, Senator John L. McLaurin, of South Carolina, was so moved by a speech delivered by a Massachusetts statesman, Senator George F. Hoar, defending the American Imperialism and its methods, that he rose to thank his colleague from the Bay State for his "complete announcement of the divine right of the Caucasian to govern the inferior races."

The Atlantic, noting the application of the harsh and frankly disfranchising Mississippi plan to the Philippines, said: "If the stronger and cleverer race is free to impose its will upon 'new caught, sullen peoples' on the other side of the globe, why not in South Carolina and Mississippi? The advocates of the 'shotgun policy' are quite as sincere, and we are inclined to think quite as unselfish, as the advocates of 'benevolent assimilation.' "

The two phrases are, in fact, two names for the same thing. Southern reaction, especially on the part of those engaged in disfranchisement, was one of almost incredulous joy at their good fortune. The business of disfranchising the Asian and African Americans went forward simultaneously.

In the South there was some opposition from Populist groups. Many individuals spoke out against it. Of these, John Spencer Bassett, historian of North Carolina, said of his state's brazen disfranchisement law: "At best, it is an enameled lie...one more step in the education of our people that it is right to lie, to steal, and to defy all honesty in order to keep a certain party in power."

Professor Bassett was prophetic. Having assumed the

burden of a lie and of dishonesty clad as truth and virtue, the South, and the nation, moved from 1900 into a decade of savage violence. Race riots were many. Lynchings multiplied in numbers and brutality. Southern politicians, of whom Ben Tillman is perhaps the best example, lectured under the banner of Chatauqua, declaring the Negro to be sub-human and shouting "To hell with the Constitution if it says we cannot lynch to avenge crimes against womanhood." Racist extremists reached a wide audience North and South. Edgar Gardner Murphy, then an Episcopal minister in Montgomery, Alabama, and one of the really remarkable men of his time and region, denounced this brutal and inhuman trend, saying that racist extremists had "proceeded from an undiscriminating attack upon the Negro's ballot to a like attack upon his schools, his labor, his life——from the contention that no Negro shall learn, that no Negro shall labor, and (by implication) that no Negro shall live." They ended by preaching, he said, "an all-absorbing autocracy of race," an "absolute identification of the stronger race with the very being of the state."

It is the fall-out from the decisions of this period in American history that slowly has poisoned and sickened the nation, and, more particularly, the South. The burden of guilt and fear, the acceptance of a system immoral and expensive in human and economic terms, made inevitable a lack of first-rate educational opportunity for the average Southerner. It doomed most of the people of the rural South to an existence so meager and unrewarding as to bring on, and yet be unable to sustain, the Populist revolution. The sharecropper tenant statistics of the 1930's revealed how great had been the cost in things temporal and spiritual.

That cost continues. In my opinion it will be paid over and over for at least a generation to come and it is perhaps fitting that it must be borne nationally. But, the South, inevitably, will pay the heavier share of it.

One illustration will suffice. It applies to Georgia. Its findings can, with very little alteration, be applied to any

Southern state. It now is the custom for rural counties with eroding economics to join together in an effort to attract industry and find jobs. Recently ten such counties in South-Central Georgia so agreed. They asked the Georgia Institute of Technology's Industrial Development Division to research their area and give them the facts of it. (The counties, for the record, are: Bleckley, Dodge, Johnson, Laurens, Montgomery, Pulaski, Telfair, Treutlen, Wheeler and Wilcox.) Until they knew what had happened to them in the past decade to so deplete their economy, they clearly couldn't plan to meet the needs of the next decade. There was reason to be disturbed. The median family income in Georgia is $4,200. This is below the national average, but it represents substantial advance. But in the ten counties seeking information about themselves, the median income ranged from one half to three quarters of the state average.

The report pulled no punches.

These were the facts. The 10-county area had lost 12,215 farm jobs between 1950 and 1960, a jolting decline of 62 percent.

Another 824 jobs had been lost in forestry. More than 13,000 jobs representing over 30 percent of the total persons employed in the area in 1950 had evaporated.

New jobs, primarily in manufacturing, opened up for 8,000 persons during the same time. But this still was a net loss of 5,000 jobs in one decade for this 10-county area. That was an 11 percent loss of jobs in a period when Georgia as a whole gained 10 percent.

Moreover most of the manufacturing jobs were in apparel, wood products, textiles and food products. The Georgia Tech study noted that in the national context these are low-wage, slow-growth industries with a comparatively unfavorable outlook for future employment. Yet, such industries account for 90 percent of the area's manufacturing jobs.

With farm jobs disappearing and unreplaced, it was not surprising that every one of the ten counties except Bleckley lost population. This county had more manufacturing jobs. But even so, 25 percent of Bleckley workers commute across county lines to work, chiefly in Houston County, where there is a large Federal depot, and in the metropolitan area of the city of Macon.

What's the outlook for the ten counties? The Georgia Tech study gave answer: "The increasing importance of technical skills and of basic aptitudes for training will have a crucial bearing on the area's ability to compete successfully."

The study then emphasized that at present each of the ten counties falls below the average educational level achieved by Georgians as a whole. And the state's nearest vocational-technical schools will be at Macon, Albany, and Swainsboro——forty to fifty miles away.

This 10-county area isn't much different from many others in Georiga or those in neighboring states. It can respond as others will to drastically improved education, individual initiative, imaginative enterprise, and federal aid like the job retraining program which was really designed not as a socialistic spending plot, as the right wing conservatives have insisted, but to help Americans as they equip themselves to make a living.

Whether these and other similarly depressed Southern counties will reverse their course will depend on those who remain as the population decreases. It will require a change of mind from that of the present time. The ten counties are a stronghold of the status quo in racial attitudes. In all past elections, a majority of these votes have gone for the most blatant of demagogues. Many of their residents have not yet learned the price their grandparents, parents, or they, themselves, have paid, and are paying, in resisting changes necessary to free them from an impossible economic dilemma. They cannot advance without ridding themselves of the conditions that have brought them to the present emergency.

There are other measurements of the daily cost of the folly of a plan which was meant to disfranchise, exclude, and exploit a minority but could only debase the educational, cultural, spiritual, and economic base of the entire region.

238

The National Education Association estimates of school receipts per pupil in daily average attendance in thirteen Southern states for 1960-61 reveal seven states with less than three hundred dollars per pupil against a national average of $445.31. Of the seven, two are below $250. They are Mississippi at $231.85 and Alabama at $286.70.

In sixteen Southern states the percent of population twenty-five years of age and over with four or more years of college show the four highest with percentages ranging from Delaware's 7.4 percent to Texas with six percent. Four of the sixteen states have percentages here below four percent. They are Kentucky, Mississippi, Alabama, and Arkansas. Further pursuing this aspect of educated leadership, in and out of teaching, the table of earned doctorates, in all fields, for sixteen Southern states, for the twenty year span from 1936 to 1956, show a high total of 2,045 in Maryland, 1,994 in North Carolina, 1,993 in Texas, and 1,015 in Tennessee. We then have a precipitous drop to 754 in Virginia, 631 in Louisiana, and 553 in Florida. The four states with the lowest totals are Mississippi with 23, South Carolina with 24, Arkansas with 45, and Alabama with 65. There has been improvement in more recent years, but the total remains low.

The Southern Regional Education Board, in projecting future problems, said: The growing enrollment and replacement of faculties will mean a need for about 50,000 new college teachers in the next ten years in the South... The outlook for college presidents trying to hire faculty members, particularly in chemistry, physics, mathematics, and other science fields is dismal indeed... Southern salaries are lower than in the rest of the country... Though average salaries have risen, the South still lags behind the rest of the United States by from $1,000 to $1,500. We are not catching up..."

Against the lacks of education, skills and jobs, there is everywhere the spectre of automation. The opportunities for jobs for the functionally illiterate are disappearing. Here again, the South is paying heavily for the more than sixty years of segregation, disfranchisement and isolation of the Negro and much of the rural white South from the cultural and political life of both the region and the nation. The white Southerner is just learning what his forefathers did to him.

The slum ghettos of poverty and color in the large Eastern cities are largely a product of migration out of the South. What their cost has been, and what it will be in the future is now impossible to calculate. We know only that it has been great and will continue.

Perhaps the real phenomenon of the population since 1945 has been its mobility. A recent report by the U.S. Census Bureau said: "About 35.5 million, or 20.0 percent, of the 177.4 million persons one year old and over who were living in the United States in March 1961 has moved at least once since March 1960. Although this overall mobility rate has reflected to some slight extent some of the postwar changes in business conditions, it has remained relatively stable in the fourteen successive surveys conducted since 1948...

"Of the 35.5 million persons one year old and over who were living in a different house in March 1961 from that in 1960, about 24.3 million, or 18.7 percent of the total population one year old and over, had moved within the same county; 5.5 million, or 3.1 percent had moved between counties in the same state; and 5.8 million, or 3.2 percent, had moved between states.

Not all the slum disadvantages are Negro. There are enclaves of white persons, also functionally illiterate and unskilled. These slums of the last half of our century are not stopping places as they were in the old days when the great waves of immigration came to America. Few persons are leaving those of our time. They grow, glacier-like. And they fester.

It has taken us almost a decade to see that the U.S. Supreme Court decision of May 1954 was merely the opening of a door through which the whole problem of discrimination, injustice and deprivation has been brought to the center of the national stage. It will be there for some time.

The decade has not been without progress. In fact, it is accurate to say that actual advances in political power, economic opportunity, education, and standard of living generally, are unparallel. Yet, they have served to put into perspective the long, calamitous record of injustice and denial and to make more unpalatable and unacceptable the state-proclaimed defiance in Mississippi and Alabama and that of single communities in other states. We now have added from the new governor of Louisiana a promise that he will, in imitation of Alabama's George Wallace, "Stand in the door" of any school ordered desegregated.

The symbolism of these governors is so obvious one wonders why they are not embarrassed. Governor Wallace, when he attempted to prevent lawfully qualified students from entering the University of Alabama, actually had painted a small circle in which to stand. Having drawn himself into a confining circle, he then barred two young Alabamians from the door to education. It is a melancholy commentary on the quality of invention in Louisiana that it can only imitate this grotesque symbolism.

Reporters who were in Mississippi for the Beckwith trial report that police in that state are very heavily armed and that even peaceful demonstrations will be regarded as unlawful because they may bring on disorder. The mayor of Jackson confirms both reports. There is to be a voter registration campaign in Mississippi this summer and many college students will assist in it. Yet, we see Mississippi leadership, confronted with the desire of qualified persons to register to vote, adding to armament and to an inflamed state of mind. It seems at times, looking at Mississippi's actions, as if there is a morbid wish to force the Federal government again to send troops to that State. As of this writing, there is no word from the new governor of that state welcoming the voter registration drive and assuring it of all necessary cooperation and protection. This would be, in the United States, a reasonable thing to do. And, yet, to those who look fearfully toward the state of Mississippi, the only answer now seems to be more shotguns, tear gas, and the setting up of concentration

241

pens. The nation might well ask if it is impossible for Governor Johnson to announce that the state will protect the right to encourage and assist the registration of voters.

Mississippi, and other states and communities that have made no concessions whatever——and which have records such as the Oxford riots, in which two men were murdered and Federal marshals subjected to attack and a constant tirade of filthy abuse; and Birmingham where Sunday school children were dynamited to death——inevitably create demonstrations, resentments, protest marches, boycotts, and complaints from Negroes in America and in other regions of earth. It is human enough for others to say that there are too many demonstrations and marches, and that the pace of change should be slowed. But, incidents such as the murder of Medgar Evers, the need to call troops to assure a native Mississippian the right to enter this state university, the bombings, and the harassment of those seeking to register to vote, have enough emotional meaning to make the pace of progress seem slow.

Progress——and let it be repeated, there has been, and is progress——also is blurred by economic events. There are now more jobs for Negroes. The door of job opportunity opens wider and wider. The Negro knows this and welcomes it. But the opportunities merely serve to highlight the educational lacks and deficiencies that have been a part of the history of the Negro. This deprivation has been more especially true in the small towns and in the rural communities of the South, many of which had few elementary schools and no high schools at all until comparatively recent years. Hence, those Negroes who today are educated and trained make rapid progress. But the real story is in the files of the U.S. Department of Labor. Unemployment in America is largely Negro. As an economic group, the Negro has not moved forward.

Out of this frustration comes acts and words often irrational and bitter and out of it is generated a mood of distrust which is heavy and disturbing.

There is a guild feeling in the South and in the nation. Only the more obtuse fail to see that the folly of the disfranchisement period and all the injustices that grew out of it have now caught up with us.

The civil rights bill, now being irrationally and demagogically filibustered, is long overdue. It is, in fact, a reasonable bill. It takes away no rights, despite the filibuster propaganda claims to the contrary. Letters come asking if some of the "rights demanded by Negroes do not mean taking rights away from white persons." So deeply fixed is acceptance of the status quo that those asking such a question do not comprehend that if a right belongs to all citizens, then being sure all have it does not take it away from anyone.

The public accommodations section of the bill is especially needed. In many Southern cities, hotels and restaurants serve without restrictions. But, there are always some who cannot afford to take a temporary loss if his nearby competitor does remain segregated. Last summer in Atlanta, one restaurant man saw his business fall off by some forty percent for three months because a racist competitor arranged to have pickets march daily before his place of business with signs reading, "This place serves Negroes. Don't eat with him." He lasted it out. He now is doing well.

"I keep reading the book of Job," he said, "and you know what——Job ended up making more money than he had before."

So separated were the races in the South that few white Southerners ever thought of the psychological effect of not being able to take one's family out to a decent, down-town restaurant. They did not think how it felt not to be allowed to attend a theater, movie, or concert without sitting in a segregated second balcony, or in a partitioned-off area of seats in some far corner. Few realized the indignities encountered when traveling by automobile and having to go off the main road seeking some wooded area when restrooms were denied. Or, of sleeping in the car at night when motels were declared sold out, even though the vacancy sign was on, or when the more callous said, "We don't accept Negroes." And these things happened——and still happen——outside the South as well as in it.

It is difficult to believe that a person who has a license to do a public business can, at will, declare it a private business and turn away decently clad, orderly customers because he does not like their color. That there must be legislation is plain. In many cities, hotels and most restaurants have acted voluntarily. But, always there are some who seek to profit at the expense of those who have acted on their own. And in at least two states there have been no concessions whatever. Here again, we may see that progress is fogged by the emotional resentments aroused by those who perpetuate indignities and discriminations.

But, in conclusion, let us understand that the civil rights bill can be nothing more than a beginning——a legal pivot toward equality in education, politics, housing, and jobs. The vote and education will be the more powerful tools. What we have come to call de facto segregation is, for example, a problem of housing, and yet we have tried to burden school administrations with it. De facto segregation will begin to erode when progress may be made in the areas mentioned——at the ballot box, in jobs, housing, and so on.

So, in a very real sense, the civil rights bill cannot be compromised... If the Congress depletes the essential features of the proposed legislation, then they will find it necessary to put them back. Individual rights cannot be compromised out of existence. The filibusterers would do well to understand that basic fact. It ought to be a relatively simple task for some 172 million Americans to do what is right. That it isn't possible to move steadily toward this objective is an indictment that will not be *nolle prossed* for a long time to come.

NATIONAL EDUCATION ASSOCIATION
Miami Beach, July 30, 1966

This address came during the one hundred and fourth annual meeting of the National Education Association at the large Miami Beach Convention Hall. More than 6,500 of the 7,460 available seats were occupied by delegates from nearly all states and several foreign countries. I saw McGill address this education-conscience audience for about thirty-five minutes without notes.

Delegates at this convention were largely concerned about racial desegregation, federal aid to education, and the extension of education. Probably the delegates were more interested in financial support than any other topic. A check of the official *Proceedings* of the NEA revealed a constant concern for local, state, and federal financial support. This year was no different. The day after McGill's speech, the convention passed an official resolution calling for "substantial federal contributions" and "teacher pay starting at $8,000 a year."[1]

Racial desegregation was an issue before the educators but one should consider the motivation behind this discussion. Careful study of the NEA's official *Proceedings* vividly demonstrates that, *as a body*, that group did not serve as an early impetus to social reform. Only after the federal government had enacted laws did the NEA, *as an organization*, give serious thought to desegregation in public education. Not until the Supreme Court decision of 1954, for example, did the NEA pass even its vague "fair play and good will" resolution as to the "matter of integration in the public schools."[2] Three years later George M. Snyder, of California, told the delegates "we have all sinned... I propose that we do not ignore this momentous issue by an innocuous resolution but that we resolve as teachers to do something about it."[3] The old "fair play" resolution stood.

[1] *Miami Herald*, July 2, 1966, p. 13A
[2] *Proceedings of the Ninety-second Annual Meeting*, 1954, Vol. 92, Washington, D.C., 124-125.
[3] *Addresses and Proceedings of the Ninety-fifth Annual Meeting*, 1957, Vol. 95, 192-193. (for further comment about McGill's delivery of this speech and the audience reaction see Chapter 8.)

After decades of inaction, and nine years of circumvention, finally, in 1963, the NEA passed a proposal with teeth. But it took until July 1, 1966, the day after McGill's address (there was no apparent connection), for the NEA to warn state affiliates who were still segregated "to integrate by next June or face expulsion from" the association.

McGill's audience, then, was interested in education, personal income, and desegregation. Audience action, however, probably was determined largely by a desire for more money. Having tasted the 1965 support from the federal government, the delegates were quite willing, now, to activate so-called human rights programs which had been bred by judicial courts and given life by massive aid. Consequently, if McGill planned to convince or actuate delegates attending the NEA convention in 1966, he had better draw his supporting materials from the purse and the pocketbook. (Speech taken from taped recording.)

President Batchelder, officers of this association, ladies and gentlemen. I appreciate your president's gracious introduction. I must say to you in all candor that I appreciate the opportunity of speaking to this organization and this convention more than any other invitation I have had.

I have a feeling always that a responsible newspaper writer, editorial or editorial columnist is in some sense occupying the role of a teacher. I am not saying they are teachers but that they fill a somewhat similar role, in that what they write I think should stimulate discussion, inquiry, more reading, more study, a seeking for more information, and it is in that sense that I mean a responsible editorial writer or editorial columnist should, I feel, occupy the role of a teacher.

When I was a boy of about eleven my father, who had moved from a farm in——north of Chattanooga, Tennessee, where he had got all the schooling he could get——which was about four or five months each year in a small one-room school building which I had the opportunity to see later on when it was abandoned and being used as a place to keep hay. He moved, when his first two children were born, to get where there were some schools. He had of that——that generation had a great passion for education, and a respect, and an admiration for it which he transmitted as best he could to his children.

When I was about eleven he took me on an excursion train from Chattanooga to Louisville, Kentucky, to see if he could get in to see Henry Waterson, then the editor of the *Louisville Courier Journal*. My father had been reading that paper and had formed a great admiration for Mr. Waterson.

I remember we got in, and I remember the dark desk and the old furniture and the short figure of Mr. Waterson with his goatee beard. I remember my father talking. I don't remember what they said, but I remember a motto which was on Mr. Waterson's desk, and it read thusly: "Lord, give me this day my daily idea, and forgive me the one I had yesterday." (laughter)

In a time when things are changing so rapidly, this is not a bad motto for any of us. But I think it is especially a good one for one who has the temerity, anyone who has the temerity to write daily and to sign his or her name thereto.

I use this as a sort of text frequently because, and I use it tonight because I would not have you think that I am presumptuous enough to stand here in any——with any idea that I am an educator or that I really know anything about education. It is something that has been close to my heart and interest. I have tried to learn something about it. I have traveled a great deal visiting schools and trying to inquire into problems and to learn them.

I am proud of the program which is before you, the extension of school, but I wanted to talk——I wonder——I remember talking with the historian Toynbee when he came to my city on a visit and he had written something in one of his [b]ooks about, as a young boy, watching the Diamond Jubilee of Queen Victoria——and of how to him as a boy, it seemed that history was something glorious; it was something which he felt made Great Britain at that time just standing at the peak of the world, and everything was wonderful and glorious and nothing would ever change it.

247

He said he had no sense of history happening, even though he lived under this queen who had done so much to make history happen. But he said he felt that if he had been a small boy in the United States and in the Southern part of the United States in 1897, he would have felt that history had happened, and he would have felt that it had happened to him and his region.

And yet, I somewhat doubt if the small Toynbee, had he been there, would have felt this. In 1897, we were moving toward a war with Spain. In February of 1898, a battleship was to be blown up in the placid, peaceful harbor or seemingly so at Havana. And within days, history had taken another turn.

Somehow I think we might quote another line from Robert Frost, [President of American Legion had quoted from Frost earlier.] a line in which he said, "Two roads diverged in the wood, and I, I took the less traveled one, and that has made all the difference."

Somehow I think this is what we have done in this nation with regard to much of our education, and I think it important that we comprehend, as I am sure we really do. But I would like to review something that I have seen and watched happen and puzzled over and wept over and thought over.

I can remember the boll weevil decade. Nobody pays any attention to that much today but I can remember how the cotton sharecroppers and tenant cabins, emptied, some of them burned, leaving the chimneys there like silent sentinels representing something gone never to return.

I saw the others, many of them, hundreds of them, emptied, their wooden windows sagging, the doors sagging, window——, the roof broken in, the old hearth places where people had dreamed and thought and perhaps sorrowed, and turned over, animals moving in through the buildings——1920's.

And out of the South in that decade there moved over 100,000 persons, because their way of life was gone. And I remember people trying to poison cotton for the boll

weevil and seeing in the fields grandmothers and grandfathers and wives and husbands and little children even,
with a bucket of poison syrup and a stick with a rag on it,
touching a drop of this poison syrup to each plant.

And still they went and away went and we didn't pay
much attention to it. The depression came, the
outmigration slowed till the latter part of that decade; and
the great war was coming, and I remember watching the
labor recruiters get their crowds together in country towns
and in cities and seeing whole trainloads and busloads of
people move out, mostly Negroes, but not all, always a
mixture of the poor white farmer who was going. I don't
know how many of us comprehended at that time that in
all of this country, oh about seventy-two percent of all of
its Negro population was in the southern states, that about
three-fifths, almost three-fifths of all the farms in this
whole great rich nation were in the southeast and this
meant that most of them were small and that most of
them, when the great change came, had been committed
always to cotton and cotton as a way of life had ceased. A
man with a plow and a mule was no longer an economic
unit that could compete. And he had to go, and he went
and began to go to all the great cities. And when the
tragedy of December 7, 1941, came and it became necessary for this nation to build up and down its West Coast
the great factories of war to build ships of all kinds——
transports, liberty ships, landing craft——thousands of
aircraft, weapons, materials of war, never have I witnessed
such a migration.

I suppose when historians look back at this nation they
will say that one of the great phenomena of it was its
mobility, the mobility of its peoples. We got used to trailer
camps and we got used to people on the move in
thousands by the thousands.

And so changes came. I remember one of our writers
watching trainloads of people leave off of these small
farms, out of these emptied cabins, out of the small towns.
He wrote of them that they left and he seemed to see that
their hands were still curved to fit a plow handle or a hoe

handle, and that he felt like weeping because all they were taking with them was the small skill of a small farm.

They had not had much chance at education. They had not had much chance at learning anything else but this narrow field of making a living on a small farm. And there they went and the war ended and they were distributed. One example will do.

The beautiful city of San Francisco, their great cosmopolitan population, and with a history of this sort of population, found itself in 1940, '38, with a population of about five thousand Negroes. The war was ended, it was somewhere near sixty thousand.

Boston, Chicago, Detroit, Pittsburgh, Tacoma, Seattle, Atlanta, all over the country, this was the story; and no longer was it just a Southern story. And now we find ourselves with the great cities, with so-called flight to the suburbs and in our inner cities, there is no longer any real choice of housing. Either the very poor live there or the well-off fill in the high-rise-luxury apartments.

And America has become urban. Most of our people live in cities or in urban communities about cities, and this is an old story but it has happened. And in the last three or four years, I have spent some time and weeks going to the great cities and seeing what is happening in these areas.

Not bad people, some bad people, but a lot of lost people, so to speak, who lost their ties to the land which they could never get back again because their way of life was gone, who were picked up by the great engines of war so to speak and put down, and there they are, white, Negro——great white slums too——15-,20,000 in one I have in mind, all with a great deal of pathos.

They are not well educated. They don't have skills, they are middle-aged. Their children, many of them, have not done well in the very poor schools they are attending.

And we in this time begin to be conscious of this gap. Mr. Francis Keppel, the former Commissioner of Education, wrote in the Harvard Graduate School Bulletin last year an article and in it he said that he thought there were four significant figures in the great educational revolution of the past fifteen years.

250

And he started about fifteen years ago with the great conservative figure Senator Robert Taft, the last Senator Robert Taft of Ohio, who was certainly in the great and true conservative tradition, which makes me wonder, if you will pardon a personal expression, what has happened to the great personal tradition as he represented it. And he introduced legislation, this great conservative, to spend federal money in elementary and secondary education. He was defeated. But the idea was introduced from the conservative side that the federal government had an obligation to education and that money ought to be spent, and the idea persisted.

Mr. Keppel listed next Nikita Khrushchev who, as premier, had put up the first great startling Sputnik in orbit about the earth and had frightened us about our schools and had put us to examining whether they were good enough and what we had to do in this area of education.

And then he thought that Pope John, the last Pope John, by calling attention to the fact that people were divided, and that religion had an obligation to be——to make itself relevant to the lives of people, and that education must be improved——and he started, called for movement which is already beginning to help his own——the parochial schools of his own churches. But more particularly Pope John because he said there ought to be a united——that the church——the people who worship Christian, in Christian churches should have more unity and should approach the problems of their communities in a greater unity.

And then he thought his fourth one was President Lyndon Johnson who, after other Presidents had failed, had managed to get through the Congress a really massive federal aid bill and a civil rights bill which was so closely tied to educational bill because of need.

And he commented, as you and I would that these were four very varied characters, an odd assortment. And you might have other figures but he rather thought these four stood out in the past fifteen years.

Now, certainly, as a Southerner, born in Tennessee, in Atlanta, Georgia, for almost thirty-seven years now, I have known nothing else insofar as birthright is concerned but the South. I have a great love for that region, I have a great respect for its progress, but I must most earnestly say that we have far to go, far to go.

I listened as the Commander of The American Legion spoke and I agree that under this nation we must allow every person to have his dignity, human dignity. And I don't think it is fair that all of the burden should be put on education. But most of it is going to be put there.

I don't know how we will do it——how you will do it, unless you could somehow summon up more help. But it is true now that we see, I think, clearly and painfully how ugly and what a great weight and burden this policy of segregation put upon the Southern people, and now by the great dispersal toward the——into the industrial areas and into the great industrial cities, upon the whole nation. The price will be heavy. It is not yet paid, and I hope that somehow education can speed up the process of acceptance of what must be done morally, religiously, if you want to put it that way, and legally——and what ought to have been done long ago without all the pressures.

We see now that in my region which has exported so much——so many people who never had a chance at education, who never had a chance at skills, who never had a chance to learn to be a voter, who never had a chance to participate in community affairs and learn something of citizenship——we learn, I hope we see, very plainly indeed, that this produced the harvest of today, or much of it. And that in this region where we had not enough per capita income, being largely agricultural, for one good school system, at a time when we had seventy-two percent of all the Negroes in America in our region, we chose, out of heaven knows what disaster of decision, to try to have two systems when we couldn't really afford one good one.

And now today we see still not only in the little Southern towns and the big Southern cities where still there are some white toughs who will jeer and curse and hurl rocks and stones——we see in some of the great cities in the expansion and breaking out of riots in those intolerable slums that there is a lot to be done, and that the evil of the past has been exported nationally and put down nationally.

We have discovered in this time of self-examination how very wide the gulf is between the schools of some of our inner city situations and those of the suburbs. We know the inequities of tax support, and we are beginning to see what a tremendous job it is. Head Start, a great drama. Upward-Bound, another one. We are seeing, and I visited two of these last summer, how young Negro students out of schools which are not up to standard, because they never have had the money, brought in for summer sessions and intensively prepared to enter college and perhaps stay there. When I look at Georgia Tech, for example, perhaps the best engineering school in the Southeast and getting better all the time and I know that every year roughly forty percent of its students drop out because they are not prepared to stay in this engineering school, and that about forty-six percent of the high schools in my state——and I think we are a cut above some of the others——forty-six of the high schools, roughly that, I am told by the State Department, cannot prepare a youngster to get into Georgia Tech because they don't offer the advanced high school math, or the advanced chemistry, advanced physics, high school.

I look at that and see that so much of this has been spread over the nation. I wish we could take our minds off of the violence, off of the theatrics of protest, and bring and keep them fixed always on the great job that exists. Wherever you may think, the great job is there.

A generation of children in many areas have been sacrificed to very poor quality of schools. This has reached up into the inner cities so-called of most of the cities of this nation, the effect of it, the presence of it is there.

It thrills me and excites me that education is recognizing this, and that education at least is aware of it and that the nation, I believe and hope, increasingly has this on its conscience.

History keeps on happening. It is only about 33½ years since Franklin D. Roosevelt was first inaugurated as President, a short time, and yet when we look back at how much has happened to us in this nation in those thirty-three years, and when we consider that it is only a little more than thirty-three years until the year 2000, and we can wonder, "What changes will happen to us in the thirty-five years ahead? Will they be as much? Will they be as great? What are we going to do?"

We were poorly prepared when we looked upward out of the depression of the first years of the thirties. We were——that first decade of those thirty-three years we were poorly prepared.

I sometimes wonder now, I wonder in my own profession, which I think has done on the whole a very poor job of interpreting this to the nation, with certain notable exceptions.

It seems to me that organized labor, with certain notable exceptions, has not done all it should have done.

It seems to me that the church, with many notable exceptions, has not done all that it could have done to look ahead and to plan for this next year, this next thirty-five years, when we begin the third millennium.

So what will we do? And it's going to be put more and more upon your shoulders to do it and my——I wonder and hope whether you will and I hope and pray you will have enough help.

It seems to me that we ought to begin to say that taxes are the price you pay for civilization. (applause)

And yet, there is growing in this country a petty, niggardly mean attitude about voting school taxes, school bonds. I wish another Senator Taft would speak out in that area. We find ourselves looking at something else. The Bureau of the Census lets us know that sometime next year, 50 percent or a little more of all the people in this country will be 30 years old or younger. And if the present trend continues, five years after that, in '72, half the people in this country will be twenty-five years old and younger.

What do we do about that? How do we plan for that? We haven't done much. I am ashamed of what my profession has done.

We have seen two magazines, supported by teen-agers, *Seventeen, Mademoiselle.* We have watched great national manufacturers become wealthy manufacturing clothing, cosmetics for teen-agers. Yet we have paid very little attention to what impact this will have on politics, what it will have on the economy, what it will have on education, what it will have on religion, the church.

Again, I am here as just a working newspaperman. I don't know the answers. I can't find them yet. I keep looking, but I don't see many people except those manufacturers who knew they could start a great new market selling clothing and cosmetics to teen-agers——I was looking at a magazine coming down; there was a great new cosmetics for teen-agers and the name of it is "Going Wild"——this was a——perhaps——so what do we do in politics? How do we think? Or do we think about it? How will it affect us: homes, schools, churches?

All of these things are coming and what I am trying to say is that history is happening to us, and we sometimes notice it and sometimes don't. But we know or should know, I hope, that we cannot move forward as a nation until we really quit this foolishness of trying to resist what is bound up in the civil rights laws and to go ahead and do what is pretty simple to do if we will just do it. (applause)

It's worked pretty well everywhere people have gone ahead and done it. And I think not until we get this ugly aspect out of our lives will our future begin to brighten and we will be able to turn our minds and hearts to the great necessary thinking of a nation that is getting more young in one respect and yet its other division is of people getting older and living to older ages. So that we——those in the middle age, they are not going to be so many in the future. At any rate, it is a very exciting, thrilling time to be alive. And I wouldn't miss it, especially when you consider the alternative to missing it. (laughter) But I just simply wouldn't want to miss it. It's too exciting to contemplate, but there it is, the history happening to us. I don't know the answer. They are going to turn to you more than anyone else. And we are probably going to do not much more for you and we will do that reluctantly unless we can somehow get the people to seeing what the future demands of us and what must be done.

I again want to thank you for asking me to be on the program and to say what an honor it has been for me to speak to you here this evening. Thank you. (applause)